WRITING IRRESISTIBLE PICTURE BOOKS

INSIDER INSIGHTS INTO CRAFTING
COMPELLING MODERN STORIES FOR YOUNG
READERS

MARY KOLE

GOOD
STORY
PUBLISHING

"Writing Irresistible Picture Books"
By Mary Kole

1. Reference / Writing, Research, and Publishing Guides / Writing

FIRST EDITION
Ebook ISBN: 978-1-939162-04-5
Print ISBN: 978-1-939162-07-6

Cover Design: Jenna Van Rooy
Editing: Amy Wilson
Printed in the United States of America

For Theo, Finn, and Ella (again): You're the three precious reasons my house is stuffed with picture books, and I wouldn't have it any other way.

CONTENTS

ABOUT THE AUTHOR

A former literary agent, Mary Kole knows the ins and outs of the publishing industry. She founded Mary Kole Editorial in 2013 to provide consulting and developmental editing services to writers across all categories and genres. She started Good Story Company in 2019 to create valuable content like the Good Story Podcast, Good Story YouTube channel, and the Writing Craft Workshop membership community. Her Story Mastermind small group workshop intensives help writers level up their craft, she offers done-for-you revision and ghostwriting with Manuscript Studio, and marketing services with Good Story Marketing. She also develops unique and commercial intellectual property for middle grade, young adult, and adult readers with Upswell Media and Bittersweet Books, the latter with literary agent John Cusick and #1 *New York Times* best-selling author, Julie Murphy.

Mary has appeared at regional, national, and international writing conferences for the SCBWI, Writer's Digest, Penn Writers, Writer's League of Texas, San Francisco Writers Conference, WIFYR, Writing Day, and many others. Her guest lectures have taken her to Harvard, the Ringling College of Art and Design, the Highlights Foundation, and more. Mary's recorded video classes can be found online at Writing Mastery Academy, Writing Blueprints, Udemy, and LinkedIn Learning.

Mary holds an MFA in Creative Writing and began her publishing career with a literary agency internship and the Kidlit blog, which she started in 2009. She has worked at Chronicle Books, the Andrea Brown Literary Agency, and Movable Type Management. Her books are *Writing Irresistible Kidlit: The Ultimate Guide to Crafting Fiction for Young Adult and Middle Grade Readers* from Writer's Digest Books/Penguin Random House, and *Successful Query Letters*, *Writing Irresistible Picture Books*, *How to Write a Book Now*, and *Writing Interiority*, from Good Story Publishing.

Originally from the San Francisco Bay Area, she lives with her three children, husband, two pugs, and a cat, in Minneapolis, MN.

MARY KOLE

"Receiving Mary's feedback on my novel has been one of the best things that has happened to my writing in recent years. Thanks to her, I see the possibilities in my book and also feel like a fire has been lit under me to continue. I know the work is not yet done, but today—*today*—I feel like it's possible."

ANONYMOUS

facebook.com/goodstoryco
x.com/goodstoryco
instagram.com/goodstorycompany
linkedin.com/company/goodstorycompany
pinterest.com/goodstorycompany
tiktok.com/@goodstoryco
youtube.com/goodstory

INTRODUCTION

Picture books for today's young readers are vivid, imaginative, heartfelt, and a whole lot of fun to create. But the traditional publishing marketplace has also seen tremendous growth over the last quarter century, and aspiring modern picture book writers need to get up to speed with the contemporary publishing landscape—or risk being left behind.

Though I have spent over a decade working with picture book writers, I continue to be surprised when I hear, "How hard can it be? A picture book is *only* 600 words![1]"

Well, the truth is, writing an *irresistible* picture book is hard, but that's what makes it challenging, worthwhile, and very intriguing to learn about. *I'm* still learning.

I don't begrudge anyone the assumption that picture books are simple to create, but this is the first myth I want to bust.

---

1. The sarcasm is heavily implied with the "only," because the art and craft of picture books is far from simple. And, truthfully, most aspiring picture book writers don't even know that picture books are generally 600 words or fewer. We'll learn later that 600 is actually the upper range. A lot of draft manuscripts I see from beginners come in between 1,000 and 2,000 words.

Writers who have the opinion that picture books are either less complex than longer works, or somehow child's play (since they're intended for children), will have a tougher time thriving in today's picture book market. I probably don't have to convince you of this, because you've chosen to read a picture book guide and educate yourself, but I do want to set a very clear intention for our time together.

It's very possible to write irresistible picture books. In fact, with the research I offer here, I hope you'll see many opportunities to make original contributions to today's shelves. In that spirit, if crafting picture book stories at the highest level possible is your goal, consider making the following mindset shifts. They are:

- A deep and profound respect for—and understanding of—your target readership;
- A deep and profound respect for—and understanding of—the power of character and plot structure for young readers;
- A deep and profound desire to tell a good story, first and foremost; and
- The humility and maturity to:

>   learn new things;
>   play and experiment;
>   take feedback and advice;
>   revise and reframe;
>   pivot and cultivate perspective;
>   and finally, let go and move on, if necessary.

Why am I talking about letting go and moving on in the introduction to a writing and publishing guide? Shouldn't I be hyping you up to go on this tremendous journey with optimism and excitement?

Yes.

But.

As I hope you'll discover in these pages, there is so much richness and nuance in the picture book space that it demands richness and nuance from you as well.

About This Guide

To put this guide together, I analyzed 90 narrative picture books, 45 concept books, and 19 nonfiction picture books, for a total of 154 published books from shelves that I use as case studies and to support various craft lessons. How did I select these? Some of them were personal favorites I had lying around the house. I'll be perfectly honest, my bias as a parent and industry professional definitely played a role. But I also wanted to showcase very recently published projects, to make the ideas in this guide as contemporary and relevant as possible. So I did exactly what I'll advise you to do in Chapter 2 and headed to libraries and bookstores.

I looked at prominently displayed books, and those that caught my eye in other ways (everything from illustration style to title to the premise communicated by the marketing). This was not a very scientific process, I just checked stack after stack of picture books out until I felt like I had enough of a sample. I stayed mostly away from bestselling titles, as longevity on a bestseller list is not necessarily a guarantee of craft or quality. As such, I've missed some pretty obvious books, and also hit some unexpected "hidden gem" projects that I wouldn't have otherwise discovered.

To be clear, I was very methodical about my analysis of each work, but my project selection rubric was looser, and reflective of my own personality. I do bring over a decade of children's publishing experience to the process, but I can only describe this part of my research as, "Whatever caught Mary's eye." Whether that makes it less or more useful is up to you. I'll tell you one thing for certain—I had a blast doing it.

But analyzing already-published books was only the first component of my original research. Because I'm also very curious about the upcoming picture book market that we might expect to see in the next few years, I then read through and evaluated 1,000 picture book deal memos for titles that were acquired by traditional publishing houses between May 2022 and May 2023. These books will be released in 2024 and beyond.

With this methodical review of picture books, past and future, which I will dissect in great detail throughout this guide, I hope to present one of the most comprehensive discussions of the picture book market and writing craft for *today's* aspiring children's book creators.

I want to help you create actionable goals as a writer and a potential published author, and I think setting expectations is crucial, too. The sooner the better. This includes setting expectations for this book you're holding in your hands. My primary target audience with this guide is people who are writing (or interested in writing) children's picture books. There is a heavy fiction focus, though I do discuss concept books in Chapter 7, and nonfiction picture books in Chapter 8. A lot of the advice here slants toward traditional publishing, though self-publishing is explored in Appendix A.

My reasoning for these choices is simple—most of the writers I talk to about picture books are writing fiction and aiming for traditional publication. There are many ways to craft content for children, and there are more publishing options available now than ever before. But fiction manuscripts geared toward traditional publication are going to be my main focus here, and I hope that's yours as well. If not, or you're approaching the market from a different angle, I still think you will learn a lot.

Together, we will explore every major topic relevant to picture book writing and publishing in at least some detail, and we will do a deep dive into what I've identified as the most important craft components.

Who am I to guide you on your journey?

I started out in publishing over a decade ago, as a lowly slush pile reader at a boutique literary agency in Tiburon, California. From there, I got my foot in the door as a reader, and eventually a literary agent, at one of the nation's leading children's book agencies, Andrea Brown. There, I got to learn from some of the greatest names in the business. I started blogging about children's writing and publishing at Kidlit.com in 2009 and am a published author myself. *Writing Irresistible Kidlit: The Ultimate Guide to Crafting Fiction for Young Adult and Middle Grade Readers*, geared toward the middle grade and young adult markets, was released in 2012 by Writer's Digest Books, which was later acquired by Penguin Random House. I published *Successful Query Letters: 40+ Real World Query Letters With Literary Agent Feedback* in 2023.

When I left agenting, I started Mary Kole Editorial, and have been advising writers and authors in all stages of their careers as a private editor since 2013.

In 2020, I began developing projects in the IP (intellectual property) space, meaning that I originate and refine book ideas, from concept to publication. I am partner at two separate "IP development" or "book packaging" companies and sit on the board for a third.

We come up with concepts for stories in a collaborative "writers' room" setting, flesh them out into comprehensive outlines, attach a writer for hire to create a partial proposal or complete manuscript, and submit projects to publishers to attract book deals.

My partners have been literary agents, *New York Times*-bestselling authors, film and television entertainers, publishing house executives at the director level and above, as well as many, many aspiring and published writers. We've done adult, new adult, young adult, middle grade, chapter book, and, yes, picture book projects in collaboration, and have sold over $1M worth of properties, as of this writing.

I've also done "white label" IP development internally on a for-hire basis within major publishers. This means a publisher approaches us, looking for development help on an idea that they can't seem to get off the ground. This way of creating stories has taught me as much—if not more—than all my years in the writing, agenting, and editing worlds.

By approaching projects from a premise standpoint first, I've learned that there are many ways to get an idea into print, and that collaboration is key to doing this successfully, on any kind of scale. This work has also taught me that open-mindedness, curiosity, and the ability to *pivot* are key to making a real go of thriving in today's publishing and entertainment industries.

Make no mistake, books are entertainment, competing for the same hours and eyeballs as Netflix and social media. (Picture books deal with this competition a bit less acutely than other book categories because your target audience members don't yet have smart phones, but the distractions vying for their attention are still very real.)

Books are also products. There can sometimes be an uneasy dissonance between the ideas of art and commerce. Certain aspiring writers don't like to admit that they want to be commercially successful, in addition to creating beautiful masterpieces of the heart. Others couldn't care less about the book—all they see are dollar signs. (These creators are likely to be disappointed in the picture book publishing business, alas.)

The perceived difference between art and business is a false dichotomy, and you risk hurting your future career chances by buying into this mentality of "us" (the artists) vs. "them" (the sell-outs). Thinking like this, or clinging to anything stubbornly, without keeping your mind open, will only hurt you in the end.

In my editorial questionnaire, which I send to all potential inquiring clients, I ask the following:

If you allow yourself to dream, what does success look like for you with this project?[2]

Would you believe it? Most of the people interested in paid editorial services want a few very specific things:

1. *New York Times* bestseller status
2. To quit their jobs and write
3. A film deal, preferably with an A-list actor attached or producing

Am I here to talk you out of dreaming big and having robust goals? Absolutely not. But I *am* here to unpack what these goals actually mean in reality, and what it might take to achieve them. There is often an acute disconnect between writing expectation and publishing reality, which we will need to bridge.

---

2. I phrase this question very specifically because, as we're learning, writing dreams can be relative.

Working on IP book projects from within the industry, I can tell you that when a good idea hits the submission wire (or the publishing director's inbox), there is no barrier to entry. There is no rejection. There is no "no," or form letter, or doubt.

Literary agents, traditional publishers, and the book-buying public are hungry for marketable, contemporary, commercial work.

The Writing Journey

When I first got my book deal for *Writing Irresistible Kidlit*, I read the email from the acquiring editor, had a little cry, and called my boss at the time, the legendary Andrea Brown. (I called her even before I called my mom or partner!) I paced along my gingko-tree-lined block in Brooklyn, my heart thrumming, and told her the news.

Now, the thing about Andrea Brown is that she has done it all, seen it all, and she'll explain it all … even things you're not prepared to hear.

"That's great," she said, "but don't expect it to change your life."

I stopped pacing. *Huh*? A book deal had been my lifelong dream. Achieving it *would* change my life. That was the point.

To be clear, Andrea wasn't being cruel or even insensitive. She was being honest. And she was right. Writing that book and having it available for purchase so that a printed version of me could advise thousands of writers—*did* change everything. I am immensely grateful that I've had the opportunity to live on people's writing reference shelves and counsel them about story, character, and the publishing landscape.

But it didn't actually *change my life* to have a book published. I am still an aspiring writer in my head. (Multiple people, over the years, have had to remind me that I'm actually a published author.) I still drink too much coffee and shop compulsively and experience challenges in my personal relationships. Some days, I still don't see myself as a creator. I've been personally involved in *millions* of dollars' worth of book deals with almost every major publishing house. Yet I still doubt myself and my work.

Selling my own book didn't change my life in the sense that it was a one-and-done pursuit, a box to check, or a goalpost that never moved again. Instead, it was just the beginning of a much longer, bigger, and more interesting journey than I could've ever imagined. Now I'm sharing what I've learned specifically about the children's book publishing industry and the category[3] of picture books.

Reframing Success

"Success" can be a tricky notion, and it means different things to different people. It also changes from project to project, which I didn't realize until I'd seen the publishing process in action over many years, in the careers of friends, clients, and colleagues.

In writing—and publishing, specifically—there is no destination, there's only the journey. You need to decide what you want from your writing life. Is it going to be a hobby? Do you write primarily for yourself? Will you produce self-published projects for a small group of friends and family? Or are you gunning for a traditional publishing contract, and then another one, and then another one, until you're Jane Yolen?

---

3. This term is also used very intentionally. Read on to find out why in Chapter 1.

All of these goals are valid. They can also evolve gradually. Sometimes they change from one project to another. Sometimes they take a complete and sudden left turn. If you want to have a long life in letters, that's completely up to you. But if you want to have a writing career validated by traditional publishing gatekeepers, you need to learn your craft, read widely, practice your writing and idea-creation skill set, and continually level up. There will be highs and lows, but perhaps the most important decision you must make at this point is to *commit*.

I suggest that you dream big, but also keep your short-term, medium-term, and even long-term goals flexible. All the while, strive to be open-minded, open-hearted, and confident that you can write, as long as you're willing to put in the work and remain nimble and curious.

In fact, I got my graphic designer to make me a sticker, which you will see below. (All of the merchandise in the Good Story Company store starts as some kind of inside joke, then I go overboard and make a shirt or sticker. I don't expect to please anyone but myself, but sometimes, I hit on something that has legs.)

I've shared this image at writer's conferences and put in on slides while presenting talks and webinars. Once, I even got a group of mostly Mormon writers to wear this image on buttons. (Some attendees crossed the swear word out with Sharpie, which made it even more fun to see this modified slogan floating around the conference on people's lanyards.) This is the sticker:

I love it when writers can buy into this ethos and take themselves less seriously, even if they're deeply devoted to their craft. Too often, I see creators clinging to a project—or to the execution of an idea—when it's clear that something isn't working. Writers who clutch their original vision without any possibility of outside feedback, who struggle with marrying the concepts of art and business, who think picture books are "only 600 words" and therefore easy, and who believe they already know everything ... might not enjoy this guide.

But if you're intrigued to learn all about writing irresistible picture books, read on. I promise that I will honor your artistic integrity, while also making a case for a writing career where you can be successful and still surprise yourself along the way.

Our journey starts with learning the market, inside and out. Let's go!

ONE
CURRENT PICTURE BOOK MARKET OVERVIEW

THE GREAT—AND sometimes frustrating—news about the picture book market is that it is very specific. Did you catch that I intentionally called picture books a "category" in the introduction? When you start learning about the children's book publishing landscape, the last thing you want to do is call every book intended for young readers a "children's book." Why?

There are at least six major categories of books for children within most publishing programs. They are:

- Board book
- Picture book
- Early reader / easy reader / stepped reader
- Chapter book
- Middle grade
- Young adult

For our purposes, we will be focusing primarily on picture books, but for the sake of comprehensiveness, I'll touch upon the bordering categories of board books and early readers toward the end of this chapter. For now, let's establish a foundational understanding of the picture book market.

To set the tone, I want to share this lovely quote from *Show & Tell: Exploring the Fine Art of Children's Book Illustration* by Dilys Evans:

Children's books have never looked better or been more important. They are one of the few quiet places left where a child can go to be alone, and to travel worlds past, present, and future. They are often the first place children discover poetry and art, honor and loyalty, right and wrong, sadness and hope. And it is there between the pages that children discover the power of their own imaginations.[1]

Picture Book Basics

You're about to read a lot of rules about this category. This part doesn't feel very fun, but I do want to caution you against ignoring the foundational guidelines of the children's book market, especially if you're just starting out.

Why? Isn't creativity the driving force behind writing a book?

Yes.

But.

Ideally, you will learn the rules first, internalize story structure, and then, if you have a very good reason for doing so, break those same rules intentionally. Breaking rules out of

---

1. Dilys Evans, *Show & Tell: Exploring the Fine Art of Children's Book Illustration*, 7. Full citations can be found in Appendix C.

stubbornness and ignorance is very different from breaking rules out of a sense of innovation.

The guidelines for children's books exist because we are working within some very specific parameters. Picture books are either **read aloud by adults** or **read independently by novice readers** who are not yet confident in their skills.

This idea informs everything from character age to word choice to word count to page count in this category.

Picture books are, as mentioned in the introduction, usually fewer than 600 words long. There is furious debate about this, but if you're getting into longer word counts, I'd strongly suggest either streamlining your idea, leaving room for illustrations in your writing (which we'll discuss in Chapter 15), or pivoting into another children's book category.

Your target age groups for picture books are:

- **Younger**: ages zero to two (overlaps with board books)
- **General**: ages three to five
- **Older**: ages five to seven (overlaps with early readers)

There are always exceptions to these basic guidelines, of course. For example, I'm an adult, and I read picture books all the time.

In general terms, your readers (or listeners, and we'll dive into this distinction shortly) are kids, which means your characters are also kids. Or childlike kid analogues (animals and objects who behave like children). Adult protagonists, perspectives, and points of view are very rare in contemporary fiction picture books.

Picture books are generally 32 or 40 pages long, including front matter and back matter, as well as endpapers, whether self-ended or pasted down. (This has to do with how the book is printed, and we'll dive deeply into the logistics in Chapter 16.) This generally leaves most 32-page separate-ended books with approximately 14 usable spreads, or 28 pages. Most 32-page self-ended books have about 12 usable spreads, or 24 pages. Similarly, 40-page separate-ended books offer 18 usable spreads, or 36 pages. Self-ended versions have 16 usable spreads, or 32 pages.

Where did 32 and 40 come from? Why is the total number of available pages not 21 or 37? Traditionally, picture books are bound in "signatures," or folded bundles of paper that have eight spreads each. These are folded in half, creating 16 pages, and two of these bundled together equal 32 pages.

That means we can go down to 26 pages, though this is quite rare, or up to 40, 48, 56, or 64 pages, in eight-page increments. You will see some nonfiction picture books intended for older readers clocking in at 64.

But generally, 32- or 40-page projects are the gold standard, so I'd stick to these lengths when you're developing your first few ideas. Books in these formats look "friendlier" to an acquiring editor who's considering how much it'll cost to produce each copy, and to the literary agent, who wants a more attractive pitch.

Books with more pages per copy are:

- more expensive to produce, especially since full bleed color printing is expected;
- wider on shelves, meaning bookstores can stock fewer books—or sales opportunities—per inch of space; and
- more costly per copy to ship and warehouse.

I'm not trying to be a buzzkill or force anybody into a creative cage. You can, of course, write a 500-page picture book for middle-aged cat lady audiences, but will it be considered a picture book, in that case? Or is it simply a book with pictures? And what are your odds of traditionally publishing such a manuscript within the established market?

Try a picture book story that's intended for a 32-page format first, and then deviate from that if you absolutely have to. You can also gain credibility for yourself after publishing a few projects successfully, which makes it easier to argue for a different format or premium options like glitter printing, box sets with merchandise, the use of die cuts or paper engineering, etc. (See Chapter 7 for more on this.)

Every one of these very desirable things is expensive, and if you require any or all of these extras to pull off your idea, you're giving publishers reasons to say "no," especially if you are an aspiring debut.

A lot of writers interested in self-publishing are attracted to creative freedom, as they don't want anyone telling them what to do. This is totally valid. However, the standard reading experience that audiences expect from picture books has been set by traditionally published works. You are competing with those expectations when you intentionally or unintentionally deviate from them, even in a self-published project. Sometimes this will be widely accepted, sometimes not.

There's consensus, more or less, about standard target audience age, book format, and page count in the picture book world.

The ongoing controversy?

Word count, as I've alluded to a few times already.

Here are the standard word count guidelines for picture books, and a few adjacent categories, for good measure:

- **Board Books**: 100 words or fewer
- **Young Picture Books** (ages three to five): 400 words or fewer
- **Older Picture Books** (ages five to seven): 600 words or fewer
- **Nonfiction Picture Books** (ages five to seven): 1,500 words or fewer, excluding the back matter, glossary, teacher/parent/author note, etc.
- **Nonfiction Picture Books** (ages seven to nine): 3,000 words or fewer, excluding the back matter, glossary, teacher/parent/author note, etc.
- **Early Readers** (ages five to seven): 1,500 words or fewer (this seems to take a step back in word count, which I'll explain later in this chapter)

This is where a lot of aspiring writers wail and gnash their teeth. But it's also a hill I will choose to die on, because it really is *that* important.

In fact, my original research uncovered the following word count totals:[2]

- The shortest was a narrative picture book, at 21 words (*Meow!* by Victoria Ying, and get ready to hear about this one a lot)—I excluded all of our wordless books from word count analysis, so as not to skew the averages;
- The longest was a nonfiction picture book, at 1,842

---

2. If you're curious, I've included a list of the word counts for every published project I analyzed, found in Appendix C. Yes, I sat there and counted words. As such, a few of the numbers might be off by one or two, because it's really strenuous and mind-numbing to sit and count hundreds of picture book words. But I can tell you with 100% honesty that this represents my best good-faith effort to get accurate numbers. There isn't a centralized database of published book word counts out there, alas, or I would be all over it.

words (*Mother of Sharks* by Melissa Cristina Marquez, illustrated by Devin Elle Kurtz)—I excluded the back matter word count here, so the complete text is longer, more on that in Chapter 8;

- 34 books had word counts over 600 (6 of those were nonfiction), or 22.8% of the total books analyzed. I separated my word count averages into two categories:

> Books with fewer than 600 words, and
> Books with more than 600 words;

- In books with fewer than 600 words, the average word count was **317.21 words**; and
- In books with more than 600 words, the average word count was **876.41 words**.

Let's pause here for a moment. The average narrative picture book length from the cohort of manuscripts with 600 words or fewer?

317.21 words!

Look at that number again!

That's right. I have already been preparing you to mentally embrace a 600-word manuscript, and now I'm telling you to halve that number. And I sleep just fine at night.

The Main Types of Picture Books

There are also four distinct types of picture books to consider, and it's important to remember that, for our purposes, this guide will primarily be talking about narrative stories.

Aside from narrative projects, there are picture books called concept books (discussed in Chapter 7), which don't generally feature a traditional character-driven story. There are also nonfiction picture books (discussed in Chapter 8), which sometimes don't take a narrative storytelling approach—but sometimes they do. There can be considerable overlap between these types of ideas, as narrative picture books can also teach or have a concept element to them. It helps to become familiar with these frameworks as you learn about the picture book landscape, since this is how a lot of industry professionals discuss the manuscripts that they acquire and bring to market.

The majority of projects bought and sold today, and what we think of as standard picture books are, indeed, traditional character- and plot -driven narrative picture books. But let's also define three more types of picture books that you might encounter or want to write.

Craft Definitions:

Narrative Picture Book: A story-driven fiction picture book with character, plot, and theme. This is also the primary type of picture book discussed in this guide.

Concept Picture Book: A picture book that expresses a specific concept, or presents an idea, sometimes with a narrative element, but often without. We'll dive into this category in Chapter 7.

Nonfiction Picture Book: A picture book that explains a specific topic in detail. There is an organizational structure, but often no narrative element.

Narrative Nonfiction Picture Book: A picture book that explains a specific topic in detail, using narrative elements for organizational purposes, and applying fiction storytelling tools to a nonfiction topic. We'll dive into both nonfiction types in Chapter 8.

Does learning these guidelines—and that most picture books are the narrative type, formatted for 32 or 40 pages, aimed for ages three to seven, and containing 600 words or fewer—take all of the creative fun out of it for you?

You might find yourself wondering if the picture book market is, indeed, the right fit for your self-expression dreams. What about those board books and early readers I mentioned earlier? Good question. Let's explore these categories briefly so that you can make more informed decisions when you sit down to write a children's book.

Board Books

One of my favorite consulting jobs involves helping aspiring writers target the correct category for their work, or potentially offering a gentle redirect if they *believe* they've written one thing, but their manuscript is actually a stronger fit for a different target audience or format.

Since publishing *Writing Irresistible Kidlit,* which tackles the middle grade and young adult fiction markets, I have probably been asked "Is my project MG or YA?" thousands of times. And I love this question, because it allows me to bring my market knowledge to bear on the writer's vision, and help them pick the right category to pursue.

I strongly believe that there are a few crucial choices that all writers must make about their projects, and the sooner those decisions crystalize, the better. Target category *can* change during revision, but switching horses after the first draft can create enormous ramifications. If you can nail down the following points before you start writing, or during your initial drafting phase, your life will be a whole lot easier. They are:

- Target audience and category (this will give you clear guidelines to follow, especially about character age and development, language, and word count);
- Tense (present or past are your main options in most children's books); and
- POV ("point of view," generally first person or close third, though sometimes a different perspective is used, like second-person direct address, as we see in *Your Alien* by Tammi Sauer, illustrated by Goro Fujita).

For picture books, the consequences of changing POV or tense after the first draft aren't terribly dire. If you change tense while revising an 80,000-word novel, you're in for a slog. But you might still want to consider making solid choices about the above, sooner rather than later. (I'll discuss tense and POV more in Chapter 14.)

Zeroing in on your intended target audience is a more consequential decision. My favorite anecdote about matching target audience to book content involves a writer who approached me with an alphabet book verging on 3,000 words. I'm not joking.

If you don't realize why this is funny, consider the general age of the child who is learning the alphabet. They can't read yet. Most alphabet books—board books, especially—are 26 words long and feature a lot of pictures. The kid who's capable of reading a 3,000-word manuscript, or sitting still and focusing long enough to have one read to them, is absolutely not the same child working on their alphabet skills. An ABC book should not be 3,000 words because there's a huge disconnect between content and audience.

So what's appropriate for those youngest readers?

The category below picture book is board book, and it is very rare to debut with a board book original. A lot of picture book writers dream of having their work printed on solid board and gummed on by babies, though, and they often see popular picture book titles in this format. So why is it hard to get there?

Overwhelmingly, these books start out as picture books first and are acquired and initially published as such. In fact, most picture book publishing contracts will have provisions for putting the property into board book format, too, but it'll start out as a picture book.

Original board books are rarer, unless you're writing a concept book that is exceptionally tailored to the board book audience. For example, short primers—on the alphabet, shapes, or colors—are a natural fit for board book publication because they teach very simple concepts and are appropriate for the age of child they're targeting.

Board books can sometimes also have different formats and layouts. Board originals can have fewer pages, while picture books translated into a board format can resemble a separate-ended 32-page picture book. (We'll learn more about picture book layouts in Chapter 16.)

It's also important to note that a lot of original board books are developed in-house. Why pay an outside creator to choose stock photos to represent each color of the rainbow when a publisher can get an intern or salaried graphic designer to do that without paying an advance?

This might seem mercenary, but publishers have tremendous overhead—which is one of the biggest issues with the traditional publishing business model. I'm here to give you a realistic sense of the industry, even if it means bursting a few bubbles. Most board books are either adapted from a picture book, or developed internally.

If you aspire to board book fame, Sandra Boynton-style, your route forward will likely be through selling picture book publishing rights with a board book clause included, developing a relationship with your editor, then pitching some original ideas intended for board.

Early Readers

The category above picture book is the early reader, easy reader, or stepped reader. All of the major children's imprints have a dedicated program for these books, and each has a brand name, hence the interchangeable and confusing terminology.

If you've been looking at these tiny spines in your bookstore or library and getting excited to develop a slightly older (in terms of audience) and longer (in terms of word count) manuscript from your picture book idea, I have some more shoot-the-messenger news for you.

It can be exceedingly tough to debut in the early reader space as well, especially if you're coming off the street with an original idea. There is a very specific route into this market that some writers take, and it's not the standard traditional publishing path of getting an agent and making a sale, which I describe in Chapter 18.

The issues that plague the board book space are very similar to those in the early reader market. Namely, the ideas for these books tend to come internally from the publisher, or from licensing partners.

You've maybe noticed that a lot of early readers feature beloved media characters, or are yet another installment of a long-running series like *Fancy Nancy*, originally by Jane

O'Connor, illustrated by Robin Preiss Glasser. Yes, these ideas were unique, standalone brainchildren once, but now they're multimedia properties that have all kinds of TV shows and merchandizing attached to them.

Will a publisher want to acquire (and pay for) an original early reader manuscript from a debut author with an unproven concept, then try to market it and potentially turn it into a series? Or will they stick to a tried-and-true license?

There are a number of obstacles to successfully breaking out an original early reader:

- The spines on these books are very narrow, and the titles do not tend to stand out on shelves as a result;
- their retail price points are very low; and
- they have very specific (and much stricter) word count guidelines, language restrictions, and syntax expectations, as discussed in Chapter 14.

This last point merits attention. Early readers are really where academic reading and writing standards like Lexile scores come into play, as books in this category are very tightly graded in up to six individual reading skill levels. Every house has their own criteria and style guide for them. Like picture books, they are generally 32 pages long, but some can go up to 48 pages, or even 64, by the final "step" of the publisher's early reader framework.

Publishers must put in a lot of effort to screen for, acquire, and invest in an original early reader property. Or they can go back to the well and exploit their low-hanging fruit. Specifically, various publishing and media conglomerates might already have a license for *Dora the Explorer*, for example, and can easily print yet another familiar adventure from a beloved character.

Instead of contracting with a new writer and training them up, publishers know they can instead get this new installment written in-house—by someone fully versed in the guidelines, who is already being paid a salary—or by a trusted freelancer they've contracted with before.

There is some opportunity for writers to break into this category via a freelance pool. But you would need to be very well versed in the writing guidelines for early readers, and comfortable engaging on a work-for-hire basis. Some writers get connected to opportunities while employed in staff positions at houses, and others are approached with jobs by their agents. Otherwise, the early reader category, and finding a viable route into it, can be quite opaque.

All this said, most children's writers don't break into the industry with board books or early readers. Instead, they keep their mortgages and rent paid by picking up ad hoc writing projects in these categories, or they expand into these markets by selling a picture book property that's subsequently translated into different formats.

Board books aren't simply short picture books (unless they are literally adapted picture book titles) and early readers aren't simply slightly longer picture books or "a great way to repurpose my picture book text if I simply can't get it under 600 words." These are distinct publishing categories, yet they don't provide a lot of vibrant opportunities, especially for debut writers.

I consider both of them working harder, not smarter, especially if you're looking to sell your first book.

Picture Storybooks

You may have also heard or seen reference to the "picture storybook" publishing category. Writers will sometimes pitch their project as a "storybook." Both of these terms refer to longer manuscripts of up to 2,000 words, and layouts that combine full-page illustrations with text on the opposite side. (We'll talk more about illustrations and text configurations in Chapter 16.)

Sometimes the manuscript is within that shorter 600-word range, but the separation of text and illustrations, as well as more image-driven or descriptive writing, are hallmarks of this category.

This explanation appears in the picture book guide, *Writing with Pictures: How to Write and Illustrate Children's Books* by Uri Shulevitz, which was geared mostly toward aspiring illustrators and published in 1985:

> A *story book* tells a story with words. Although the pictures amplify it, the story can be understood without them. The pictures have an auxiliary role, because the words themselves contain images.[3]

Madeline by Ludwig Bemelmans is a great example of this style, as are many Dr. Seuss books. Both of those franchises are classics, so what's the problem?

Unfortunately, this format has gone out of favor in the last few decades. As you'll hear over and over (if you haven't gotten the message already), word counts are shrinking. Picture book layouts are also being designed in such a way that the text is overlaid on full-bleed art. If you pitch your project as a "picture storybook," you might unintentionally

---

3. Uri Shulevitz, *Writing with Pictures: How to Write and Illustrate Children's Books*, 15.

send up a red flag to agents and publishers that you are operating with an outdated idea of the market.

I'd strongly suggest aiming for a more contemporary format, and getting that word count down, rather than trying to pitch a category, like "storybook," that publishers have largely abandoned, aside from legacy properties or projects by well-known authors. (I'll discuss other reasons you might sometimes see exceptions to these and other guidelines in Chapter 6.) Your case might be stronger if you assume that these options and alternatives aren't open to you as an aspiring debut.

Adhering to Guidelines

So let's say you're now convinced that you'll pay more attention to target audience, category, word count, and all of the other nitty-gritty rules of picture books. But you're starting to feel creatively stifled by it all. Why can't you just tell a great story and let the world fall in love with it?

Great question. I don't like handing down unilateral information without explaining myself, so let's dig a bit deeper here. In the picture book category, you are limited by:

- the **attention span**
- **breath capacity**
- **reading ability** of your target audience (and their caregivers)

First, young kids are notorious for having short attention spans. Toddlers, preschoolers, and early elementary students have a naturally tough time concentrating on something, even if they love it. This is developmentally appropriate, but it also means that they aren't able to focus for a long period and retain information, especially if they are being read to, rather than doing the reading themselves.

When we read a story firsthand, we tend to be more grounded in it. When it is read to us secondhand, it's a distinct experience, and the information is processed differently. This relates to an individual's preferred learning style, as well. This is why illustrations are a core component of picture books—they reach readers via a different channel.

I once talked to a very notable publishing insider (a literary agent) who wrote a bestselling picture book. She, with some chagrin, confided that she always told writers to keep it to 600 words or fewer. But with her own book, she simply couldn't trim the story down. The manuscript clocked in at 1,100 words.

And the takeaway?

She realized that this was far too long, and that she could've made many small (and a few large) cuts and still maintained the story's integrity.

How did she learn this?

After doing her first book reading at a bookstore (!), once the book was already published (!!), as she kept running out of breath (!!!), and watching her audience start to squirm by the story's midpoint (!!!!). There's a reason I suggest reading your work aloud in Chapter 14.

So, can you write a 10,000-word picture book? Sure thing. You can literally do whatever the hell you want. Will it be as potentially traditionally successful as a 600-word one? Probably not. This has to do with the scope of your idea, how the story is expressed to and internalized by a child in your target audience age range, and the publishing format of a standard picture book.

Once you get over the initial overwhelm and knee-jerk reaction to such a restrictive word count, you'll see that there is real intentionality and logic behind this advice, and it's not done to alienate writers or punitively curb anyone's enthusiasm.[4]

There are always going to be exceptions to any rule. I'll sit here and wait while you go find them on your very own bookshelf. I know them, too. I love them. They are traditionally published, and some are very successful, despite breaking Rule Y or Rule Z.

But if you're really interested in pursuing your picture book writing dreams in a strategic way, and working smarter, not harder, you will want to at least try writing a few manuscripts that fit the guidelines I'm discussing here.

We'll build on all of these foundational ideas throughout this guide, but I wanted to get on the—bad publishing joke incoming—same page on some of these more important elements, sooner rather than later.

Let these concepts percolate for a while. Learn the lay of the land of picture book publishing. Consider the confusing but also formative life experience of your target reader. Dwell on these things, and see how they might come together into a unique understanding of the picture book story (or stories!) that you want to tell.

Then … spend your lunch hour banging out a picture book manuscript. And make it 601 words, because you're reasonable and want to succeed, but also a bit of a rebel.

Well, no. Not quite yet.

First, you'll want to gather up the whole magical brew that's

---

4. Can you tell I have this conversation/argument a lot?

happening inside your head and take it to a library or independent bookstore. Don't actually think about doing it and then never get around to it. Don't just think it sounds like a good idea and then go back to writing a picture book the hard way.

Actually do it.

Now.

TWO
READ BEFORE WRITING

THE PICTURE BOOK landscape has changed a lot in the last twenty years, and especially in the previous decade. We're practically in a different picture book universe that existed when the mainstay in everyone's nursery, *Goodnight Moon* by Margaret Wise Brown, illustrated by Clement Hurd, was published by Harper & Row (now HarperCollins) in 1947.

Don't get me wrong, that book was groundbreaking when it came out, and it heralded the start of an entire industry.[1] But if your knowledge of the market is limited to *Goodnight Moon*, or if you last read a picture book when your own kids or grandkids were in diapers, it's time to get reacquainted with this category as it exists now.

---

1. For some really great historical insight into the children's book publishing industry, check out Leonard S. Marcus's *Dear Genius: The Letters of Ursula Nordstrom*, a collection of letters from Ursula Nordstrom, the editor who championed books like *Goodnight Moon* and *Where the Wild Things Are* by Maurice Sendak. Some would say that she launched the entire children's book market as we know it.

Ideally, you'll do this *before* you write your own manuscript. Because we ain't "in the great green room"[2] anymore.

Contemporary picture books are lively, creative, *beautifully* illustrated (ahem, unlike *Goodnight Moon*, ahem) and speak to contemporary issues experienced by contemporary children —though in a subtle way, of course, as we'll discuss in Chapter 5.

Have I said "contemporary" enough? Are you catching my drift?

The only way to get access to this playing field is to know what the field is doing. And the only way to know what the field is doing is to read books that have come out in the last few years. If you're still resonating with '70s, '80s, and '90s standouts like *Elizabeth and Larry* by Marilyn Sadler, illustrated by Roger Bollen, *Martha Speaks* by Susan Meddaugh, *Imogene's Antlers* by David Small, or the oeuvre of Dr. Seuss, that's fine. Me too!

But I'm also making a concerted effort to analyze the current market, because even books being published *today* were acquired two or three years ago. That means publishing industry tastes and trends have already moved on by the time first editions of the most current stories arrive on shelves. Publishing has an incredibly long lead time, especially for heavily illustrated projects, like picture books. Patience is a virtue to learn early on if you're hoping to play this game successfully. You will need it.[3]

---

2. Margaret Wise Brown, *Goodnight Moon*, 2-3.

3. If you figure out how to deal with this excruciating pace of doing business, please tell me how you did it. I am still constantly amazed by how slowly things move in this industry, especially compared to other sectors, like tech. Yes, I grew up in the Silicon Valley and rejected the career path that most of my peers chose. (Sorry, Mom!)

Am I suggesting that you only study the current market and try to copy what you see there?

Should you subsume your creativity and chase trends instead?

Are you not allowed to have a unique idea?

Am I peddling groupthink?

What kind of monster am I, anyway?

No, no, no, no, and you'll have to ask my husband for a detailed analysis on that last one.

I'm not saying that market trends are the end-all, be-all. But we *are* going to be talking about the traditional publishing landscape, and making intentional decisions based on certain guidelines. In essence, I've already outed myself as a rule-following automaton of Big Publishing.

That's simply because I know a lot of writers are interested in traditional notions of success—ideally with a literary agent and major house—and for that, you will want to at least track what the big players are up to. This is a good time to reiterate that there are many paths to success. There is no one roadmap, and your creative strategy can change from year to year, and even book to book.

I generally recommend a website called Publishers Market-place when writers are researching literary agents and approaching submission, but you can access it whenever you want a straight shot of publishing news, gossip, and the most comprehensive deals database available. A lot of industry professionals, like agents and editors, check PM every morn-ing, looking at what their peers and competitors are doing—or will be doing within the next few years. It's not perfect, but there's no better insider resource available. This will become very relevant in Chapter 6, and my analysis of upcoming picture book topics.

Your job now is to learn a little bit about picture books, whether you take the obsessive path and dive right into Publishers Marketplace, or you do a reconnaissance trip to read what's on shelves today. In the broadest possible terms, educating yourself and seeing what your published peers—who are a few steps ahead of you—are doing is never a bad thing. So head to the library or independent bookstore. The great news is twofold:

- There are people out there who specialize in what's being published *right now* in any given category. They're called booksellers and librarians. (If you want a bit more guidance or to bring them a list of books to start the conversation, you can't go wrong with the most recent ALA award winners!); and
- Picture books are delightfully easy to read—even a stack of 50 shouldn't take you more than a few hours.

That's honestly what I suggest doing, too. Go to your local independent bookstore or library, grab a huge pile of picture books, and go through them. (Just make sure to clean up after yourself to the best of your ability, and if you're in a store, buy something. You don't want to do this and then leave a Leaning Tower of PB for some poor librarian. What would a wise old finger-wagging adult in an outdated, moralizing picture book say about this kind of behavior?)

A few pretty obvious realizations will emerge when you do this (not *if*, *when*).

First, you will be enthralled by the colorful, vivid, imaginative, and very robust art form that is the contemporary picture book. I challenge you to read a stack of these things and walk away unimpressed. There are true geniuses working in this format. They are at the top of their game. Some of them are one award nomination from children's book superstardom.

In my editorial work, I'm always shocked to meet aspiring writers who do not read. This doesn't just happen in the picture book space, but I've noticed this phenomenon in this category. These well-meaning writers often look and sound like reasonable humans. But then they invariably say the thing about not wanting "to pollute their creative well by reading books," and I begin to doubt whether we really occupy the same reality. Are we on a show? Am I being pranked? I understand this attitude in theory, but not in practice.

Read in your own category and outside of it. There's no excuse for not reading. Absolutely none. Especially when sitting down with a trove of picture books is such an utterly delightful way to spend an afternoon.

Second, when you read picture books, you will start to internalize their flow and structure. (That's why I analyzed so many when putting this guide together!) Even though picture books generally clock in at only 600 words or fewer, most manage tight, expansive, and multilayered narratives. Great picture book characters are fully realized humans (or human-analogue animals or entities, which I'll talk about more in Chapter 9). You'll also be treated to a depth of feeling and theme and universal resonance, as discussed in Chapter 4.

There's no better way to experience these craft concepts firsthand than to crunch through a big pile of published examples. You'll find yourself falling into a rhythm, recognizing some of the structural scaffolding that you'll read about in Chapter 12, and otherwise noticing patterns and moving parts in action.

Finally, you will also start to train your ear in picture book voice. While it's true that there isn't just one type of picture book voice, there are some common elements of writing for young people that we'll explore in Chapter 14. You'll notice humor and pathos and tone. You will see rhyme (a controversial topic also covered in Chapter 14) and rhythm (appropriate for prose as well), word choice, syntax, sentence length, dialogue, description … and a lack of description, too. The latter is what I mean when I'll tell you to leave room for illustrations in Chapter 15.

You shouldn't just be passively reading when you do this exercise. You should be trying to read like a writer—noticing things, figuring out the craft skills operating underneath the surface, and wondering how you might apply the same ideas to your own work. Picture book writers often generate many manuscripts in their lifetimes (not all of which will be successful, more on that in Chapter 18), so you never know when you'll want to use a writing idea, technique, or tool that you've discovered by doing this exercise.

Reading like a writer takes experience, and there's no better time to start than today. You should be studying the market before you participate in it, and you should then keep up with changes in the market once you learn it, even as a published author.

Your ideas will be your own, don't get me wrong. The voice and writing craft you hone will be unique to you. But it would do your potential readership a disservice if you didn't also pay attention to what publishers and peers are doing, because generations of kids might miss out on your creations, unless you work to be more informed.

In summary, it's very fun to learn the picture book market, it can happen quickly, and this research can be absolutely free, if you go to the library.

For bonus points, you might want to attend a few story hours to see picture books in action on a grand scale. (Libraries and bookstores often have programming and interactive story times for young readers, though it might be weird to attend without a child, so be sure to kidnap one from the grocery store parking lot first and BYOB.[4])

Think critically about what you're seeing as you interact with published works, especially if you have a rare opportunity to watch how a book lands with eager kid audiences. Which jokes hit, if applicable? When did the group's attention seem to wander? Which parts of a story seemed to engage young listeners? Where did the reader (usually a librarian, bookseller, or visiting author) stumble over their words or run out of breath?

You can and should use what you learn when crafting your own picture book stories, and we'll continue to deepen your understanding of the market in the next chapter.

---

4. Bring Your Own Baby, obviously. And I'm just kidding. Don't call the FBI. You should absolutely *not* kidnap a child. Ever. If you choose to kidnap a child and this book is in your purchase history, I want to clarify that I am joking. All this *hilarity* aside, if you do want to go to some bookstore or library events for young readers, you may want to tag along with friends who have young kids or grandkids. Don't wear a trench coat and dark glasses. Parents tend to be quite nervous, for good reason, so exist in these spaces respectfully.

THREE

READER RELATABILITY, CONNECTION, AND GATEKEEPER ISSUES

A LOT of the information in this chapter will hook into Chapter 1, where we learned about picture book market guidelines, Chapter 4, where we'll discuss theme, Chapter 6, which offers a giant list of topics, and the self-publishing conversation in Appendix A.

Hold onto your hats, because we're really doing a holistic overview of the entire category, including readers, writers, publishing gatekeepers, and the buying and reading end users for picture books.

Did you think children's books were all about pigeons driving busses and fancy little princesses? Here's where the rubber meets the road, and I hope you're excited, because thinking critically about your choices is what it's all about if you want to have a career (or a robust hobby) in this space.

Reader Relatability

First, let's talk about your readers. The kids you're writing for are your guiding lights (theoretically, more on this in a moment). Most of us have core memories of either cuddling on a loved one's lap with beautiful art spread in front of us or doing the same with our own children or other kids in our lives.

The experience of sharing a picture book with an excited youngster—or one who's desperately fighting bedtime—is one of the most pure and magical things that we're lucky enough to do as human beings. And how cool would it be to have your creation at the center of it all?

In order to take a very concerted shot at picture book success, you need to consider reader relatability. I'll walk you through some thoughts about what your target audience is experiencing in their day-to-day lives.

Picture books are all about character, and there's no better way to foster a positive reader-character relationship than by deeply understanding the mindset of your audience, first and foremost, then presenting a character they'll recognize.

Connection, relatability, and empathy are crucial picture book ingredients. If you've ever met a five-year-old, you know that they tend to care very deeply about the things they like. And dislike, too, even if it's just the blue water glass at dinner which, up until this moment, was their absolute favorite.

You have a story you care about, and likely a character who has inspired you to start writing. But you care about it because it's *your idea*. This is your creative baby. The caring and relatability are already baked in.

For you.

This is the same pivot I talk about with my memoir clients— you know the story, you relate to the story, you have made a lot of meaning from your story. (And in the case of memoir, it's literally *your story*.)

But at some point, if you want to share it with the world, you will have to turn *your story* into something that engages an outside reader. You need to connect that reader to your story and character in a way that makes *them* care.

The problem with picture books is that it's been a while since you were a five-year-old (I'm guessing), so it might be harder to remember the thoughts and feelings involved. And yet your goal is to eventually connect with young audiences, so character relatability is a priority. That's why it's so important to put yourself in a preschool mindset as you prepare to write for this age group.

Your Reader's Life Experience

Let's take a moment and think about what it's like to be a toddler, preschooler, or early elementary-aged kid. There are amazing parts to childhood, but there are also some thorny things that adults tend to forget with time.

Kids are told what to do all day long, by parents, grandparents, teachers, tutors, doctors, religious leaders, older siblings —hell, even younger siblings (if my own kids are any indication). They don't have the power to make many autonomous decisions, and this point will come up pretty frequently in this guide.

There's obviously a good reason for this. If kids called the shots, they'd skip school and eat marshmallows for dinner, then stay up all night playing video games. The guardrails and boundaries in a child's life are largely necessary. (If you're frustrated, as a writer, by being told to follow guidelines, channel that white-hot rage into a kid character who hates adhering to the rules!)

Even though grown-ups mean well with their guidance, this imbalanced dynamic between kids and the other people in their lives can leave children feeling disempowered. They want control over their environment and existence, but they don't often get it.

If you need a vivid example, try to pick out a toddler's outfit. If you get past the Gauntlet of the Socks, I cordially invite you to come help out at my house on busy weekday mornings. And may God have mercy on your soul if you put the Cheerios into the purple snack container instead of the green one.

For many reasons, books that talk down to or preach at these young readers are dead in the water (a lot more about this in Chapter 5). As are passive characters, and the wise adults/magical beings that solve all of their problems for them.

Young readers want a safe and playful—but also empowering —way to explore their feelings and conflicts. This is the foundation of a lot of the character and plot advice that will follow, starting in Chapter 9.

Furthermore, kids this age are exploring their personalities and identities, and getting their footing in a very interesting, complex, yet confusing world. They struggle with self-regulation and naturally want a lot of understanding and validation —even when they seem to push those very things away during a tantrum.

If you've missed the SEL (social-emotional learning) cultural movement because it was before your parenting or grandparenting time, you might want to read up on the basics. A lot of picture books in today's marketplace take a very intentional approach toward how children are portrayed, how themes and lessons are expressed, the process of rendering character thoughts, feelings, and choices on the page, and much more.

If you firmly believe that children are empty vessels that need to be filled with adult wisdom—I urge you to either throw this guide out of the nearest window, or open that window and let some fresh air into your thinking.

Anyone looking to be successful in today's picture book marketplace needs to respect their audience and be able to inhabit a young child's mindset.

Speaking of mindset, it's important to notice that your readers are no longer looking for mundane validation of their spark or greatness. "You're awesome!" isn't the final revelation of today's picture books.

It's the starting point.

Don't get me wrong, kids still struggle with all kinds of issues, including insecurity, a lack of courage and confidence, social trouble with their peers, or a turbulent home environment. However, today's picture books take the conversation beyond reinforcing that children are loved and unique. Your readers will know there's a bright light inside them, and contemporary picture books will focus on what to do with that light, ways to make it glow brighter, and how to shine it onto others.

Since I'm making a lot of generalizations here, remember that not all kids are the same. It is always frustrating to teach writing because every writer, project, and reader are different. Some of these broad-strokes thoughts are included here because I'm working to be comprehensive and useful to as many writers (and, eventually, audiences!) as possible. But do keep in mind that not everything I say will apply to you, and not everything might resonate.

We tend to talk about the picture book audience in the broadest terms, but children don't develop at the same rate (and this includes their reading skills, so a lot of picture books work to include reluctant readers or neurodivergent kids who have cognitive or learning differences). Children don't all feel the same way about everything. They don't make the same choices, or all need to learn the same things.

There are as many picture book ideas, characters, plots, and themes as there are children in the world. In order to write a compelling entry into this market, you will want to come up with an idea that's specific (rather than generic) and one that's compelling to a child as they learn and grow in these formative years.

Just as you can't be all things to all people in terms of premise, you also cannot please all kid readers or adult gate-keepers.

And in traditional picture book publishing, there are two types of gatekeepers, which a lot of writers don't consider.

Picture Book Gatekeepers, Part I

Many aspiring picture book creators think they're writing for children.

Oh, honey. That's cute.

There are actually many gatekeepers between you and kids: literary agents, publishing house editors, publishing house sales and marketing teams, book buyers at various resellers, and, finally, family members and educators.

Pay careful attention here. Publishers don't actually sell books to readers (though all do some form of direct-to-consumer sales). Publishers' customers are libraries, schools, museums, doctors' offices, and, of course, bookstores.

So let's talk about this first layer of gatekeepers, those who stand between you and seeing your picture book roll off the industrial press, illustrated, designed, printed, and bound.

Namely, literary agents and acquiring editors. (You'll have less direct access to sales and marketing teams, designers, and all of the other lovely people working within a publishing house. Your editor is really going to be your direct liaison, and your agent, if you have one.)

When they realize that gatekeepers stand in their way, some frustrated children's book writers gripe that they're not writing for children at all. They feel like they're trying to impress a bunch of publishing executives (a majority of them, white women in their thirties, forties, and fifties) who are many layers removed from the picture book target audience.

I've been asked the following question more than once: "Am I writing for kids, or am I writing for a bunch of adults sitting around in an office?"

It's a very insightful question, even if it can sometimes be tinged with bitterness after a rejection. I'm not sure my answer will be pleasing, though.

To get to those kids, through all the gatekeeping strata, you will need to gather allies in that office building first. (If your goal is to publish traditionally, of course.) And even though those agents and editors are decades removed from preschool, remember that they have chosen to work in children's publishing for a variety of reasons. They are likely more attuned to what kinds of books kids like than you might think.

In fact, that was one of the things that attracted me to publishing for young readers initially, in 2009, when I started blogging about children's book writing, submission, and publishing. There are surprisingly few true assholes in the kids' book business, and most people you'll meet are intensely mission driven. I was working in mobile gaming when I made the jump to children's books. Instead of peddling mindless entertainment, I wanted to help create tangible, beautiful, and important projects. Kidlit publishing people are, by and large, working to inspire generations of readers and shape art and letters for years to come.

In short, you *are* writing for kids, and your ideas for that specific audience should be your absolute north star, guiding the heart and soul of your work. But you're also writing for the people who make children's books happen—the literary agents, editors, and other publishing professionals.

That's not all, though. You're also targeting the sales and marketing representatives within houses, and then the book buyers at bookstores, libraries, and schools. Those are the people who actually place the orders and tell publishers what they'll stock.

All this is a very detailed way of saying that it's important to keep an eye on the industry itself. While it can be soul-crushing to chase trends, and impossible to try and forecast the next big thing, you shouldn't ignore the hidden layers of the picture book landscape.

You probably shouldn't resent them, either. Instead, try and gather intel into what these gatekeepers are looking for as part of your due diligence.

Picture Book Gatekeepers, Part II

Once we get past the production side of things, we can think about the dissemination of picture books to the end user. In this category, you're also writing for the people who make retail buying decisions. In no other publishing market is there such a profound disconnect between those who pay the bills and those who enjoy the product.

So as you develop a picture book idea with your target audience in mind, and start to inhabit the life experience and mindset of a preschooler or early elementary student, you also need to consider the decision-makers surrounding that child.

These are parents, grandparents, teachers, therapists, pediatricians, etc. In other words, all of the folks who can connect your book to young readers or block it from ever reaching them (as the Keepers of the Cash or Credit Cards).

In the picture book world, these adults are the ones handing books to kids. I don't suggest writing books that are only meant to please adults—that would be rather beside the point, and some very specific character and plot issues arise from this wrongheaded thinking, which I will discuss in Chapter 5.

But you need to be at least distantly aware that your book should be somewhat appealing to adults. *The Young Arsonist's Guide to Getting out of School … Forever* can only ever be an *ironic* picture book or gag gift, for example.

Sometimes, picture book writers put their kid characters into dangerous situations or include content in their work. By "content," I mean anything that would take a movie rating into PG-13 or R, like drug use, sex, violence, etc. You might not think that people are putting content in picture books, but you would be surprised.

This is not to deny that troubling situations happen to kids of all ages, and this is not to suggest that you should make everything sunshine and rainbows when writing children's books, but how you handle content on the page needs to be extremely light.

For example, the suggestion of a parent with problematic drinking habits can absolutely be included in a picture book, but it's done with a few words in the text or an empty bottle in illustrations. It is more implicit than explicit. (We'll dig into "issue books," or picture books that are primarily intended to deal with social and family issues, in Chapter 6.)

Let's take a less extreme example, though, to make this point. If your picture book shows kids modeling name-calling or sneaking out of their houses at night or doing something else that parents, grandparents, teachers, and doctors aren't going to love—even if actual kids do that activity all the time—you might struggle to place your book.

Even if the book's takeaway is that you shouldn't do this kind of thing.

Frustrating? Absolutely.

Let's imagine that you have written an anti-bullying book where the bully calls the protagonist names. The protagonist decides to avenge themselves and be proactive,[1] so they sneak out at night to execute a prank and teach the bully a lesson. The bully sees the error of their ways, and the moral is that bullying is bad.

So why are you having trouble getting traction with this manuscript?

Well, you're modeling name-calling, even if the villain character is doing it. You're also modeling sneaking out at night, taking revenge, and the unreasonable outcome that the bully learns a lesson once, and will never be mean to anyone again, ever. Even four-year-olds know life isn't so simple. Gatekeepers are going to look at this project askance because, while it has a moral high ground, sure, it is also unintentionally showing kids doing several bad behaviors, and it sets unrealistic expectations.

Is the protagonist supposed to just roll over and take the

---

1. Ordinarily, a proactive character is a great choice!

name-calling? No, that's not the solution, either. But they shouldn't be taught any unsavory self-defense strategies, as parents and teachers won't want even villains doing things that explicitly or implicitly model bad behavior. (I will gently suggest that the idea described here is past its expiration date, anyway, even if bullying is still at crisis levels. I'll discuss morals more and explain why in Chapter 5.)

Gatekeepers will examine your work very closely, and if it has —even unintended—negative elements associated with it that parents don't want to introduce to their young charges, they will not buy it. And they'll get on their Facebook mom groups and raise a stink, to boot. (I categorically disagree with book banning, to be clear, but it's at a fever pitch now, so to imagine that this phenomenon would never impact your well-intentioned but subtly problematic picture book manuscript is naïve.)

Another thing to notice is that many parents, grandparents, teachers, therapists and other decision-making purchasers in this gatekeeping layer are paying close attention to picture book topics, which we will discuss in Chapter 6.

A lot of parents, for example, shop for picture books to help them address common family and childrearing challenges. A new sibling, potty training, separation anxiety—you name it. There's opportunity there for you to present a fresh take on a useful family-oriented concept, sales hook, or story topic. Consider search keywords. If your book lends itself to being purchased to address a certain behavior, for example, you could build a keyword into your title, so that gatekeepers might find it more easily.

You obviously cannot and will not please everyone. A cogent discussion of whether or not today's climate of "cancel culture" is helpful to art and artists is beyond the scope of this guide. That being said, the purchasing gatekeeper layer is worth considering.

That fantasy of the easy-peasy 600-word manuscript dashed off during your lunch hour is starting to seem more and more nuanced, huh.

Well, good.

Because we're about to get right into the very marrow of the picture book craft and start developing the idea that could launch your career. And I recommend reverse engineering that premise from a writing craft term that sometimes get a bad shake: theme.

FOUR
UNIVERSAL THEMES

A THEME IS the underlying idea of a story, the focal core along which your project takes shape. Some novelists I work with don't tease out their book's theme until they've made it all the way through their first draft. This makes sense with a longer work because there are so many different strings to thread together.

Over the course of a novel, things fade in importance, or are emphasized, and the writer won't exactly know how it'll shake out until they've finished their 80,000 words. Others tell me that they don't truly figure out what their story is "about" until they write their query letter—a dreaded exercise that I'll discuss in Chapter 18.

And that's fine for novelists.

But with picture book projects, I recommend starting with theme, which is why I've laid this guide out to focus on theme as the first major craft topic.

Specifically for picture books, theme needs to be simple, clear, and universally relatable to as many kid readers as possible, even if the topic of a picture book is specific. Wait a minute, what's the difference between theme and topic or subject?

Craft Definitions:

Theme: The emotional resonance of a project. What the "book is about" on a deeper level, meant to be intuited from the story, rather than explained outright.

Topic: The literal subject of a project. What the "book is about" in an obvious way, since the character, plot, or moral of the story (or all of these elements combined) express it clearly.

I hope that clarifies things a bit. And, of course, if we go back to our discussion of the different picture book types in Chapter 1, we might also consider that some are theme-heavy (like narrative picture books) and some are subject-heavy (like concept books and nonfiction picture books). That being said, I think most projects have both.

Consider *They All Saw a Cat* by Brendan Wenzel. This amazing concept book has a narrative, sure, because it follows a boy and his cat on a walk in nature. But it also teaches a very valuable lesson (mainly via the shifting illustration style) about perspective. That is the topic. And the theme is that everyone sees things differently. That's part of what makes our world—and all of the creatures in it—amazing, interesting, and diverse.

Theme is everywhere, and, ideally, you will choose one that your readers can intuitively understand and relate to. However, the key there is "intuitively understand," because, as we'll see in the next chapter, you are not spelling your theme out. In fact, the early picture book guide, geared mostly toward illustrators and published in 1985, *Writing with Pictures: How to Write and Illustrate Children's Books* by Uri Shulevitz, has this to say:

> Just as the tip is the extension of the base [in a mountain], the obvious in a picture book stems from a broader, invisible base—the suggested. What you don't see affects what you do see. It is this relationship between the seen and the unseen that contributes to a good picture book. The whole picture, both the tip and the base of the mountain, has to be clear to you, for the unshown elements can be just as significant as those that are shown.[1]

Exploring Current SEL and DEI Themes

As you cast around for picture book theme examples, look to contemporary social movements in the childrearing, parenting, teaching, and education spaces. For example, as I mentioned earlier, SEL (social-emotional learning) topics have really come to the forefront of the conversation. So has DEI (diversity, equity, and inclusion).

While SEL is not nearly as politicized as DEI, some of the emotional awareness ideas that form the core of SEL principles can be interpreted as left-leaning. These two trends have some values in common, including a focus on honoring each human being, and self-guided personal development.[2] They

---

1. Uri Shulevitz, *Writing with Pictures: How to Write and Illustrate Children's Books*, 59.
2. I'm going to sidestep a lot of controversies in the cultural conversation about different teaching modalities like CRT and gender and all of the hot-button ideas that have made early childhood education a political minefield. A cogent discussion of these issues is beyond the scope of this guide.

also tie together two things that are undoubtedly true in today's market:

- A lot of publishers are based in coastal cities and, with the exception of imprints that have avowed a right-leaning bias, a lot of media professionals (especially those working in children's books) lean to the left, politically; and
- Regardless of your feelings about DEI initiatives, the move toward a more inclusive publishing industry—and more representation of diverse voices and creators—is here to stay.

These trends are important in the current children's book marketplace, and you need to be aware of them. Many, many books being acquired today are published in the service of either an SEL or DEI topic. I think it's incredibly important for the industry to reflect the demographic make-up of our larger world.

In fact, many of today's up-and-coming authors got into writing because they share a core memory: They couldn't find books on shelves that reflected their identity or life circumstances. With the hard and necessary work being done now, future generations will not feel so excluded.

It's important to note here that creators from certain demographic identities and lived experiences get priority in today's publishing landscape, especially when telling stories about those identities and lived experiences. The reasoning should be obvious, given the old adage, "Write what you know."

Historically, certain creators have not gotten a seat at the publishing table to directly relay their own stories. Now, publishers are looking to rectify this, and offering preferential consideration for Puerto Rican creators, for example, when it comes to telling stories about Puerto Rican characters, settings, cultural traditions, foodways, etc.

I do think that the current extreme focus on DEI may not last indefinitely. Publishing has a lot to make up for in the way of giving underrepresented creators and stories a place to shine. But is it all genuine and positive?

I remain skeptical, as there have been murmurs of diverse voices feeling like they're being exploited for optics, rather than genuinely supported. There are multiple ramifications— intended and unintended—to every trend and cultural movement.

The point remains that if you want to write modern picture books, you need to be aware that a lot of authors, agents, publishers, booksellers, librarians (all of those layers of gate-keepers that we've identified) are generally looking for books that:

- Affirm a more holistic view of validating and integrating emotions in a young child's experience (SEL)
- Include elements of DEI

If you are not interested in doing this work or you actively think that these cultural initiatives are destroying the fabric of the world, you may have a harder time placing your picture book in today's market, unless you conscientiously seek out gatekeepers and publishers who share your ideologies.

As you think about your theme and topic, also consider how you might add an emotional intelligence layer or a more inclusive worldview. These don't have to be overt ingredients, but they should be present.

Examples of Picture Book Themes

Now that I've introduced two banner thematic categories, let's explore some other universal themes that are viable options for modern picture books. Remember, a theme is the figurative and emotional answer to the question, "What is this book about?"

The below is, by no means, an exhaustive list, but here are some examples:

- Mommy/daddy/family loves you, no matter what
- I am me and that's great
- It's okay to feel your feelings
- Life takes courage sometimes
- Change is hard, but a big part of being alive
- I see my own value
- I see the value in others
- All feelings serve a purpose
- Loss is hard, but part of life as well
- Friendships take work and compromise
- Our choices and actions contribute to our moral compass
- How to develop an identity
- It's okay to make mistakes
- Conflict is part of life (a lot more about this in Chapter 11)
- Everyone has special talents and attributes
- A good life is possible when we accept ourselves and others
- How to deal with anxiety and uncertainty
- The impact of world events on children
- Overcoming obstacles

A lot of these themes have a positive bent, as you have likely noticed. They are meant to be redemptive, validating, and empowering, even if the story also touches on a tough part of the human experience, like loss or change. This is very purposefully done, because a picture book will ideally leave your readers feeling something hopeful or uplifting.

Consider your audience. Young readers and their gatekeepers want to feel a sense of possibility or opportunity when they close the back cover of your book, even though the text is not going to overtly preach any of these messages.

The theme is more of an emotional starting point, and from there, you can pair it with the topic of your story. Narrative picture books aren't the only ones with themes. Concept books sometimes have themes. Nonfiction picture books, even those without a narrative component, can have themes as well.

For example, many picture book biographies (considered narrative nonfiction) have an inspirational theme attached. *Mae Among the Stars* by Roda Ahmed, illustrated by Stasia Burrington, presents the origin story of Mae Jemison, NASA's first Black female astronaut. The voice and message are very uplifting, and it has the additional selling point of celebrating an underrepresented STEM innovator from history. (We'll talk more about how to intentionally select competitive nonfiction picture book topics, especially for biographies, in Chapter 8.)

After you decide on your theme, the subject or topic is the next choice you need to make.

Examples of Picture Book Topics

A project's topic is the literal answer to the question, "What is this book about?"

There was an imprint at Random House, several corporate lifecycles ago, called Dragonfly Books (there is currently a small publisher called Dragonfly Books, but they are not the same). They published my paperback edition of *Imogene's Antlers*. In the back, there's a list of the picture book topic categories that they produced. A lot of these still hold true:

- Classics (Including Caldecott Award Winners)
- Concepts (Alphabet, Counting, and More)
- Cultural Diversity
- Death and Dying
- Family
- Fascinating People
- Friendship
- Growing Up
- Just for Fun (*Imogene's Antlers* fits into this category)
- Myths and Legends
- Nature and Our Environment
- Our History (Nonfiction and Historical Fiction)
- Poetry
- School
- Sports

As you can see, this is a nice little broad-strokes overview of picture book topics. It's a great starting point, and even though this list was created decades ago, you'll see that a lot of these ideas track all the way into today's picture book landscape.

Here are some more specific examples of picture book topics, with a more contemporary slant:

- A child's friendship story
- A child's family story
- Sibling relationships
- Parent/child relationships
- Bedtime stories
- Fantasy worlds and creatures
- Stories about holidays and traditions

- Emotions (defining, expressing, or grappling with them)
- Acceptance and inclusion in a specific situation
- Exploration of a setting
- Stories about imagination or creativity
- Teaching a specific skill or subject area
- Stories about competitions, talents, and achievement
- Stories that unpack specific childhood experiences (starting kindergarten, going to the doctor, etc.)

Hold on to your hats, because I am going to present and analyze almost 80 distinct picture book topics in Chapter 6.

It's important to acknowledge that there can also be some overlap between theme and topic. Note that a narrative picture book can have a theme of self-acceptance, or embracing your shyness, and a topic of speaking up in class, for example. Here, the theme and topic overlap.

However, this might not be a very marketable idea without additional elements layered onto it, as it is quite straightforward. We'll discuss how to add nuance to your big picture ideas in the next few chapters.

Going back to *They All Saw a Cat*, the topic (a child and cat going for a walk and imagining how different animals see the world) also aligns with the theme (everyone has a distinct and valid perspective). But in other cases, theme and topic can diverge.

Contrasting theme and topic can be done for an interesting effect. In fact, two concept books I analyzed—*The Monster Parade: A Book About Feeling All Your Feelings and Then Watching Them Go* by Wendy O'Leary, illustrated by Noemie Gionet Landry, and *The Color Monster* by Anna Llenas—both present emotions as monsters (largely friendly ones) in order to personify, and therefore humanize, them.

As you can tell, it's important to make these choices deliberately, as they will form the primary foundation of your story.

Picture Books 2.0 and 3.0

Now that you might have some ideas about themes and topics that you want to explore, let me throw another curveball at you: There have been a lot of children's books published since Ursula Nordstrom broke the market wide open in the late 1940s. A *lot*.

Picture books are published by imprints at all of the major houses in the U.S. market. They're published abroad. They're published by small presses. They're self-published. They're sitting in a writer's drawer, never to see the light of day.

Though I've spent over a decade in children's book publishing, I can confidently say that I've probably read less than a small fraction of .01% of all picture books that have been published, an even smaller percentage of all the picture book manuscripts ever written, and an even smaller number of all the picture book ideas ever dreamed up.

There are no new ideas, truly.

But there are some old ones, which are getting left behind in the dust.

This is where my idea of Picture Books 1.0 vs. 2.0 and 3.0[3] comes in. Picture Books 1.0 are pretty straightforward. Think about *Llama, Llama, Red Pajama* by Anna Dewdney.

Llama is chilling upstairs (a bedtime topic) and suddenly needs to see Mama Llama *right now*. He's struggling with separation anxiety (topic). Mama Llama is doing the dishes

---

3. These are my own terms that I use to talk about changing trends in the picture book market, rather than official industry terms.

and talking on the phone, so Llama escalates dramatically (causing "llama drama,"[4] which is a great line). Mama has to reassure Llama that she's there, even if she doesn't come right away (theme, even though it's stated outright), and Llama is pleased.

This is a very clear story that works with the topics of bedtime and emotions (impatience, fear, and insecurity), and the theme of separation being healed by love and acceptance between a parent and a child. And it's a huge hit that has spawned a mini empire.

But it's also incredibly linear. Child has an experience, Adult reassures the child, Lesson is learned, and that's it. This makes *Llama, Llama, Red Pajama* (published in 2005) an example of Picture Book 1.0.

So are a few other titles I analyzed for this guide, including *Monster & Son* by David LaRochelle, illustrated by Joey Chou (2016), *Grandfather Twilight* by Barbara Berger (1984), *Beaver Is Lost* by Elisha Cooper (2010), *Race!* by Sue Fliess, illustrated by Edwardian Taylor (2017), *Take a Ride by My Side* by Jonathan Ying, illustrated by Victoria Ying (2018), *Smashy Town* by Andrea Zimmerman and David Clemesha, illustrated by Dan Yaccarino (2020), and *Dragonboy* by Fabio Napoleoni (2021).

To my eye, the recent focus on SEL and DEI has ushered in Picture Book 2.0, as well as more layered themes and topics. What does this mean?

In Picture Book 1.0, the child is more of an empty vessel. They don't have a lot of their own tools or resources until someone comes along and contextualizes the story topic for them by expressing the theme. Then they feel better. In Picture Book

---

4. Anna Dewdney, *Llama, Llama Red Pajama*, 30-31.

2.0, the child has more substance and, more importantly, confidence in themselves as a starting point.

Think about it this way—in Picture Book 1.0, we end on the uplifting note of the child being made whole. In Picture Book 2.0, that synthesis is the *beginning* of the story, not the *end*. In Picture Book 2.0, the child already realizes their worth or inherent spark. They know that being different is important, or that bullying is bad.

Now, from this foundation, the Picture Book 2.0 story takes that more evolved child on a different journey, which uses their emotional intelligence and sense of worth as a starting point.

The child doesn't doubt their spark. They use that spark to make a difference, pull together their community, come at a familiar problem from a new angle, or inspire another child.

The Picture Book 2.0 protagonist is not a blank slate waiting for wisdom before they can "come online" and live a full life. They are already online (in the identity sense, not in the YouTube sense). And now what?

This pivot is at the heart of writing modern picture books, and it is the framework we'll use to discuss contemporary character and plot going forward. But what about Picture Book 3.0, which is mentioned in the heading of this section?

Well, that's the next iteration of the picture book marketplace. And now that the SEL and DEI approach is becoming saturated, I'm already asking myself, "Well, what's next? What's the evolution going to be?"

The point is, it will be tough to launch a Picture Book 2.0 idea in the Picture Book 3.0 world, which is right around the corner. It's going to be even tougher to enter the Picture Book 3.0 world with a Picture Book 1.0 concept.

That's why it's so important that you learn how to build a picture book idea from the ground up, using theme and topic and strong market knowledge as your launchpad. No matter what happens next in the picture book space, you will be ready, and dreaming in the right direction.

All this said, there's nothing that sinks a picture book idea faster or more catastrophically—be that a 1.0 idea or a 3.0 idea —than a heavy moral. Before we dive into character and plot, I have a bit more soapboxing to do about, well, soapboxing.

FIVE
MORALIZING AND THE MESSAGE

AN OVERT PICTURE BOOK MORAL, or the explicit statement of your picture book theme, is perhaps one of the most toxic traits that can sour an aspiring children's book project in any category—whether aimed at picture book readers or young adults.

Remember when we discussed a child's daily life experience? And how they spend their time hearing from people around them, who believe they know better about pretty much everything?

Well, books are one place where kids can escape. A safe place, if you will, from overt explanations, rules, and slogans. You need to be that safe harbor for your readers, unless you want your book to be relegated to the donation bin, if it makes it into print at all. Publishing gatekeepers find little as repugnant as overt preaching.

What's the difference between a moral, a theme, and a topic? Theme and topic were both defined in the previous chapter. Theme is the covert subject of the book, and topic is the overt. So is moral, defined below.

Craft Definition:

Moral: A story's lesson or takeaway, stated outright.

Pushing a Picture Book Agenda

Remember my discussion of bullying in Chapter 3? I made a strange point: Explaining that bullying is bad in a picture book is undesirable. On what planet would a book that holds such an obvious moral high ground be problematic?

Don't get me wrong, most preachy books mean well.

But when a picture book only exists to serve up a moral, it is too obvious. Condescending. It doesn't take a kid's life experience into account. Most of your readers, by the point they encounter your picture book, will have at least been to some daycare, preschool, or kindergarten.

This means that, if their teachers participate in the current SEL education model, they probably know that sharing is good, bullying is bad, everyone is special in their own way, there is value within all of us, we shouldn't judge others, and any number of reasonable, helpful, and perfectly boring lessons that educators cheerfully espouse.

So now what?

A great book about sharing and rivalry, which never truly explains itself, is *Knuffle Bunny Too: A Case of Mistaken Identity* by Mo Willems. Trixie takes her presumed one-of-a-kind bunny to school, only to discover that another girl has one just like it. Being preschoolers, the girls immediately begin to fight about whose bunny is better. At no point do the parents or teacher step in and say, "It doesn't matter, both bunnies are special, and so are you."

That would be a very Picture Book 1.0 treatment of these topics, and it would present an obvious moral. Instead, the girls accidentally switch bunnies, realize they both love their bunnies equally, and intuit that there's no need to compete. They only develop this empathy when they are each deprived of *their* bunny, and now they see the "wrong" bunny within a context of mutual understanding.

That's a function of characters experiencing a plot firsthand, not a wise teacher or parent lording an explicit moral secondhand.

Similarly, the wordless *I Walk with Vanessa: A Story About a Simple Act of Kindness* by Kerascoët is a modern take on an anti-bullying book. Sure, bullying is bad, and the project doesn't glorify it, but it also doesn't spend a lot of time postulating that bullying is hurtful, we shouldn't bully, and that it is painful for the victim. Instead, it shows a classroom of kids banding together without saying the obvious (and literally without saying *anything*) to make the new student feel welcome and supported.

Both books elevate explicit morals into stories. Nothing you want to tell kids outright is really new information. These foundational ideas already exist in a young reader's world. It's not an issue of them never having heard before that bullying is bad, that they shouldn't tease their siblings, or that it's a terrible idea to bite their daycare friends.

They know.

And if a book also drones on to them about the same topic, they might tune the message out, just like they're able to ignore that long-suffering teacher.

If you want to moralize, go into the bumper sticker industry.

Writing a picture book solely to push a message isn't going to get you anywhere in today's market. Preaching in picture books also doesn't engage your reader. From a craft perspective, this isn't ideal, either.

Moralizing doesn't make kids feeling anything—other than, perhaps, annoyance. It puts them in an imbalanced power dynamic that they're all too familiar with, that of student (them) and master (you). It treats your young reader as a vacuum to be filled with knowledge, usually by a wiser, older character. Which is unflattering for them, and very self-congratulatory for the wiser, older character, who is often a very obvious avatar for the author.

Though you would never dream of condescending to a child on purpose, dear reader, know that I have actually edited projects where the writer and the Adult Fountain of Wisdom[1] share the same name. I've seen drafts that are titled something like *Grandma Betty's Wisdom* by Betty Smith. Agents, editors, and readers see right through this, I'm afraid.

Power Dynamics

I have mentioned the idea of power dynamics several times. While it might seem weird to talk about this in a picture book writing guide, this concept goes back to reader relatability.

When one character has all the answers, and another character has none, not only is there a clear "winner" and a clear "loser," which lacks nuance, but the plot can only take one possible shape: The character with all the answers gives them to the character with none. It's a one-way street, with no interplay.

If you don't have a lecturing parent in your project, you might be tempted to skip this chapter. (You might even see

---

1. Patent pending.

this chapter as talking down to you, but the soapboxing is done intentionally.)

But guess what? The wiser and older character isn't always a parent. They can be a teacher, religious leader, grandparent, paranormal creature, anthropomorphized animal, or Adult-like Idealized Child.[2] The latter is a character who is technically a child but has never made a mistake in their lives and is playing the role of the child every adult wishes existed, because it would make parenting and teaching a lot easier.

This type of idealized child shouldn't feature in picture books, especially as a protagonist, because it lacks all the qualities that make children real, flawed, wild, and wonderful.

The *modern* picture books best practice, then, is to put most of the characters on the same power-dynamic playing field. This means casts that consist of kids, classmates, siblings, or anthropomorphic animals who are similar in age to your target audience. There are absolutely ways to include older, wiser characters, but they shouldn't lord their knowledge, experience, or power position over the child characters.

When you're choosing who to include in your picture book, make sure that most of your characters are on even footing with one another, unless you are specifically writing about birth order and sibling dynamics, for example, where imbalanced relationships are part of the story conflict. I'll talk more about secondary characters in Chapter 13.

Revisiting the Bully Story

Nobody needs an entire picture book manuscript to convey a familiar lesson. Everyone knows the moral already. However,

---

2. Patent also pending.

if you use your book idea as a base and think about a universal theme, as discussed in Chapter 4, this can be a starting point for a bigger and more layered story.

Let's take another run at our hypothetical bullying book. The message the writer wants to convey is "bullying is bad." But that's something everyone already knows—*including the bully*, believe it or not.

So let's use that as a jumping-off point:

Bullying is bad.

And? So?[3]

Well, we should discourage bullying.

And? So?

So that everyone feels like they have a place in the classroom.

Well, now we're suddenly facing something uncomfortable.

What about the bully?

If "bullying is bad," then we can't have a truly inclusive classroom, as it would exclude the bully. (Yes, I'm playing devil's advocate, but stick with me for a moment.) Now, to tease out a more modern idea from this beginning, let's search through some of our SEL ideas and themes.

How does the idea of "bullying is bad" dovetail with

---

3. This is a question that I ask all the time with my novel editorial clients. They arrive at one layer, and I help them tease out more nuances in individual scenes or story moments, as well as bigger plot points. This line of questioning can be incredibly helpful when it comes to crafting a picture book concept. Put these two words on a Post-it note by your writing station and remember to use them when you're feeling stuck or uninspired about something. These questions can be used to examine your story premise, character choices, plot points, and themes.

emotional intelligence and inclusion? If we think about it from this angle, we'll notice a subtle shift.

"But Mary, are you suggesting that we include the bully, instantly forgive their misdeeds, and force the kids they've victimized into close contact with them against their will?"

Not at all. However, as we're creating a more nuanced Picture Book 2.0+, we do need to think about the potential unspoken ramifications of our story choices.

Invalidating the bullied kids' perspectives to forcefully include the bully could potentially send the message that the victim's feelings aren't valid, and that we should just bend over and accept someone else's mistreatment of us without any self-advocacy.

However, there's this idea floating around in popular psychology that "hurt people hurt people," which suggests that a bully comes to their aggression and nastiness honestly, usually because they are being mistreated themselves.

For a child bully, that usually means they're learning their behaviors somewhere, like at home. That's not to excuse the bully or their mean-spirited choices, but it's to try and understand them on a deeper level.

We can take our "bullying is bad" idea and examine it. In addition to asking "And? So?", we can also try making a "Yes, and …"[4] statement.

Bullying is bad.

Yes, and?

We should seek to understand the bully as well as hearing the lesson

---

4. My therapist would be so proud!

that "bullying is bad," because the bully's behavior comes from somewhere.

Yes, and?

Is there a way to then navigate the bullied/bully relationship holistically by trying to represent all sides?

For this Picture Book 2.0+ concept about bullying, you start with all of the characters knowing that bullying is bad, but then working together to figure out how to move forward as a classroom. This might look like extending an olive branch to the bully and getting perspective on their life. This might look like learning about boundaries, so that the bully's behavior is discouraged and walled off, preserving the integrity of the kids that are being victimized.

It also allows the bully to realize the consequences of their own behavior, and to come around on their own accord, rather than getting a lecture. This might look like working together to change the emotional climate of a classroom instead of spinning a simplistic "us vs. them" narrative. As you'll see in Chapters 11 and 12, there are actually very few *outright* antagonists in modern picture books.

As already mentioned, the idea that kindness, understanding, and empathy can soften even the hardest heart might be unrealistic. Human relationships and feelings aren't a zero-sum, black-or-white game. "Bullying is bad" leaves no room for nuance and conveys the simplistic expectation that once the moral strikes, everyone will ride off into the sunset on a herd of unicorns. Therefore I'm not saying that this story ends with the bully having a life-changing realization. Or the idea that nobody will ever be hurt again.

But maybe the kids can find common ground and connection, and move forward in a better direction together.

Instead of absolutes, become comfortable with the gray area and use your picture books to introduce SEL concepts and teach kids how to know themselves better and function in their worlds. Instead of "bullying is bad," which applies to one situation, you can instead introduce concepts and themes —like empathy and boundaries—that will serve kids across a variety of life experiences.

Empowering Your Characters

A concept that's related to "starting at the end" is having your character actively discover the message, if your story absolutely requires a more overt moral. Not only does this honor your kid readers and how sophisticated they've become in their three or five or seven years of life, but it empowers them.

What if your protagonist already knows that "bullying is bad"?

What will that idea empower them to do in their classroom? How will they interact with their peers—including the bully?

If they aren't sure of the theme or lesson yet, they can actively learn this concept through their own exploration. Maybe the bully keeps playing jokes and pranks on the kids, and, at first, the protagonist doesn't know whether they enjoy this. After a few "funny" experiences that don't turn out to be fun at all, the protagonist can decide that they should listen to their gut instinct. It turns out they know what they want, and can confidently trust their own north star.

The theme can be that our feelings are valid, and that we are our own best advocates. This message translates to many potential situations, not just a bully scenario.

Adults can help with this exploration by making suggestions or setting up experiences for the protagonist. They should not come out and explain, preach, or make grand pronouncements, though. Instead, they can facilitate the child main character's own journey.

But here's the most important idea for you to take away from this chapter: The kid protagonist should originate the message. This includes phrasing it in their own voice (rather than in all-knowing adult language).

When the protagonist comes up with the theme or the takeaway, they are empowered. Having the character discover the lesson firsthand puts them on the same playing field as your audience. Your reader will be more receptive to learning from a character who is on equal footing with them, which is crucial to packaging any *subtle* message in a picture book.

And for extra credit?

Let your character then turn around and teach the takeaway to someone else. This truly elevates them and makes them a leader. Your readers will be much more engaged by seeing your protagonist share their wisdom with a younger sibling or classmate, a pet or a stuffed animal.

If you simply must have a strong message in your story, make sure that it's coming from a child character, rather than an adult, and that it's presented in a proactive way, as the character originates the emotional realization that underpins your theme.

All picture books are about something (theme and topic), but not all picture books have a big verbatim slogan where the message is stated explicitly. You must create this idea in your reader's mind without putting a neon sign on the page to do it. The best and cleanest way to accomplish this is by having your protagonist go on a journey that's compelling and emotionally true, and just so happens to deliver them to a place where they have a realization about their lives (and maybe to pass it on).

My favorite books, from the selections I analyzed, that land nuanced messages beautifully are *Meow!, Mr. Tiger Goes Wild* by Peter Brown, *Courage Hats* by Kate Hoefler, illustrated by Jessixa Bagley, *The Rough Patch* by Brian Lies, and *Say Hello to Zorro!* by Carter Goodrich, among others.

We'll also learn a lot more about expressing theme through conflict, turning points, resolutions, and other story beats in Chapters 11 and 12. Now, I'll turn our attention to the vast and diverse spectrum of potential picture book topics, and present some very exciting original research from the next few years of children's book publishing. This is the closest we'll get to a preview of things to come. With some learning, tenacity, and hard work, you might participate in this next phase yourself with your own picture book idea.

SIX

PICTURE BOOK TOPICS

THIS CHAPTER BUILDS on the Picture Books 2.0 discussion with a much more granular breakdown of common picture book topics in *upcoming* projects, which will be published in 2024 and beyond.

In June 2023, I reviewed the most recent 1,000 picture book deals in the Publishers Marketplace database, the most comprehensive log of book deals in the industry. It doesn't collect every single deal, but it's the best compilation of memos available.

If you want a truly cutting-edge look into what publishers are doing—or will be doing—within the next few years, I recommend investing in a Publishers Marketplace subscription.[1]

It's important to note that these deal postings highlight the intended sales hooks of each project. They are supplied by literary agents, sometimes working together with the

---

1. At the time of this writing, it costs $25 per month to be a PM member, and there's a small price break if you pay annually. You can cancel anytime. I'm a happy customer and don't benefit financially in any way from making this recommendation.

publisher, to announce upcoming books and try to drum up subrights or foreign rights interest, where appropriate. (Not all picture books are a good fit for the international or film markets, for example, so selling these rights is not always a given.)

Craft Definition:

Sales Hook: An element of the project—whether the theme, topic, character, curriculum angle, or plot—that intends to make it more marketable to retail readers or customers like schools and libraries (sales hooks for the latter are more relevant to nonfiction picture books).

In analyzing these 1,000 picture book deals, which were posted between May 2022 and May 2023, I broke them into almost 80 subcategories, by topic. I'll explain these here, as well as cite the number of projects that seemed to fit into each one.

This is an unofficial survey, and the most important thing to know is that most books have been labeled with multiple topics. In fact, the majority got at least four topics *each*, which means that these projects seemed to have multiple sales hooks and layers.

The second most important thing to know is that I did not read the books themselves—I only responded to the one- or two-sentence pitch in the deal memo. Here are a few examples of deal memos and my analysis, meant to demonstrate my thought process and how I arrived at this list of topics. All of these individual examples were taken from this cohort of 1,000 deals.

Here's a narrative picture book deal memo posted on May 6th, 2022:

THE GATHERING TABLE, by Antwan Eady and London Ladd

Antwan Eady's THE GATHERING TABLE, following a family year-round as they celebrate special occasions—a golden anniversary (love), New Year's Eve (hope), a wedding (Pride), and Juneteenth (freedom)— standing around a table in their backyard, illustrated by London Ladd, to Rotem Moscovich at Knopf Children's, in a two-book deal for the author, for publication in summer 2025, by Steven Malk at Writers House for the author, and by Lori Nowicki at Painted Words for the illustrator (world).

Here, there are several sales hooks to note, and they seem to be tied together rather brilliantly, too. As you will see, there are Queer, Black Identity, Other Holiday, Family/Home, Love, Neighborhood/Community, and Elder/Ancestor topics represented. This little deal memo touches on six identified topics, and I might either apply a Sweet/Positive or Poignant tone topic over everything, because of the signals I'm getting ("hope").

Here's another, sillier narrative picture book deal memo posted on March 8th, 2023:

THE SQUISH, by Breanna Carzoo

Author-illustrator of LOU[2] Breanna Carzoo's THE SQUISH, about a sandcastle that tries to protect itself from being constantly knocked down by all of life's squishes until it discovers the value in resiliency, rebuilding, and reaching out to others, to Megan Ilnitzki at Harper Children's, in an exclusive submission, for publication in summer 2024, by Jennifer Rofe at Andrea Brown Literary Agency (world).

I love this picture book creator, so I might be applying my existing knowledge of Breanna Carzoo's *Lou* to my reading of the deal memo. This new project seems like it can be labeled with Object Character (the protagonist is a sandcastle), Water Ecosystems, Courage/Bravery/Strength/Resilience, and Kindness topics. That's four right there. I might also add a Quirky, Funny, or Sweet/Positive tone topic, because I'm seeing both humor *and* heart in this concept.

Now let's look at a nonfiction picture book deal memo posted on March 14th, 2023:

LIVING BRIDGES, by Sandhya Acharya and Avani Dwivedi

---

2. This is one of the published books I'll analyze later in this guide!

Sandhya Acharya's LIVING BRIDGES, set in the mountains of Meghalaya, India, where one generation teaches the next how to weave the roots of their beloved Jingkieng Jri, ancient man-made bridges made of living tree roots, illustrated by Avani Dwivedi, to Catherine Laudone at Paula Wiseman Books, for publication in spring 2025, by Kathleen Rushall at Andrea Brown Literary Agency for the author, and by Shadra Strickland at Painted Words for the illustrator (world).

This is a very cool-sounding nonfiction project, which highlights topics of AAPI Identity, Nature, Neighborhood/Community, International Setting, Elder/Ancestor, and STEM—because you can't build a bridge without some kind of engineering.

As you can see, there's some good information contained in these deal listings, but not a lot. I could be wrong about the project, especially when it comes to the tone topics I've applied. With THE SQUISH, the overall effect of the book could be funny and silly, or it could be more poignant. As such, I've made my best guess about some of the more subjective categories, but I might end up being wrong, depending on the execution of the final product.

Before I present the full list of almost 80 individual picture book topics that I codified, I want to cluster them into overarching categories. These are:

- **Topic**: A picture book about a specific topic, whether a bigger category of related elements (Family Issues) or a more granular subject (for example, having working parents);
- **Character**: A topic that informs who exists within a story;

- **Attribute**: This differs from Character, in that I've used it to mean that a character's personality attribute —their humor, their kindness, etc.—seems to play a role in the story;
- **Relationship**: A topic that seems to lend itself well to interpersonal relationships or conflicts as a defining part of the story;
- **Setting**: A topic that mostly informs setting, whether physical, time (Historical, for example), or another factor of the space inhabited in the book (like Environment/Climate Change, and Weather/Seasons);
- **Tone**: As discussed above, tone can be tough to pin down. I used my best judgment to label projects as Funny, for example, or Poignant, or Quirky. These topics inform the overall vibe of a book;
- **Culture**: If the project has a cultural or identity element, I've labeled it as fitting into this broader category; and
- **Nonfiction**: These topics are commonly covered in nonfiction projects, but not exclusively.

Now let's discover how these larger categories translate into the specific topics I identified in my research. I've omitted a few that I didn't find terribly compelling or noteworthy. Here are the topics I isolated from reading 1,000 picture book deal announcements, presented in order of popularity, from most frequently cited, to least:

- **Animals** // Topic, Character (113 instances): I took this to mean any stories that either featured wild animals interacting with humans, were focused on animals as a nonfiction topic, or had animals as anthropomorphic characters who were analogues for children (more on this in Chapter 13). In hindsight, I wish I had broken this topic into these three subcategories. Animals is far and away the most popular label. Pets, Fantasy Animals, and creatures who live in Water Ecosystems have their own categories—as do books that are deeply concerned with only one type of animal, in which case, that becomes its own Specific Topic.

- **Courage/Bravery/Strength/Resilience** // Character, Attribute, Tone (101 instances): This topic fits into both character and tone categories. It's important to note that most deal memos with this topic mentioned these words, especially "resilience," as did our THE SQUISH example. I took these stories to be about a character overcoming something over the course of the story, usually by digging into reserves of courage and strength that they didn't previously know they possessed. It can also speak to the takeaway of the story, where the need for resilience is the primary theme. This is a wildly popular topic, which isn't surprising, given the focus on SEL described in Chapter 1.

- **Poignant** // Character, Attribute, Tone (100 instances): This refers to the overall tone of the story and differs from Sweet/Positive and Quirky. I determined that books fit into this category if they seemed to evoke heartfelt or profound feelings. This overlaps with the SEL topic, and some other attribute categories. To differentiate this from Sweet/Positive, I identified a sense of sadness or a bittersweet element for Poignant topic projects.

- **Sense of Self** // Character, Attribute (97): Whenever I read about a character who seemed to know who they were and were proud of that self, or discovering that sense of self in the story, I applied this topic. This dovetails with our discussion of SEL as well as the idea that, in most Picture Book 2.0 projects, kids are largely already aware of their unique spark and worth, in most cases.

- **Family/Home** // Relationship, Setting, Tone (95 instances): A child's life is generally pretty small in terms of their "bubbles," or immediate surroundings. They tend to occupy home and family spaces. There's a difference between Family/Home and House as topics. Family/Home has connotations of the people and emotions that create a sense of home, comfort, love, and acceptance. Family/Home also refers to the people immediately tasked with raising a child. In a few cases, the project emphasized the idea of "found family," or family tied together not by birth and genetics, but by friendship and love. There are separate topics for Elder/Ancestor, as well as for books that seemed to primarily focus on Siblings, as subsets within a family.
- **Neighborhood/Community** // Relationship, Setting, Tone (91 instances): With the market's focus on diversity and inclusion, this topic's popularity is not surprising. This label refers to the larger community or neighborhood that a child inhabits, which can sometimes play a role in a picture book, as if it's a character in its own right. Books that fit into this topic seem to be set in a specific neighborhood, or to center around a group of people living in proximity. An example would be a picture book about a parade or a community garden, or people banding together after a natural disaster. A great published example is *The Busiest Street in Town* by Mara Rockliff, illustrated by Sarah McMenemy.
- **Friendship/Teamwork** // Character, Relationship, Tone (82 instances): It's also no surprise that friendship topics are popular for this age group.

While a picture book-aged reader's primary relationships are within their family unit, they are also working on socializing and individuating themselves among others, which can include Neighborhood/Community members, Elder/Ancestor figures, but also friends and classmates. The overwhelming majority of these books focus on friendships with peers, however, and the majority of those friendships can be called "odd friendships," where unlikely relationships form between clashing personalities (see Prickly Character). Only a few of these books are specifically about teamwork rather than the creation or navigation of a friendship relationship.

- **Nature** // Topic, Setting (82 instances): With Animals emerging as such a hot subject matter, it's not surprising that Nature features in the top ten most popular picture book topics, too. It's important to note that all Animals books are Nature books, but not all Nature books are Animals books. For our purposes, I was very intentional about designating Animals topics and Nature topics separately, when possible. A trend definitely emerged here: trees. Fallen trees, tall trees, the ecosystems within trees, animals who live in trees, etc. Forests were also popular. I'd say north of 60% of books in the Nature topic in this sample of 1,000 deal memos had something to do with trees. It's also important to note that Water Ecosystems, Weather/Seasons, Environment/Climate Change, and certain Specific Concept topics have their own categories.
- **Elder/Ancestor** // Relationship, Character, Tone (79): The prevalence of this topic surprised me, but perhaps it shouldn't have. This topic is overwhelmingly about grandparents, with a pretty

even split between grandmothers and grandfathers. (Unfortunately, I didn't divide this topic into more detailed subcategories.) A small percentage of these projects is about elders in the community, like a neighbor who also has a significant relationship with the child character, so there's a Neighborhood/Community topic overlap. Ancestral knowledge, family legacy, and understanding one's roots seem to be major angles in these stories. There's significant overlap with the Poignant topic and the Family/Home topic, as well as Identity-specific and Cultural Traditions topics.

- **AAPI Identity** // Culture, Character (74): This topic includes picture books that specifically deal with the Asian-American Pacific Islander experience, which covers everything from Japanese, Korean, Chinese, Southeast Asian, Indian, Philippine, and other cultures, whether the protagonist has direct lived experience in that culture of origin (including active immigration from a home country, though immigration is also tracked as a separate topic under Diversity/Inclusion, Social Issues, and Family Issues, depending on the story), or claims an AAPI identity in other ways. I did not tally this topic based on the cultural identity or demographic of the picture book creator(s). I only used this label if the project seemed to deal with an element of AAPI-specific cultural identity or tradition. If I could do this survey over again, I would specifically carve out stories about Indian culture and identity as a separate topic. There can often be overlap with Elders/Ancestor, Neighborhood/Community, Food, Cultural Traditions, and Other Holidays.
- **Biography** // Character, Nonfiction (73 instances): Books with this label are nonfiction projects that focus

on a specific person or a group of people. For a more in-depth discussion of nonfiction and biography picture books, see Chapter 8.

- **Black Identity** // Character, Culture (72 instances): This topic includes picture books that specifically deal with the Black experience, which covers everything from African-American stories to those of Afro-Caribbean, African mainland, and African diaspora identities, whether the protagonist has direct lived experience in that culture of origin (including active immigration from a home country, though immigration is also tracked as a separate topic under Diversity/Inclusion, Social Issues, and Family Issues), or claims a Black identity in other ways. I did not tally this topic based on the cultural identity or demographic of the picture book creator(s). I only used this label if the project seemed to deal with an element of Black cultural identity or tradition. If I had this survey to do over again, I would separate the African-American, Afro-Caribbean, Afro-Latin, African diaspora, and mainland African projects into distinct topics. There can often be overlap with Elders/Ancestor, Neighborhood/Community, Food, Cultural Traditions, and Other Holidays.
- **STEM** // Attribute, Topic, Nonfiction (71 instances): The popularity of picture book projects with a STEM (Science, Technology, Engineering, Math) focus is absolutely no surprise. There is common overlap here with Women Heroes and Biography, as well as Specific Concept. Sometimes, the acronym used is STEAM, adding "Arts," but Art/Creativity/Imagination has its own topic. Teaching STEM and STEAM concepts has become very popular in recent years, especially when it comes to activating girl

characters in STEM. This topic applies to both fiction and nonfiction projects.

- **Diversity/Inclusion** // Character, Culture, Tone, Topic (69 instances): Politics aside, it's important to note that picture books focusing on topics of diversity and inclusion are incredibly popular, as discussed in Chapter 1. The projects categorized under this topic specifically featured storylines and characters making a concerted effort to create a more inclusive community, school, or friendship. There's overlap here with SEL, Poignant, Cultural Traditions, Neighborhood/Community, Friendship/Teamwork, Family Issues, Disability, Shy/Quiet, and the various Identity topics.

- **Cultural Traditions** // Topic, Nonfiction, Character, Attribute, Relationship, Culture, Setting (63 instances): This topic is a catch-all for any projects that described cultural traditions, but is generally exclusive of religious and holiday traditions, which have their own topics. This refers to non-holiday and non-religious rituals and ways of living that are inflected by a specific culture or identity. For example, significant garments and rituals that children and families participate in. There is a heavy focus in this cohort on Black hair, for example, though books on this topic can also overlap with Black Identity, Family/Home, Elder/Ancestor, and Neighborhood/Community.

- **Women Heroes** // Topic, Character, Nonfiction (62 instances): This topic overlaps with Biography and Specific Concept, as well as STEM and the various Identity topics. There's a very prominent trend to feature women, especially women of color, and their contributions—which have often been historically minimized—to sciences and other fields that have previously been thought of as male-dominated.

- **Quirky** / / Attribute, Tone (58 instances): This is one of the toughest topics to explain. There's some overlap here with Friendship / Teamwork, Object Characters, and Funny. This label is related to a gut feeling I got when reading the deal memo. It could mean a quirky character (eccentric older neighbor) or a particularly odd friendship (between a stick and a stone, for example). These books can be lighthearted, but sometimes quirk and humor are used to balance a profound theme (which also has a separate Poignant topic). This is known as the picture book sweet spot of "humor and heart." The deal memo for THE SQUISH sounds like it fits this label.

- **Historical** / / Nonfiction, Topic, Setting (58 instances): There are nonfiction and fiction projects with this label, but it lends itself to mostly nonfiction and Biography. There were a lot of projects about the Great Migration and WWII in this cohort, especially the Holocaust and Japanese internment camps. Basically, anything with a historical setting, or a biography about a prominent historical person, got this label.

- **Sweet/Positive** / / Attribute, Tone (57 instances): This topic differs from Poignant in that it's optimistic and uplifting, while Poignant can be a bit sad and includes elements of longing. I want to reiterate that this was my impression of the overall pitch, as all the tone category labels are. There's a lot of overlap between this topic and Quirky, Mommy / Daddy / Baby, Friendship / Teamwork, Neighborhood / Community, Family / Home, Love, and others. Most projects with this topic have other (and I would say *primary*) labels.

- **Shy/Quiet** // Character, Attribute, Tone (57 instances): The number of books with this topic surprised me. It can sometimes be seen as a bad thing to have a "quiet" book (and I'll talk about this more in Chapter 11), but the market is now acknowledging that many types of personalities exist. With the rise of SEL ideas, shy, quiet, and/or anxious characters are having their moment in the sun. This topic has heavy overlap with the Courage/Bravery/Strength/Resilience topic, as well as Friendship/Teamwork, SEL, Change/Growth, Poignant, School, Diversity/Inclusion, and Sweet/Positive. Most of these books seem to affirm their shy and quiet characters, rather than attempting to change them or have them "see the error of their ways," as our innate human qualities are not something to fix.
- **Specific Concept** // Topic, Setting, Character, Nonfiction (56 instances): This is one of my favorite catch-all labels in this analysis because it covers projects about very specific single topics. Most of these are nonfiction, but some of them are fiction. Some concepts fit into other categories as well (such as Animals, Nature, and Water Ecosystems), but others are so delightfully specific that they seem to come out of nowhere (and yet strike that note of "I wish I'd thought of that!"). Here are some selections from this cohort of 1,000 deal memos:

  Sorting and categorizing (appropriate for this chapter!);
  Noses and facial features;
  The hidden female artists behind Tiffany lamps (also Historical, Art/Creativity/Imagination, and Women Heroes);

Wind (also Weather/Seasons);

Wishes across the world (also Cultural Traditions and International Settings);

Crepuscular animals (also Animals and Nature);

The principle of nature vs. nurture as it applies to alpacas and how it influences their wool (!!!)—perhaps the most specific topic of all time (also Animals, Nature, STEM, and SEL);

Earth's atmosphere (also Nature, Environment/Climate Change, and Weather/Seasons);

Rubber;

Animals and their homes (also Animals, House, Nature, and Home/Family);

Museums around the world (also Art/Creativity/Imagination and International Settings);

The number zero (also STEM);

Chess;

School shootings (also School and Social Issues);

Rocks (also Nature);

Light pollution and its impact on bird migration (also Animals and Nature, and I noted several deals about bird migration and natal homing);

Reconciling contradictions (also SEL);

Language and culture (also Cultural Traditions and International Settings);

Ice cream around the world (also Food and International Settings);

Events of the year (also Other Holidays);

Color theory (also Art/Creativity/Imagination);

Famous trees (also Nature);

Measures (also STEM);

Wordplay, compound words, and palindromes (also Wordplay/Story)

Maps (also Historical, in some cases, and I
noticed a lot of projects about maps and
mapmakers!);

Code switching (also SEL, Social Issues, Diversi-
ty/Inclusion, and several Identity topics);

Financial literacy;

The scientific method (also STEM);

Sustainable farming (also Gardening/Plants)

Refugees (also Social Issues and Family Issues);

Manners (also Behavior, SEL, and Family
Issues);

Behind the scenes/unappreciated jobs;

Anticipation/expectation gap and waiting/pa-
tience (also Behavior and SEL);

Counting (also STEM);

Conflict resolution (also Family/Home,
Siblings, Prickly Characters, Behavior,
Friendship/Teamwork, and SEL);

Opposites;

Law, specifically the Supreme Court and
Congress;

Holes (also Nature);

Routines of one day or one season (also
Weather/Seasons);

The human body;

Wonders around the world (also Historical and
International Settings); and

Horseshoe crabs (also Animals and Water
Ecosystems).

- **Change/Growth** // Character, Attribute, Topic,
Relationship, Tone (54 instances): This is either a story
that charts obvious character change and growth, or
one that implies growth is happening. There is some
overlap with Courage/Bravery/Strength/Resilience,

as well as other family- and relationship-based topics, like Friendship/Teamwork, Family/Home, Behavior, or Prickly Characters. For this topic, I would be careful about expressing an obvious message (see Chapter 5). The implication here is that a character will learn something and grow as a natural part of coming of age, but without the idea that they must change who they are (see Sense of Self and Shy/Quiet). This topic is very closely overlaid with Grief/Healing but can be much bigger than mourning life's challenges. It can also show characters growing for the sake of self-improvement, which would overlap with SEL, Sense of Self, and Identity Crisis.

- **SEL** // Character, Nonfiction, Attribute, Topic, Tone (53 instances): This topic is covered in great detail in Chapter 1. SEL-labeled projects seem like they will pretty explicitly recognize various emotional states and deal with feelings. There's some overlap with Change/Growth, School, Family/Home, Courage/Bravery/Strength/Resilience, Shy/Quiet, Sense of Self, Identity Crisis, and Friendship/Teamwork.

- **Latinx Identity** // Culture, Character, Setting, Attribute (52 instances): This category includes picture books that specifically deal with the Latinx experience, though this term has somewhat fallen out of favor. It's generally taken to mean everything from Hispanic stories to those of the South American experience, with some Caribbean and Afro-Latin mixed in, whether the protagonist has direct lived experience in that culture of origin (including active immigration from a home country, though immigration is also tracked as a separate topic under Diversity/Inclusion, Social Issues, and Family Issues), or claims a Latinx identity in other ways. I did not tally this topic based on the cultural identity or demographic of the picture book creator(s). I only used this label if the project seemed to deal with an element of cultural identity or tradition. If I had this survey to do over again, I would separate Hispanic and Mexican identities from Caribbean, and Central and South American identities. There can often be overlap with Elders/Ancestor, Neighborhood/Community, Food, Cultural Traditions, and Other Holidays.

- **Fantasy Creatures/Spooky** // Character Attributes, Tone, Setting (47 instances): These books feature protagonists, friends, or antagonists from a fantasy pantheon. Creatures in this topic include:

  Mermaids (quite a few projects in this cohort, also in Water Ecosystems);

  Monsters (generic and tied to Other Holidays mostly, as monsters specific to various cultures are labeled Myth/Folk);

  Yetis (quite a few!) and Bigfoot (overlapping with Myth/Folk);

  Vampires (also Other Holidays);

  Ghosts (same);

  Aliens;

  Imaginary friends (also Art/Creativity/Imagination);

  Unicorns (also Fairy Tale/Kingdom, and Adaptations/Retellings);

  Golems (also Jewish Identity);

  Fairies (also Fairy Tale/Kingdom); and

  Witches (also Other Holidays).

- **Other Holidays** // Topic, Culture, Setting (47 instances): Holiday picture books can be a tough proposition in the market, as their sales window is limited to the few months surrounding the relevant holiday. Stores will put out Halloween picture books from September to October. Otherwise, they might not be shelved at most bookstores for the remainder of the year. (Though my daughter was born on Halloween, so I have a vested interest in getting her some "spooky szn" books whenever I see them!) This topic is separate from the mother of all holiday topics: Christmas. Christmas is all about gifts, and picture books sell like hotcakes in November and December. This means Christmas books have their own label. Most other holidays fall under this topic, which also sometimes overlaps with Cultural Traditions and Religion:

Valentine's Day (pretty popular, also Love);
Halloween (very popular, also Fantasy Creatures/Spooky);
Purim, Passover, and Hanukkah (also Jewish Identity)
Groundhog Day (also Animals);
Samhain (also Myth/Folk);
Tet (also AAPI Identity);
Earth Day (also Nature and Environment/Climate Change);
New Year;
Lunar New Year (also AAPI Identity);
Juneteenth (also Black Identity);
Thanksgiving;
Dia de los Muertos (also Latinx Identity);
Diwali (also AAPI Identity);
Eid (also Middle Eastern and Muslim Identity);
All Souls Day (also Religious); and
Holi (also AAPI Identity).

- **School** // Setting (47 instances): This topic refers to any project that's set primarily in school, is about school traditions and relationships, or apparently happening at a school function (a field trip, for example). This topic does not cover learning that might happen outside of school, or individual curriculum topics (that's Specific Concept). The two main sub-topics here seem to include social relationships (see also Friendship/Teamwork), managing emotions (see SEL and Behavior), and changing schools or starting school for the first time (see Change/Growth).
- **Pets** // Character, Relationship (46 instances): All projects with pet characters also got an Animals label, but not all animals are meant to live in the home (or on a farm) and offer companionship. This very popular category mostly deals with cats and dogs, but there were some more offbeat animals represented as pets, too, like chinchillas. There's a lot of overlap with Family/Home here, as well as Friendship/Teamwork, Diversity/Inclusion, and Disability (service dogs, for example).
- **Love** // Character, Relationship, Tone (46 instances): This is a tone topic, mostly, but also deals with character relationships. There's heavy overlap here with Mommy/Daddy/Baby, Family/Home, and Elder/Ancestor. Other related tonal topics are Sweet/Positive and Poignant. The word "love" was mentioned in most memos that got this label, specifically the feeling of love between characters, rather than a preference ("Amy loved kittens!").
- **International Setting** // Setting, Character, Culture (46 instances): This topic overlaps with various Identity topics, Cultural Traditions, Elder/Ancestor, Family/Home, Growth/Change, Grief/Healing, and

Family Issues. I saw entire stories set internationally, maybe with a Myth/Folk or Other Holidays slant, or the international country of origin factored into an immigration story.

- **Funny** // Attribute, Tone (44 instances): There's overlap with this tone and Quirky and Sweet/Positive, but to me, Quirky means a little odd or unique, while Funny can be broader. All kinds of things can be Funny without also being Quirky, as long as the story or writing has humor. We'll talk more about humor in picture books in Chapter 14.
- **Family Issues** // Topic, Character, Relationship (42 instances): This topic differs from Family/Home because it's less focused on the togetherness and harmony of the family (and a tone of love and community), and is more concerned with specific family issues that kids and parents might be dealing with, such as:

    Divorce;
    Military families;
    Working parents;
    Single parents;
    Immigration experiences (also various Identity topics);
    Adoption;
    Phone addiction (!) (also Behavior);
    Moving;
    Job loss;
    Foster care (also various Identity topics, Diversity/Inclusion, and Social Issues);
    Responsibilities and roles within a family; and
    Sharing a room with siblings (also Siblings).

- **Food** // Culture, Topic (42 instances): Food is incredibly important, not only to biological life, but family life and culture. There's a lot of overlap here with various Identity topics, Family/Home, Neighborhood/Community, Cultural Traditions, Elder/Ancestor, and Other Holidays. In these books, food was identified in the deal memo as playing a role in bringing people together, or as an exploration of identity.

- **Weather/Seasons** // Setting (41 instances): Weather informs setting, as well as calendar-year moments in a child's life. There is overlap with Nature and Environment/Climate Change, which is a separate topic.

- **Music/Dance/Performance** // Attribute, Topic (40 instances): Kids love to express themselves, and it's not unusual to find a story about a child whose personality is wrapped up in doing some kind of music, dance, or performance. These topics sometimes have a contest plot mechanic, overlap with Other Holidays, or bring the Neighborhood/Community together.

- **Mommy/Daddy/Baby** // Character, Relationship, Tone (39 instances): This is a very popular picture book topic, almost stereotypically so, in the vein of *If Animals Kissed Good Night* by Ann Whitford Paul, illustrated David Walker. It's the kind of cuddly book with a tone of "Mommy/Daddy loves you!" Love, Family/Home, and Sweet/Positive are overlapping topics, but I suppose the more subversive *Boss Baby* by Marla Frazee would've also gotten this label, while also slanting it in a Funny direction.

- **Verse** // Tone (38 instances): This is technically a topic that would fit in a writing style category, which I didn't create because its application would've been too limited, so I've slotted it under Tone. Any type of story can be a Verse picture book —it all depends on how a writer has chosen to express themselves. See Chapter 14 for more on rhyming picture books. I'm not sure that every use of rhyme was identified in the deal memos, but it's important to note how few instances there are, given the overall tallies. Prepare for some tough love if you're a picture book poet. This label covers both rhyme and verse projects, with rhyme indicating a more stringent pattern, while verse refers to a looser poetic style.

- **Wordplay/Story** // Topic (37 instances): Book people love books. Have you ever read a novel about a writer? A librarian? A bookstore owner? That's no accident. Bookish topics, or stories about stories, can be catnip for agents and editors. Some of these projects also seem to have a heavy wordplay or literary element.

- **Art/Creativity/Imagination** // Attribute, Topic, Tone (36 instances): As with Music/ Dance/Performance, Art/Creativity/Imagination books feature a child who loves to use their imagination and express themselves. This activity often offers not only Sense of Self to the character, but potential for their creation to inspire others and bring people together, overlapping with Neighborhood/Community or School.

- **Kindness** // Attribute, Tone, Relationship (36 instances): These stories have a tone or ending geared toward kindness for ourselves, others, and the world. There's a difference between this topic and the tone categories of Sweet/Positive and Poignant. Kindness involves something people *do* in addition to a pleasant or uplifting tone, and there's overlap with Diversity/Inclusion and Disability.

- **Adventure** // Setting (36 instances): Adventure books affect plot, but I didn't have enough distinct topics to necessitate a separate plot category. Therefore, I decided to make the odd plot-related outliers part of the Setting category. This label refers to stories that take kids or families on a more active, often outdoor, journey. There's a lot of overlap with Nature and Animals.
- **Social Issues** // Topic, Culture, Tone, Nonfiction, Character (34 instances): Just as Family Issues is a more topic-specific slant on Family/Home, Social Issues is adjacent to Diversity/Inclusion and Disability labels. As we discussed in Chapter 1, the modern picture book market is very concerned with social justice advocacy. More specific picture book stories with this topic include:

  Refugee issues;
  Synagogue vandalism (also Jewish Identity);
  Child labor;
  Housing insecurity (also Family Issues, House, and Family/Home);
  School shootings (also School);
  Socioeconomic inequality;
  War (also Historical and International Settings); and
  Disaster relief (also Neighborhood/Community).

- **Grief/Healing** // Character, Attribute, Tone, Relationship (34 instances): Grief can impact our Sense of Self, Family Issues, and Change/Growth. It often centers on Elder/Ancestor characters, or Family/Home, and demands Courage/Bravery/Strength/Resilience. There's overlap with SEL, and these projects often have a Poignant tone. Grief touches all of us, unfortunately, and there's a perennial need for books that provide perspective on it.

- **Water Ecosystems** // Nonfiction, Setting (33 instances): There's overlap with Nature and Animals here, as well as Weather/Seasons, and Environment/Climate Change. This topic relates specifically to creatures who live in rivers, lakes, or oceans, and to stories set in and around those places.

- **Siblings** // (32 instances): Some books that feature Family/Home, Sense of Self and Family Issues topics also focus on sibling relationships. Whether the sibling is a new baby, or an older brother or sister, or there's sibling rivalry—this topic affects a lot of children in our target audience. There's overlap here with Behavior and SEL as well.

- **Environment/Climate Change** // Setting, Nonfiction, Topic (31 instances): Just as children are growing and changing, Planet Earth is changing, too. While climate change and the environment have become politically charged topics, this is understandably going to be a picture book focus now, and in the future. There's often overlap with Animals, Nature, and Water Ecosystems, but books with the Weather/Seasons label are counted separately, as not all stories about weather are also about climate change.

- **Myth/Folk** // Culture, Topic (28 instances): Sometimes there's overlap with this topic and Cultural Traditions, various Identities, and holidays (Other Holidays, Christmas, etc.), Neighborhood/Community, Fantasy Creatures/Spooky, Nature, and Elder/Ancestor. This is a catch-all topic for stories that feature traditions from world cultures as well. Projects tend to either fit in this topic or Fairy Tale / Kingdom, but not both.

- **Identity Crisis** / / Character, Tone, Attribute (28 instances): This is a really interesting topic that differs from Sense of Self. I labeled projects with Sense of Self when it seemed clear that the character is proud of and secure in who they are, at baseline. With an Identity Crisis topic, the character is struggling with part of their personality. They're not exactly hoping to learn that they're worthy (that's more Picture Book 1.0, as discussed in Chapter 1), but they have big feelings (an SEL overlap) or they're grappling with Behavior, Shy / Quiet, Family Issues, Courage / Bravery / Strength / Resilience, Grief / Healing, or Growth / Change. We'll unpack this distinction more when we discuss the Had It All Along vs. Get On My Level picture book structures in Chapter 12.
- **Mindfulness** / / Topic, Attribute, Nonfiction, Tone (27 instances): There's a strong topic overlap with SEL and Growth / Change here. In stories that I labeled with the more specific Mindfulness topic, it seems that the aim of the project was prescriptive—this is *how* you can work toward mindfulness and grow as a person.
- **Jewish Identity** / / Culture (26 instances): These books specifically identify a Jewish culture or heritage. There can be overlap with Other Holidays, Cultural Traditions, Food, Family / Home, Neighborhood / Community, and Elders / Ancestor. It's important to note that not all books with this label are overtly Religious, though.
- **Disability** / / Topic, Nonfiction, Character, Tone (26 instances): Deal memos that got this label specifically identified either a character who is a person with disabilities, or were about Diversity / Inclusion,

Neighborhood/Community, Kindness, and Medical Conditions, as these elements can relate to disability advocacy. If your main character is a person with disabilities, it lends you a lot of credibility if you're writing authentically from lived experience, as discussed in Chapter 1. Examples I saw with this batch of deal memos were:

Wheelchair users
Down Syndrome
Sensory processing disorder
Blindness
Limb difference
Neurodivergence
Selective mutism

- **Personified Objects** // Character (26 instances): For more discussion of characters who are either anthropomorphized animals or personified objects, check out Chapter 9. This topic involves characters who seem decidedly not human, and not animal either. Examples include:

A robot;
Planet Earth itself (also Environment/Climate Change and Nature);
A scab (!) (also Medical Conditions);
A matzah ball (see Jewish Identity, Other Holidays, and Food);
Individual alphabet letters;
A school bus (also School);
A sandcastle (by now, you should all recognize our deal memo example);
Sticks and stones (I have a feeling I know where this one is going …);

A volcano (also, Nature, and awesome);

A mess (I love a personified mess, being one myself!);

A sponge (!); and

A credit card.

- **Prickly Characters** // Attribute, Character, Tone (24 instances): I applied this topic to a project when I sensed a character with an exaggerated Sense of Self, including both positive *and* negative attributes. The character might even be dealing with an Identity Crisis, especially when it comes to Friendship/Teamwork. This topic also touches on Behavior and Making Mistakes, and it's important to note that the prickly elements of the protagonist's personality are balanced out by positive notes, and the character will almost undoubtedly learn to embrace their big emotions (SEL) and be redeemed (Growth/Change). Sometimes a prickly character can also be matched with a Funny or Quirky tone.

- **Middle Eastern and Muslim Identity** // Culture, Topic, Setting (24 instances): I am probably unhappiest with the label for this topic, especially after the events of October 2023, as I know that not all people of Middle Eastern origin are Muslim and vice versa, but this was my catch-all for stories that involved Middle Eastern (and adjacent) settings, cultures, and religions, whether the protagonist has direct lived experience in that culture of origin (including active immigration from a home country, though immigration is also tracked as a separate topic under Diversity/Inclusion, Social Issues, and Family Issues), or claims a Middle Eastern and/or Muslim identity in other ways. I did not tally this topic based on the cultural identity or demographic of the picture book creator(s). I only used this label if the project seemed to deal with an element of Middle Eastern and/or Muslim-specific cultural identity or tradition. There can often be overlap with Elders/Ancestor, Neighborhood/Community, Food, Cultural Traditions, and Other Holidays.

- **House** // Setting (23 instances): The topic of Family/Home covers the feeling of home, as do Love and Mommy/Daddy/Baby, while the House topic relates specifically to a story that's centered on a building, whether a family's house or an apartment complex (there's overlap with Neighborhood/Community, Cultural Traditions, Other Holidays, and Christmas).
- **Gardening/Plants** // Topic, Setting (22 instances): Similarly, there are quite a few picture books about gardening, gardens, and plants grown by people. There are obvious overlaps with Neighborhood/Community, Food, and Nature.
- **Christmas** // Topic, Setting, Tone (21 instances): We've already covered Other Holidays, as well as some Cultural Traditions and holidays related to various Identity topics. While Christmas is low on the overall list of topics, twenty-one Christmas-specific picture books sold in one year is still a notable number. This is perhaps the most common holiday that has entire picture books devoted to it, because it naturally overlaps with Family/Home, Neighborhood/Community, Elder/Ancestor, Love, Religious, Food, and Cultural Traditions. It's also a gift-giving holiday with a very specific mythology that lends itself to imaginative illustrations.
- **Fairy Tale/Kingdom** // Topic, Setting (20 instances): With this label, I saw either fairies (also Fantasy Creatures/Spooky) or a familiar story that has been

adapted (also Adaptations/Retellings). If the fairy tale had a more specific Cultural Traditions or Identity focus, I generally excluded it. Projects in this category also tended to exclude Myth/Folk, as I consider fairy tales or stories set in a traditional princess/castle type of kingdom to be a distinct mythology.

- **Religious** // Topic, Setting, Tone (20 instances): A generic label for religious stories in the Christian tradition, or nondenominational stories that aren't otherwise specific to any other Identity categories, like Jewish or Middle Eastern and Muslim. There are religious publishers catering to various faiths and creeds throughout the industry. Some might be looking for widely marketable material without an overt religious slant, while others might intentionally serve certain demographics. It's worth researching potential targets if you plan to write for a specific faith-based audience.

- **Queer** // Topic, Relationship, Tone (19 instances): Queer characters fit within this topic, which has become incredibly inflammatory, especially as it pertains to books for young audiences. Generally, queer story and character topics overlap with Family/Home, Diversity/Inclusion, and Family Issues, and it's usually an adult in the child's life who identifies as queer. There are also a few instances where children themselves are exploring their gender identity, whether they have a proud Sense of Self or an Identity Crisis about it. No matter your personal feelings about queer and gender identity topics for children, you'll find that some projects run directly at this topic, while others conspicuously avoid it. The same goes for agents and publishers—they either *really* want to see queer representation in picture books, or they *really* don't.

- **Farm** // Character, Setting (18 instances): Pretty self-explanatory! There's overlap with Animals, and this topic can mean the farm animals are either our protagonists (see *More Than Fluff* by Madeline Valentine), or the people taking care of them (as in *Click, Clack, Moo: Cows That Type* by Doreen Cronin, illustrated by Betsy Lewin, and *Patch of Sky* by Nic Yulo).

- **Making Mistakes** // Topic, Relationship, Attribute (18 instances): This dovetails with Prickly Characters, Change/Growth, Friendship/Teamwork, Sense of Self, Identity Crisis, Behavior, and SEL. The thing is, your target audience has big feelings and doesn't always handle them well. In fact, I go into detail about a Character vs. Emotion conflict type in Chapter 11. We all make mistakes (even me, but don't tell my husband), and modeling how to handle them with grace and understanding is a solid picture book topic. (Sometimes it's the kid who makes a mistake, as is the case with *Meow!*, and sometimes it's the adult who makes a mistake and apologizes, as is the case with *Good Night, Little Man* by Daniel Bernstrom, illustration by Heidi Woodward Sheffield.)

- **Birthday/Party** // Setting, Tone, Topic (18 instances): Everyone loves a party, and some picture books overtly deal with birthdays or take place at parties of various kinds, with Other Holidays, Cultural Traditions, and Neighborhood/Community overlap. *Maxwell's Magic Mix-Up* by Linda Ashman, illustrated by Regan Dunnick, is a good example of a birthday picture book.

- **Space** // Setting, Nonfiction, Topic (17 instances): Whether it features in fiction or nonfiction, outer space captures young imaginations. You can see this at play in *A Hundred Billion Trillion Stars* by Seth Fishman, illustrated by Isabel Greenberg on the nonfiction side, and *Interstellar Cinderella* by Deborah Underwood, illustrated by Meg Hunt, in fiction.

- **Bedtime** // Topic, Relationship, Tone (17 instances): Another popular topic. All families with young children have to deal with bedtime. Unfortunately, it happens every night. Books are often read as part of this elaborate ritual, so the prevalence of this topic is self-explanatory. *Even Monsters Need to Sleep* by Lisa Wheeler, illustrated by Chris Van Dusen, is a great example.

- **Sports** // Topic, Attribute (16 instances): I saw more stories about creative pursuits (Music/Dance/Performance and Art/Creativity/Imagination), but sports projects also exist. These stories often have a competition plot and teach values consistent with good sportsmanship and personal growth. It's important to remember our SEL focus. Your characters don't always have to win the game or get the trophy, and it might even be better if they don't, as this opens up opportunities for Courage/Bravery/Strength/Resilience and Growth/Change.

- **Behavior** // Topic, Character, Tone (14 instances): As mentioned in Chapter 3, parents or caregivers will sometimes shop for picture books by topic. There's heavy overlap between this label and Family Issues. Behavior books, specifically, show a character (and their family) struggling with specific issues, such as:

  Picky eating
  Bath avoidance
  Not listening

Avoiding chores

Impatience

Perfectionism (also SEL, Identity Crisis, and
Growth/Change)

Not sharing

- **Native Identity** // Topic, Character, Setting, Culture, Nonfiction (14 instances): This topic showcases stories of native and indigenous identities of the Americas, whether the child has direct lived experience in that culture of origin, or claims a native or indigenous identity in other ways. This topic can overlap with Elders/Ancestor, Cultural Traditions, Neighborhood/Community, or Myth/Folk.
- **Adaptations/Retellings** // Topic, Tone, Character (12 instances): I slotted things here that didn't fit into Fairy Tale/Kingdom and Myth/Folk. See Chapter 13 for some additional thoughts on what makes an adaptation or retelling successful in the picture book market.
- **Life Dreams** // Topic, Tone (12 instances): This is an important topic to examine for all of those aspiring picture book writers who weren't paying attention to Chapter 1 and still just want to tell kids to dream big in life. Note that we only have 12 instances here. I was not surprised by how few projects I found that seemed to deal with this message. We've all read *The Wonderful Things You Will Be* by Emily Winfield Martin, and we all want our picture books to be given to teary-eyed pregnant people at baby showers. But this "You can achieve your dreams" message is not a growth area of the market because it has been done many times over. There's obvious overlap with Love and Mommy/Daddy/Baby.

- **Business/Kids in Jobs** // Topic, Setting, Character (11 instances): It's always fun to showcase a kid doing something more sophisticated than their age would suggest, like working in a business (even if it's a family ice cream stand). There's overlap with Family/Home, Sense of Self, and Neighborhood/Community here.
- **Dinosaurs** // Topic, Nonfiction, Setting, Character (9 instances): Dinosaur books will never stop being published, whether as fiction or nonfiction.
- **Trucks/Construction/First Responders** // Topic, Setting, Character (9 instances): Neither will books about trucks and construction sites and police/fire/ambulance professionals and vehicles. I should know—my machine-crazy children own most of them already. A really fresh take on this topic, which also proposes a new mythology for storms, is *Thunder Trucks* by Cheryl Klein and Katy Beebe, illustrated by Mike Boldt, and this would also fit under Weather in my rubric.
- **Metanarrative** // Topic (9 instances): This is an interesting topic that overlaps with Wordplay/Story, as well as Fairy Tale/Kingdom and Adaptations/Retellings. A metanarrative is basically a story within a story, or a story about a story, with one story commenting on the other. There's a specific Nested Story structure discussed in Chapter 12. A published example of this type of book is *Ivan the Terrier* by Peter Catalanotto, which gives us the character of Ivan, a dog who wants to make several well-known fairy tales all about himself. Others are *Violet and Victor Write the Most Fabulous Fairy Tale* by Alice Kuipers, illustrated by Bethanie Deeney Murguia, and *How to Eat a Book* by Mrs. & Mr. Macleod.

- **Biracial Identity** // Character, Culture, Topic (8 instances): In addition to all of the specific Identity topics already discussed, this one specifically features a story about a mixed-race protagonist or family. This can overlap with Family/Home, Cultural Traditions, Neighborhood/Community, and Family Issues.
- **Zoo** // Topic, Character, Setting (7 instances): Just like Farm but set in a zoo, with the relevant Animals. The book can be about the animals or the visitors (or, in the case of *A Sick Day for Amos McGee* by Philip C. Stead, illustrated by Erin E. Stead, the zookeeper, though this is rare because picture books don't often feature an adult protagonist, as discussed in Chapter 1).
- **European Identity** // Character, Topic, Setting (6 instances): It should come as no surprise that various European (and adjacent) identities are not as robustly represented in today's picture books, as diversity and inclusion efforts are aiming to balance a largely white picture book landscape and feature underrepresented creators and cultures. If you can claim a European cultural identity and you've been hoping to explore it, keep an eye out for a timeliness hook. As you can imagine, several books with a Ukrainian focus were acquired between 2022 and 2023. Notably, no picture books from a Russian perspective were sold.[3]
- **Medical Conditions** // Character, Topic, Tone (6

---

3. I am Russian and Ukrainian by heritage, so this is a fraught topic for me. Be aware that even bestselling authors are not immune to playing the optics game. Elizabeth Gilbert, who many would assume to be untouchable, announced the cancellation of her novel, THE SNOW FOREST, in June, 2023, because of its Russian setting, and the subsequent outcry about it. Her book apparently wasn't "pro" or "anti" the war, yet its announcement was still interpreted through the lens of current events. Here's an article about her decision: https://www.npr.org/2023/06/12/1181714943/elizabeth-gilbert-halts-new-book-release-russia-ukraine

instances): This is similar to books with a Disability, Courage/Bravery/Strength/Resilience, or Family Issues topic. We all inhabit bodies, and sometimes those bodies are different, get ill, or do quirky things Allergies, mental health concerns (overlapping with Mindfulness, Behavior, and SEL), hiccups, and being sick with the flu are examples from this cohort of deal memos.

- **Bullying** // Character, Topic, Tone (4 instances): For those of you who still don't believe me about moralizing, as discussed in Chapters 4 and 5, take a look at the number of bullying books in this sample. There were only four books about bullying. *Out of one thousand*. Sure, some of the School and Friendship/Teamwork stories probably feature bullies. But only four projects mentioned them overtly in the deal memos. If your picture book idea is "Bullying is bad and we need to come together," you will need to put a very fresh spin on it. Or spin it right into the paper shredder, until you find a new angle.

This is obviously a thorough list. As you're training your imagination on various picture book topics and learning the current market, I hope some of this data makes sense. But some findings surprised even me, so I'm glad to have these ideas and numbers. This was a fascinating exercise in possibilities and perceived trends.

Other Considerations for a Book Deal

Now that your head is swimming with more picture book ideas, themes, and topics than you could have imagined, let's keep a few other things in mind. Perhaps the most jarring, yet important, is that a great idea, executed well, is not the only determining factor for getting an agent and/or publisher, or of picture book success.

Oftentimes, I'm confronted by frustrated writers who ask me, in these exact words (or other, more colorful terms): "Why do so many crappy books get published?" Hey, we've all read a book at one point or another and wondered the same thing, so let's get into it.

Artistic quality and vision are certainly two considerations of getting a literary agent or a book deal. And I would argue they're the most important two.

But. The inevitable "but …"

There are other elements that can come into play, some of which merit frustration.

Sometimes these apply to debut projects, sometimes they apply to projects by established authors, sometimes they apply to projects by people who have no business writing picture books whatsoever. (You'll see what I mean in a second.)

Other considerations that can contribute to a book deal include:

First to Market: Breaking news forces a publisher's hand and they want to be part of the conversation.

- Sometimes a publisher wants to appear current and quickly put a book on shelves that responds to a perceived need, and they want to be first on the scene.
- Our planet seems to spin on the axis of a 24/7 news cycle. Trendy or interesting or relevant topics come and go, and sometimes a specific interest area takes *the entire world* by storm (say, viral pandemics in 2020, K-pop, etc.).

- Publishers will be surprised by events and want to acquire something on the fly. This explains the relative lack of polish on some timely projects. Artistic integrity and execution are nice here, but often take a backseat.

Timeliness Hook: Similar to the above, but a book is produced to support an upcoming or known event.

- A timeliness hook is very important in some types of adult nonfiction, for example, where books can be rushed into print in a matter of months. (We've all seen transcripts hit shelves with lightning speed after a congressional inquiry, for example.)
- "Rushing a book to market" is almost a laughable concept with picture books, because good illustrations take time, as does layout, design, and production. But sometimes a publisher wants a certain kind of book with a certain topic on a certain timeline. The project in front of them might not be the *best* book possible … and yet, the publisher is thinking of timing, above all.
- Sometimes a house can preempt a big event by anticipating the need for a book and doing a lot of legwork ahead of time, just as important people's obituaries are pre-written by news organizations and ready to go when the inevitable happens. I'm betting that a commemorative version of Amanda Gorman's inauguration poem, "The Hill We Climb," was already in the works before the fact. The keepsake edition for adult readers was published by Viking on March 30th, 2021, after hitting the national consciousness on January 20th. Two months might seem like a big lag to the uninitiated, but this is lightning-fast work in the publishing world.

- The timeliness angle can also present an opportunity, especially if a publisher is planning projects in advance. If you have some foresight and want to noodle around for an upcoming anniversary that might want a picture book to support it, you could land a book deal by pitching on a timeliness sales hook. Just make sure you're thinking about three years ahead to account for development, submission, and production timeframes.

Contractual Obligation: Sometimes a less-than-excellent book can be the result of very boring behind-the-scenes considerations to do with the creator's arrangement with their house.

- Some authors have options on their subsequent work from their publishers, or are trying to fulfill a multi-book deal. At times—and for reasons that are too granular and nuanced to unpack here—they might not have a great project in mind for an option or their next book.
- They might submit something to their publishers that nobody is *thrilled* by. Everyone decides to soldier on without hurting anyone's feelings, and the book is produced.
- Publishing is—oddly enough, for all its heartbreaking rejection—a surprisingly genteel business ... which also leaves a lot to be desired when more direct communication would benefit all parties.

Loyalty: A factor that's similar to the above, except it's driven by feelings, not legal status.

- A writer might not be churning out their best work these days, but they've been with the publisher for years, and gosh, everyone on staff just loves them. Is their newest effort a blockbuster? No. But sometimes books happen because nobody wants to rock the boat. Besides, what if their *next* book is a knockout?

- It's getting less and less common for a midlist author (one who publishes regularly and dependably but without any breakout hits to speak of) is strung along indefinitely just because everyone's nice, as publishers will generally want to trim any fat they find. But loyalty can explain some middling books.

Strong Prior Sales: A proven seller is often given latitude because publishers like to make money.

- This situation differs from the above, as some authors may sell incredibly well, even if there doesn't seem to be an overt reason.
- Maybe they got started in the game a few decades ago and have a dedicated, multi-generational fan base. Maybe they are sleeping with the executive editor at their imprint (we all laugh and clutch our pearls … but it has happened).
- It can be a chicken-or-egg scenario. Do they sell well because they've always sold well, or have they always sold well because the publisher has invested in marketing them?
- Whatever the case may be, authors with steady, growing sales over time are generally left to their own devices because they have a built-in audience. Historically strong sales numbers can explain many puzzling projects. Sales numbers relate directly to the below, as well.

High-profile (Marketable) Author: Big names can be a

gamble, but agents and editors tend to rally around the promise of big sales.

- If a debut project seems like it's being marketed left and right but is maybe not the strongest in terms of groundbreaking vision or execution, look at the name on the jacket. Is it a celebrity? A TikTok influencer? A lifestyle blogger? Sometimes past sales pave the way for publishing longevity, and sometimes the notion of future sales can explain an underwhelming book.
- Having worked on some celebrity projects behind the scenes, I can confidently say that celebrity "authors" exist in a "yes" bubble. (Some of these personalities don't write a word, and instead simply communicate a half-baked pitch to a ghostwriter through several layers of agents and managers). Not because they're bad people, but because it takes a lot of effort and self-awareness to counteract the daily "you're a genius, and everyone is so excited about everything you say, so please keep paying us commission" messaging they get from their underlings.
- Famous authors, whether they're famous for being authors or famous for being famous, often get a pass on the content of their projects. A lot of celebrities get the notion to write a picture book because it's such an adorable brand extension, and someone will probably publish it if it's even remotely legible. Big names bring sales, though sometimes these projects fizzle out and are swept under the rug, because the "yes" bubble can be fickle.

Publisher Focus: Not every book is for every reader.

- Sometimes, a smaller, niche, or regional publisher can turn out projects that puzzle the average reader.

That's okay. They are likely not for the average reader, but for a very specific subset of the book-buying public.

- Before you judge a book from a small or unknown publisher too harshly, look up their mission statement. That might answer some questions or add some context.

Something in Retrograde: Astral mischief.

- A strange alignment of planets at the time of acquisition, or some kind of past life bargain with a mythological entity.[4]

This chapter is, overall, meant to be encouraging. Look how many different topics—and subtopics, and slants on topics—are possible in the picture book market! As you can see from the quick discussion on why else a picture book might get acquired, there are also other forces at play, aside from a brilliant idea, done brilliantly.

Writing and publishing can seem very complex, and there are often many factors involved (the aforementioned planetary alignment being only one example). This also means there's a lot of opportunity for all kinds of writers and ideas to participate in the marketplace.

Let's continue to explore the landscape by talking about concept and nonfiction picture books.

---

4. Just kidding. Maybe.

SEVEN

CONCEPT PICTURE BOOKS

WE FIRST UNPACKED the difference between narrative, concept, and nonfiction picture books in Chapter 1. But the category of concept books, especially as it differs from nonfiction, can be tough to understand.

Stick with me for a moment:

- Both concept and nonfiction picture books *teach*.
- Both concept and nonfiction picture books *explore a topic*.

"Huh? Well what kind of nonsense is that? Why are you confounding me, Mary Kole?"

I get it. I have to admit that I didn't understand this distinction at first.

When you think of picture books that teach something, you're probably thinking of nonfiction projects, which break down a specific topic in a lot of detail. But concept books can blend a nonfiction topic (or one that could be done in a more straightforward nonfiction style, which we'll discuss in Chapter 8) and a narrative storytelling approach. But only sometimes.

And other times, they focus on one very clear topic and nothing else. Yep, that's clear as mud.

Concept books are the weird limbo category between fiction and nonfiction, and sometimes they're neither. This is an incredibly slippery, well, *concept* for many writers to grasp. With concept books, you are often choosing one specific topic to teach, but adding some narrative structure, maybe some characters, and at least a beginning, middle, and end to the book.

We'll talk a lot about narrative structure in Chapter 12, but in a concept book, you can often get away with introducing the concept in the beginning, demonstrating or deepening readers' understanding of the concept in the middle, and reinforcing the concept at the end.

If there is a story, there won't be a deep or layered one. In fact, repetition generally bears the concept out, more than anything else.

Here are some examples from shelves, organized into several categories:

- **Topic**: In its most basic form, a concept book teaches a topic in a fresh or interesting way. *Alphabet Boats* by Samantha R. Vamos, illustrated by Ryan O'Rourke, is one such example. It highlights the ABCs of words and phrases related to boats. Who knew? *Wheels* by Sally Sutton, illustrated by Brian Lovelock, lists off popular vehicles. *Holi Hai!* by Chitra Soundar, illustrated by Darshika Varma, is about a popular holiday in Indian culture, with a light narrative wrapper that is mostly meant to explain the various events of Holi. *Look* by Fiona Woodcock is structured around a day inspired by words with an "oo" sound (they read a book and go to the zoo, of course). *The*

Lights that Dance in the Night by Yuval Zommer is a lovely rhyming meditation on cold climates and Northern lights.

- **Public Domain Material**: Adaptations of folk tales, classic stories, familiar songs, and / or nursery rhymes can fit the concept book category as well, though you will have to add enough to the existing idea to make sure that you're innovating (see Chapter 13 for thoughts on adaptations and retellings). A retelling of a folk story can be rather straightforward, like *The First Fire: A Cherokee Story* by Brad Wagon and Alex Stephenson. Or the adaptation can put a new spin on a familiar tune or pattern, like *The Rice in the Pot Goes Round and Round* by Wendy Wan-Long Shang, illustrated by Lorian Tu, which gives us a new cultural twist on a well-known (public domain[1]) song. *Still This Love Goes On* by Buffy Sainte-Marie, illustrated by Julie Flett, is an original song about love, beautifully illustrated.

- **Reversal or Twist**: A clever and unexpected reframe can sometimes make a concept book. *Even Monsters Need to Sleep* is predicated on the idea of a monster who needs his dad to read him a bedtime story. We then go into the tales themselves, and they feature all kinds of familiar monster characters getting ready for bed (Yeti, a bridge troll, the Loch Ness Monster, etc.). This is a metanarrative (a story within a story) and operates with a reversal—the monster wants his dad to check beneath the bed for humans. But because the central character (the monster going to bed) is largely off the page, there's no character growth arc, and no

---

1. Before you adapt a song or story and hinge your entire creation on someone else's intellectual property, make sure you have the legal right to do so.

plot to speak of, which makes this is a concept type of book, rather than a narrative type. *Ivan the Terrier* is very similar. The *Little* series of books by Amy Krause Rosenthal, illustrated by Jen Corace, like *Little Hoot* and *Little Oink*, play on common childhood complaints (not cleaning, wanting to stay up late, etc.) with simple twists. Little Hoot is an owl who wants to go to bed. Little Oink lives in a pigsty but wants to clean up. *How Do Dinosaurs Say Good Night?* by Jane Yolen, illustrated by Mark Teague, tackles the perennial problem of bedtime by putting powerful dinosaurs in the kids' shoes—only the dinosaurs don't dare disobey their parents. The logic is that if a T-Rex can go to bed without whining, so can a child.

- **Repetition**: Repeated instances or ideas often play a big role in concept books. *Thank You, Omu!* by Oge Mora, and *Little Bitty Friends* by Elizabeth McPike, illustrated by Patrice Barton, aren't narratives, per se, but they explore their topics (sharing in the community and love of small animals, respectively) through multiple examples that riff on one idea.

- Some concept books take a familiar phenomenon or idea and attempt to explain it in a clever way. *Thunder Trucks* claims that storms happen whenever a bunch of big trucks get together to have fun in the sky. This makes extreme weather less scary and is a crowd-pleaser for kids who love powerful vehicles.

- **Humor**: Jokes and funny ideas are a great way to present a concept, too. *Rhyming Dust Bunnies* by Jan Thomas features four dust bunnies who "rhyme, all the time."[2] Their names are Ed, Ned, Ted ... and Bob. As you can probably guess, Bob did not get the memo about the rhyming shtick. Readers are then treated to

---

2. Jan Thomas, *Rhyming Dust Bunnies*, 4-5.

several instances of Bob getting the rhyme wrong, with hilarious results. However, Bob also sees something the others don't, and it turns out he isn't messing up the rhymes on purpose. His garbled messages are a warning about a looming threat. The subversion and reversal of expectations here makes for a very fun read-aloud experience for both kid listeners and adults, which I'll talk more about in Chapter 14. But we're also introduced to simple rhymes as we're laughing.

- **Good Vibes Only**: Some concept books do express a positive message, but in an engaging way. Sometimes, publishers want to reinforce a loving or inspiring tone without too much preaching. These stories feel good to read and make great gifts. *All the World* by Liz Garton Scanlon, illustrated by Marla Frazee, *So Many Days* by Alison McGhee, illustrated by Taeeun Yoo, *Dear Boy,* by Paris and Jason Rosenthal, illustrated by Holly Hatam, *What the Road Said* by Cleo Wade, illustrated by Lucie de Moyencourt, *Maybe* by Kobi Yamada, illustrated by Gabriella Barouch, and *All Kinds of Awesome* by Jess Hitchman, illustrated by Vivienne To, are some examples. *The Joy in You* by Cat Deeley and Laura Baker, illustrated by Rosie Butcher, is one that falls flat to me, though the author's celebrity profile likely explains this, per Chapter 6.

- **Moral-driven**: Sometimes—*big sigh*—the lesson is more overt. Without it, there would probably not be a book, but the takeaway is so universal that publishers feel duty-bound to issue new material that services it. *Tell Someone* by Debra Kempf Shumaker, illustrated by Tristan Yuvienco, is about finding a safe adult and telling them when abuse is happening. This type of book needs to exist in our world, unfortunately. Other examples are *Dolls and Trucks are for Everyone* by Robb

Pearlman, illustrated by Eda Kaban, which is about gender identity and expression; *How to Hug a Pufferfish* by Ellie Peterson, which is about body boundaries; and *I Am One: A Book of Action* by Susan Verde, illustrated by Peter H. Reynolds, about making change in the world when problems feel insurmountable.

- **Current Events**: Other types of concept books exist because they're timely, as discussed in Chapter 6. A concept with a timeliness hook tackles the topic of community policing in *Can We Please Give the Police Department to the Grandmothers?* by Junauda Petrus, illustrated by Kristen Uroda. Without some of the previous decade's police brutality events and resulting social justice action, this book would likely not exist.
- **States of Mind**: A subcategory of concept books features writers who want to tackle the idea of creativity and demonstrate it, while also inspiring readers. Sometimes the characters involved try to combat another favorite childhood topic: boredom. *What If…* by Samantha Berger, illustrated by Mike Curato, *Violet and Victor Write the Most Fabulous Fairy Tale, Parker Looks Up: An Extraordinary Moment* by Parker and Jessica Curry, illustrated by Brittany Jackson, *How to Eat a Book, The Boring Book* by Shinsuke Yoshitake, and *What to Do with a Box* by Jane Yolen, illustrated by Chris Sheban, are examples.
- **Big Feelings**: SEL ideas, first discussed in Chapter 1, are also often expressed using the concept book format. Examples can be anything from *They All Saw a Cat* and *Duck! Rabbit!* by Amy Krouse Rosenthal, illustrated by Tom Lichtenheld, which both reinforce the idea that everyone has different perspectives, to the many books about feelings, like *Alphabreaths* by

Christopher Willard and Daniel Rechtschaffen, illustrated by Holly Clifton-Brown, *The Monster Parade: A Book About Feeling All Your Feelings and Then Watching Them Go, I'm Going to Have a Good Day* by Tiania Haneline and Scarlett Gray, illustrated by Stephanie Dehennin, *In My Heart: A Book of Feelings* by Jo Witek, illustrated by Christine Roussey, and *The Color Monster. The Invisible String* by Patrice Karst, illustrated by Geoff Stevenson, is about maintaining a loving connection between people, even if they're not together, with a slight undertone of grief as well, since the "invisible string" can reach everywhere, including Heaven.

- **Packaging**: Sometimes paper engineering elements or other interactive features make a concept book. *Under the Ocean* by Anouck Boisrobert, illustrated by Louis Rigaud, *Never Touch the Monsters* by Rosie Greening, and *In My Heart: A Book of Feelings* are some examples that likely wouldn't be engaging enough without their pop-up, touch-and-feel, and die cut elements, respectively.

- **Premise**: And sometimes a concept book is just plain fun, with a premise that hits a market zeitgeist or is otherwise irresistible. *The Day the Crayons Quit* by Drew Daywalt, illustrated by Oliver Jeffers, is a great idea—crayons rebelling against their usual roles—and provides entertainment, so it got to be a book. There's set-up and an ending, but the bulk of the story features letters from individual crayons, which don't necessarily evoke a larger narrative.

Some of these projects also have a story component, but their "plots" tend to be very loose. In Chapter 11, I'll unpack the types of conflicts that appear in narrative picture books, and in Chapter 12, I'll offer some structure options. In a narrative picture book, the narrative is *the point of the book*. In concept books, the narrative is almost beside the point.

For example, *Duck! Rabbit!* has the technical narrative framework of an argument between friends. The monsters in the *Never Touch the Monsters* do activities where they disappear one by one (lending the project a light counting element), then come back together to see a movie. There's also a subtle addition and subtraction dynamic in *Ten Little Zombies* by Andy Rash, which my children love, even though it's … well … downright violent. *Guyku: A Year of Haiku for Boys* by Bob Raczka, illustrated by Peter H. Reynolds, features adventure-forward, boy-friendly (whatever that means) haikus that are organized according to the familiar flow of the four seasons.

A lot of concept books tend to be short and more appealing for the younger end of the picture book target audience spectrum, as the subjects they cover are quite simple. Older readers might find concept books amusing or fun to interact with, but aren't going to necessarily be gleaning knowledge from them as actively as kids who don't yet know their ABCs.

Whether it's teaching numbers or seasons or colors or a simple idea—like the fact that everyone has big feelings (*In My Heart*) or different perspectives (*They All Saw a Cat*) or creativity (*What If…*)—these books all present a fresh spin on a universal point.

Setting Expectations About Book Format

For a debut picture book in the traditional publishing market, the simpler, the better. You'll especially want to be conservative in your ambitions if your idea demands a non-standard format.

Books with die cut elements, touch-and-feel sections, and other paper engineering requirements fall into this category.

Yes, there's usually a story present in these types of projects, but the other tactile elements of the book tend to overshadow the narrative. If a specific book has a non-standard format, that means it might be produced on board (if it's a board book, per Chapter 1), or support touch-and-feel panels, or have fewer pages, if there's hardcore paper engineering that goes into each page. For this latter type of concept book, like *Under the Ocean*, you might have a very tough time getting one acquired as a debut, because each copy costs an astronomical amount of money to produce, compared to a more straightforward format.

Any time you need something extra to make your project work, prepare for some serious resistance. This is even true of innocuous-seeming elements like the glitter swirls in *Plant a Kiss* by Amy Krause Rosenthal, illustrated by Peter H. Reynolds. Each page has the delightful distinction of being "kissed" by glitter ink.

Well, that means each page also goes through a separate printing pass just for this element, and the ink and glue or ink/glue combination itself costs money. The die cuts in *In My Heart: A Book of Feelings* also require more labor and careful attention to produce each page of the final book.

Sometimes, publishers will initiate these more elaborate projects themselves, rather than acquiring them from independent creators. (They seem much more willing to spend money when it's *their* idea!) Debut picture book writers don't seem to understand this very important point very well, either. Before we continue our conversation about concept books, I think it's worth mentioning some issues that are very relevant to the publishing business model.

A lot of writers shake their heads at this and wonder if I'm secretly some kind of dream-killer posing as a supportive guide. "Mary, that makes no sense," they might tell me. "If we attach a plushie to each book, and a craft kit, and a bubble wand, that'll be ~brand synergy~ and then we'll get a ~movie deal~ and build a ~theme park~! It'll make a bajillion dollars because we'll sell the plushies and craft kits and bubble wands at the park, too! And, besides, who doesn't want *a bajillion dollars*?"

I often make this point when it comes to a novel series, but it applies to picture books (and the idea of picture book series) as well: You're not in a power position if you *require* anything special. Demands are, in fact, a liability for an aspiring debut author. Of course you want your picture book to come packaged with some kind of merchandise. Who doesn't? But that kind of buy-in from a publisher asks the house to invest in intellectual property that isn't proven in the marketplace yet.

You are obviously going to think your work is amazing.

But a publisher will have to buy in *big* to your premise before they add a plushie, craft kit, bubble wand (a very unlikely choice because these things will break and leak in shipping and ruin entire cases of books at a time), pop-up panels, lift-the-flaps, touch-and-feel, or, yes, even glitter ink.

And if a publisher spends that kind of money on a debut and it doesn't perform to expectations, or earn back the money invested (and it'll be harder to earn out a project that was more expensive to produce in the first place), then they are going to be less enthusiastic to work with you again *and* you might never see a dime in future royalties. Furthermore, you'll have underwhelming sales numbers attached to your name forevermore—and all other publishers can see these, and judge them, when considering your next project.

Yes, the rumor goes that between eight and nine projects out of every ten acquired by publishing houses don't earn out their advances. (This statistic is largely anecdotal and not specific to picture books.) The publishing business model could use some help in this area. But you don't want your publisher to be shaking its collective head about *your* book in particular, thinking, "Oh, no, don't remind me of that puppy project with the bubble wands. What a disaster. They had to hose down the entire warehouse, and the suds still wouldn't come out. Kathy slipped, and we had to settle that workman's comp claim, to boot. We lost our shirts on it. Never again."

The power position with a series or any kind of special format is to have the publisher *come to you* with the idea, instead of the other way around. They might see great sales buy-in from their accounts before publication, or a tremendous response from readers once the book is released. Then, they might approach you or your agent and say, "Wow, your book did so well that we're thinking of turning it into a series (or issuing it as a board book, or making a plushie, or whatever). What do you think?"

In that case, they are willing to play ball, and nobody has to convince anybody of anything risky. They might even offer a more serious advance, or become more open to trying a special design element. (Well, maybe not those bubble wands —poor Kathy—but you can always ask.)

Take, for example, the fan favorite *Little Blue Truck* by Alice Schertle, illustrated by Jill McElmurry, which has had an interesting life. The first book was released in a standard picture book format in 2008, which is about what a writer can expect. It was initially either a one-book or a two-book deal for the creators, and the follow-up, *Little Blue Truck Leads the Way,* was released in 2009. The board books for these titles were issued within a few years of the jacketed picture books. (The board edition was rereleased when HarperCollins acquired Houghton Mifflin Harcourt, the original publisher, so I'm only finding the second publication dates.)

When this title went into board book format, sales apparently exploded. As you can imagine, the publisher was then much more eager to leverage this market excitement. Since then, the franchise has grown exponentially, despite illustrator Jill McElmurry's death in 2017. (Any new projects published in this series are illustrated "in the style of McElmurry" by John Joseph.[3])

There are now, as of this writing, five books in the core series, several editions each of various board book versions (including padded cover and large format options), Spanish translations, seasonal books with lift-the-flap elements, novelty books (including an audio-enhanced title and a sticker book), and, yes, of course, plushies. The brand has also entered into partnerships for branded pajamas and other licensing opportunities.

A success story, right? Well, it has been fifteen years in the making and survived the illustrator's passing. Notice that this "runaway hit" started out as a regular picture book publishing deal and ramped up over many years.

While the *Little Blue Truck* franchise is not a concept book, as the first installment has a strong narrative, future projects in the series can be considered concept books, especially the season-specific lift-the-flaps and the sticker edition.

It may be tough to break into the market with a concept book premise, but you might not be locked out of this space forever. It's a hard play for a debut, though. If you're curious about writing a concept book, you might want to practice a narrative story first, or write a narrative story in addition to a

---

3. Raugust, Karen. "A Long-Awaited Bedtime for Little Blue Truck." *Publishers Weekly*, publishersweekly.com/pw/by-topic/childrens/childrens-book-news/article/81495-a-long-awaited-bedtime-for-little-blue-truck.html. Accessed November 4, 2023.

concept book. While concept books are undoubtedly popular, their narrative cousins can be slightly easier to sell.

With a concept picture book, after all, someone will either like the concept, or they won't. With a story, you have a lot more creative control over the elements that you include, and their execution.

But before we dive into narrative picture books for a much more comprehensive look, let's round out our broad categories and discuss nonfiction picture books, where the market is robust, and the barriers to entry can be lower.

EIGHT
NONFICTION PICTURE BOOKS

DURING THE CORONAVIRUS pandemic from 2020 to 2022, publishers grew their nonfiction book lists by leaps and bounds. Why? More and more parents were having to deal with distance learning and wanted to supplement education at home. Sales of materials that could help in this overwhelming new reality skyrocketed. The market has somewhat leveled out in the "new normal," but nonfiction books have always been steady sellers. They tend to be bought *en masse* by schools and libraries, and circulate for years. Having a strong curriculum tie-in is essential for books geared toward the U.S. market, as I'll discuss shortly. But having a logical hook into what's taught in elementary schools is no longer enough.

Even before the pandemic, a sea change had come to nonfiction picture books, which is worth noting. Gone are the days when you can simply type up a basic primer on Benjamin Franklin and call it good. That has been done, and done, and done to death already. Now, if you're a historian and have uncovered an amazing new fact about Ben Franklin which nobody has explored in picture book format before (and it's significant enough to merit a book-length treatment), or you discover that Ben Franklin, and another historical figure had an unexpected friendship and would garden together on the weekends, you might have a unique angle on your hands.

The Contemporary Nonfiction Market

Nonfiction picture books do tend to be more timeless and have backlist staying power because they sell to schools and libraries. That being said, it can't hurt to educate yourself on the cutting edge of this category, such as it is.

It's important to note that your starting point, at least for nonfiction picture books geared toward the U.S. publishing marketplace, should be an understanding of what is taught in elementary schools, and when. Tying your topic into some-thing useful for schools and libraries, which can be bought by educators and taught year after year, is a great strategy.

The Encyclopedia of Writing and Illustrating Children's Books by Desdemona McCannon, Sue Thornton, and Yadzia Williams, published in 2008, says this:

> Information books that follow the school curriculum will be more likely to sell than those that do not. Your pet idea about aboriginal peoples in Southeast Asia is less likely to be considered, no matter how interesting, than one about the Civil War or the Industrial Revolution.[1]

That said, I do think that there's more room now than ever before for books about indigenous peoples, or wider angles on global topics. The decade-and-a-half that has passed since

---

1. Desdemona McCannon, Sue Thornton, and Yadzia Williams, *The Encyclopedia of Writing and Illustrating Children's Books*, 107.

the above reference guide was written has ushered in a more diversity-conscious perspective. Remember the large number of International Setting and Identity topics referenced in Chapter 6. Plus, there are already many, many nonfiction picture books published about the Civil War and the Industrial Revolution.

Keeping the above idea in mind—about wanting your idea to be useful in the classroom—you will now want to choose your concept from a more modern viewpoint.

Nonfiction picture books for today's market should ideally hit some or all of the following points in order to stand out. Note that your focus can look backward to the past, examine timely issues related to the present, or telescope forward in time to an anticipated future (especially true of books about technology, science, and medicine).

Here are examples of contemporary nonfiction picture book topics that have been chosen in an intentional way, with an eye on the market:

- A new person from history, especially if they're from a diverse or underrepresented background and you share that background—for example, women of color in STEM/STEAM;
- A person from current events who might make a big splash in the future, or is already doing so;
- A newly discovered or contextualized event in history that has contributed significantly to other well-known historical events (to tie into core curriculum standards);
- A newly discovered or contextualized event in history that has contributed significantly to the events of today;
- A new perspective or viewpoint on an event or

historical figure that everyone already knows—or thinks they know;

- New information or a new angle on something "familiar";
- A topic that ties into common core standards for different grade levels and can be used in the classroom or as library reference material;
- A topic in a field that is evolving, like artificial intelligence; and
- A specific focus on one element of a broad topic, like a single step of the water cycle or the Monarch butterfly life cycle.

Agents and publishers aren't likely to get excited for a nonfiction book about bugs. But if you stumble upon the "Charles Darwin of bugs," who catalogued most of the species we know, and they don't have a picture book yet? That'd be interesting. You could also focus on bugs that are only active at night. Bugs that eat poop (gross-out humor is a perennial crowd-pleaser with the age group, after all!). Bugs that make their home in the ecosystem of a fallen tree. Bugs, like mosquitoes, that depend on water for reproduction. Bugs that carry diseases. A scientist working to help bugs adapt to ecosystems affected by pollution. All of these are specific treatments that can exist within one broader topic.

The goal is to get more granular about a subject, while also zooming out and considering the ramifications of your nonfiction picture book, and any cultural relevance. Note that a lot of publishers have been characterized as having a liberal bias, which means that they are more likely to support books about politicized issues like climate change (see Chapter 6 for more on the market for this subject). You can get into your feelings about various topics in a narrative book, if you want. But if you are specifically writing nonfiction, make sure that you take an approach founded on facts, especially if you have qualifications that allow you to speak authoritatively.

Choosing a Nonfiction Topic

Think of issues that kids might be concerned about in the next 20 years or so in our changing world. How might you be able to weave that forward-looking focus into whichever topic you choose for your nonfiction picture book?

First, you want to do some serious market research. I generally advise aspiring picture book writers to spend some time learning their competition and what has already been published in their chosen category. This is doubly important for nonfiction writers, because once a topic is covered, it's covered. The only entry point into that same topic, then, is some kind of new spin or perspective, per the bulleted list in the previous section.

Note that nonfiction picture books tend to stay in circulation longer than narrative picture books. Libraries buy and hold them, and teachers keep books on their syllabi for years until a better or more accurate option emerges.

Remember, we don't need 30 books about Ben Franklin that all say the same thing. Or even three.

Here's an example of how you might want to approach a contemporary nonfiction picture book project with a STEM slant. Let's say you happen to be very passionate about manufacturing because you come from a long line of proud factory workers. As an adult, you worry that these jobs are either being outsourced, or will be replaced by machines. (If you're a writer looking at generative AI and worrying the same thing, I have some thoughts for you.[2])

While this is an extremely valid topic, your adult perspective on it (and any associated anxiety) might not make for good nonfiction picture book fodder, because you're not directly relating to your target audience on their level. Remember, your primary readers are young people, so you have to figure out how to slant your topic for early elementary students.

Given the above, you could take a historical approach and track how automation has been used in the factory setting since Henry Ford's time. What have the major innovations been? How have those spurned other growth in this sector? What kinds of changes has industrial manufacturing undergone since its inception?

You could also take a present or future view and unpack some recent innovations in machines and manufacturing, as well as how humans tend to liaise with these inventions. Do robots and humans ever work together on a factory floor? Are tasks completely automated, or are there still some functions that humans perform? How humans and technology interact is going to be a perennial topic of interest moving forward, so you can find your own angle within this space.

Depending on your own opinions about the topic, you can end on a hopeful note (there will always be something for people to do, even in manufacturing) or issue a warning, but with a proactive element (manufacturing as we know it might be changing, so it's worth diversifying your skill sets). I'd avoid outright doom and gloom.

In addition to having a specific and timely topic, today's nonfiction picture books also tend to have a takeaway, much

---

2. If you're interested, you can read more here: https://www.marykole.-com/will-ai-replace-creative-writers

like narrative picture books have a theme. Keep this in mind as you consider what you might want to say about a specific topic, and how you intend to treat your subject.

Picture book topics can be universal, like numbers, but these projects still do better when the writer chooses a specific focus or unifying idea. *A Hundred Billion Trillion Stars* does a great job of condensing a universe of (pretty unfathomable) numbers into a fun explanation, with a bit of an inspirational message folded in. Numbers are personified in *Zero the Hero* by Joan Holub, illustrated by Tom Lichtenheld, which also teaches other related concepts, like Roman numerals, tied together with a light narrative.

Bigger Than You by Hyewon Kyun gives readers a very easy and breezy comparison of relative dinosaur size, with a very loose narrative wrapper of dinosaurs competing with one another on the playground. *On Gull Beach* by Jane Yolen, illustrated by Bob Marstall, explores the specific environment of an Atlantic Ocean beach with some light poetry and a child character, though the bulk of the book's substance is actually contained in the back matter material.

As our planet grapples with changes and pollution, a timeliness angle helps some nonfiction projects stand out. *I'm Trying to Love Garbage* by Bethany Barton is about a narrator character trying to understand and appreciate garbage, and all of the systems that go into its processing and disposal. There's a section of empowering ideas for individuals who want to consume less, recycle more, and otherwise make small lifestyle changes.

Oil by Jonah and Jeanette Winter is a more literary entry about oil spills (and oil infrastructure) and how they affect nature and animals. The writing and art set this project apart. In different creators' hands, it would've fallen flat and been much less impactful.

In fact, a nonfiction picture book can be more lyrical than substantial, depending on how well it's executed. *Thank You, Earth: A Love Letter to Our Planet* by April Pulley Sayre is an example of a photo-illustrated nonfiction picture book with a tone of gratitude, which showcases some of the wonders of the world, without overtly imparting a lot of information.

As you can see, having a topic isn't enough. The topic must be made specific or timely, or it should be executed in a fun or interesting way, or both. You also need to be selective about the facts you choose to spotlight. If you're writing a book about ocean animals, how are you going to choose which ones to feature? With *A Hundred Billion Trillion Stars*, how did the author decide which numbers to talk about? The universe is literally made up of numbers (I think, I am not an astrophysicist). At some point, you need to narrow down the information you'll tackle, but within a cohesive framework. With this book, all of the featured numbers are either mind-bogglingly large, quirky/interesting, or superlative in some way.

Bigger Than You could've easily been a different book. The author/illustrator might have chosen other species of dinosaurs in every size category. Or they could've selected dinosaurs from only one period of prehistoric time. Sometimes, the individual facts and tidbits don't really matter, as long as they come together to support the overall concept. Sometimes they matter quite a bit.

For every fact you include in a nonfiction book, regardless of your topic, you need to be intentional and understand why you're making the choices you are. Develop an internal guiding rubric, and follow it.

Sometimes, of course, the topic dictates the content pretty neatly. *Platanos Go with Everything* by Lisette Norman, illustrated by Sara Palacios is a story about *platanos*—plantains—

and all of the ways in which they can be cooked and eaten. But it's also about Latinx identity, cultural foodways and traditions, and one family's Dominican Republic immigration story, told through dishes that remind the characters of various people, places, and events. Without these additional narrative layers, this could've easily been a Caribbean cookbook.

Characters add depth and richness so that the topic doesn't just stand by itself. In fact, there's generally nothing more interesting to children than other people (which is why I say that children often use character as an entry point into story in Chapter 9). Therefore, a lot of the nonfiction picture book market is populated with biography and autobiography.

Picture Book Biography

No discussion of nonfiction picture books would be complete without a mention of the picture book biography format. These projects usually use a lot of narrative-inspired stylistic and storytelling techniques, which make them read more like narrative picture books than nonfiction books or concept books. You can get a bit more creative and literary in picture book biography or autobiography, as you're presenting facts alongside narrative.

Hooking back into the list of topics and angles at the beginning of this chapter, notice that today's nonfiction tends to be more specific than a 30,000-foot overview of one board topic. "Bugs" is out. "Diverse and pioneering female bug scientists"[3] and "Bugs reacting to climate change" are in.

The same goes double for picture book biographies. You're not writing a summary of Ben Franklin's life from cradle to

---

3. "Entomologists," technically, and not related to "etymologists," who study the origin and history of words!

grave. You are choosing a newly discovered or unexplored thread from Ben Franklin's life and encapsulating that into its own narrative. Maybe you're focusing on his humanitarian interests. His inventions. His weekend gardening with friends. His relationship with his mother. (I am very clearly *not* a Ben Franklin historian.)

You'll want to think about theme as well as present-day relevance. The more undiscovered the element you're highlighting, the better. Instead of dealing in dry facts, you want to string together a story. This can sometimes include dramatizing your subject, inventing dialogue, or taking artistic license—as long as you stay faithful to the spirit of the law of your chosen topic, if not the exact letter of the law[4].

Books about a famous or historically important person's coming-of-age years are a natural fit for the nonfiction picture book biography format. Examples like *Me … Jane* by Patrick McDonnell, *Alabama Spitfire: The Story of Harper Lee and To Kill a Mockingbird* by Bethany Hegedus, illustrated by Erin McGuire, and *Mae Among the Stars*, imagine how events from the subject's early life might've played out, then flesh those into scenes. These books feature an obvious link between the person's childhood and how they ended up making a difference in their adult lives.

You will absolutely want to draw on primary sources as much as possible, but don't let that stop you from making narrative choices that tease out a cohesive story. Think creatively in terms of your storytelling, including pushing beyond linear chronology to unlock a modern picture book biography sensibility. The Harriet Tubman biography, *Before She Was Harriet*

---

4. For a great discussion of facts as they relate to memoir (or, for our purposes, to your picture book biography or autobiography), read *The Art of Memoir* by Mary Karr.

by Lesa Cline-Ransome, illustrated by James E. Ransome, is told in reverse chronological order, for example.

As we discussed in Chapter 1, publishers are putting a premium on underrepresented people from history or our current age for picture book biographies. This goes double when the project's writer and/or illustrator share a demographic profile with their subject. Consider *To Boldly Go: How Nichelle Nichols and Star Trek Helped Advance Civil Rights* by Angela Dalton, illustrated by Lauren Semmer, about pioneering Black actress Nichelle Nichols, written and illustrated by Black women. *Hidden Figures: The True Story of Four Black Women and the Space Race* by Margot Lee Shetterly, illustrated by Laura Freeman, showcases four Black women who worked largely behind the scenes to make the U.S. space race a reality, and both the author and illustrator are Black women as well. This kind of synergy really helps unlock opportunities in the picture book market for underrepresented writers, and to showcase unexplored true stories.

Sometimes the subject of a picture book biography isn't human, or the project otherwise offers a twist on the expectations of the category. *Sergeant Billy: The True Story of the Goat Who Went to War* by Mireille Messier, illustrated by Kass Reich, offers the story of a goat who "served" on the front lines of WWI, though he was more of a mascot or emotional support goat, long before we had conclusively identified the phenomenon of PTSD (then called "shell shock").

Yes, this biography is technically about a goat, not a person, but it also weaves in European history, some American history, and explores—in pretty light but impactful terms—the toll of war.

Narrative Nonfiction Picture Books

Sometimes you will want to write someone else's story, or discuss a topic or time period at arm's length. Sometimes, you will know the subject of your nonfiction picture book more intimately ... because you see them in your mirror every day. Narrative nonfiction, or picture book autobiography, can be a strong choice if you happen to have some interesting or timely lived experience to write about.

An autobiography is a rather straightforward portrayal of your own life, from cradle to the present moment. On the other hand, a memoir, sometimes called "narrative nonfiction," uses the same storytelling techniques that a fiction piece does to frame a curated selection of your life experience in a dynamic way.

While it can be difficult to publish and market an adult memoir (the category is very saturated, and celebrity memoirs tend to sell much more robustly than memoirs by relative nobodies, even if they have great stories to tell), you can still sell a picture book narrative nonfiction piece without being a Kardashian.

However, every narrative nonfiction project needs to have a hook, and to let readers into an exclusive, rare, or relevant world or life story. *Mother of Sharks* is a beautiful book that does just that by blending autobiography, a fiction narrative (the child version of the writer meets her adult self by swimming in a magical sea), and nonfiction with a women-in-STEM focus (marine biology). It also has the distinction, at 1,842 words (not including back matter), of being the longest project I analyzed for this guide. Not bad for several interweaving narratives that come together into an inspiring message.

The diversity and inclusion push discussed in Chapter 1 is a boon for memoir writers who can share experiences of immigration, being from a different culture, integrating with American society, or proudly standing apart from it. Books like *Priya Dreams of Marigolds & Marsala* by Meenal Patel, and *From the Tops of the Trees* by Kao Kalia Yang, illustrated by Rachel Wada, deal with immigration. In the former, the character is learning about a cultural homeland that she hasn't visited, and in the latter, the dangerous act of immigration is the plot of the story itself. *Eyes that Kiss in the Corners* by Joanna Ho, illustrated by Dung Ho, is about AAPI cultural identity and affirming the character's culture. At the time it was released, in 2021, there was mounting post-COVID anti-Asian sentiment in the United States, unfortunately, so it had a timeliness hook and was a response to a shift in the national conversation.

Some projects fictionalize an author's experiences or attach them to a folktale element, making them seem larger than life. *Sulwe* by Lupita Nyong'o, illustrated by Vashti Harrison, is a celebrity project, but also does a lovely job of dissecting society's attitudes toward different Black skin tones (as darker skin tends to be seen as less desirable than lighter skin in a lot of African and AAPI cultures). This story draws on the award-winning actress's experiences growing up with darker skin, and reframes darkness using an original myth about Night and Day, who are sisters.

The same effect happens in *The Range Eternal* by Louise Erdrich, illustrated by Steve Johnson and Lou Fancher, where a centerpiece stove in a cabin on the prairie becomes an autobiographical metaphor for growing up poor on the frontier, but how these memories connect the characters through the years and seasons. This is not technically revealed as an autobiography, but the book's setting, Turtle Mountain, aligns with the Ojibwe lands where the author grew up.

Some autobiographies are about social issues, and these are very marketable in the current publishing landscape. Others tackle socioeconomic concerns, societal expectations, and even family expectations. *Growing an Artist: The Story of a Landscaper and His Son* by John Parra does all three. A Latinx boy grows up alongside his hard-working father, who owns a landscaping business. There is some friction in his life because he worries that other kids will see him helping on job sites or riding along with his dad, and make assumptions about him based on his race and perceived social standing.

Yes, landscaping can be seen as blue-collar work, but it is also a creative vocation, and this book does a lovely job of dispelling some false narratives. However, even more interestingly, the boy has other reasons for not wanting to be a landscaper: He wants to be an artist instead, and he acutely feels his father's expectations that he will go into the family business.

The resolution isn't set in stone, as he's still living his story. It's not like he ends up becoming a famous artist, or his family members fall to their knees and apologize for wanting him to be a landscape architect when he grows up. The book makes no value judgments. What the father does is valid, what the son wants to do is valid, too. This isn't a fairy tale. But the author/illustrator has chosen details and set up specific contrasts to make a focused point. Beautifully, the book resolves as readers realize they're seeing the boy's artistic creation in action. After all, they are holding it in their hands.

The popular wisdom with memoir is that you must be someone extraordinary or have lived an extraordinary life. In the picture book market, you can tell an autobiographical story that makes a more subtle point, as long as you intentionally select your topic and angle.

Here's a lovely overview of these ideas from *The Encyclopedia of Writing and Illustrating Children's Books*:

> Writing creative nonfiction properly requires a level of empathy and research similar to that demanded by historical fiction—in fact, the genres are remarkably similar. The main difference is that the creative nonfiction writer must stick rigorously to portraying real people and events, while the fiction writer can be more creative with both their characters and the known facts.[5]

I would be remiss if I didn't also address the issue of fiction-nonfiction hybrid projects, which I see attempted frequently at the idea or manuscript phase.

Fiction-Nonfiction Hybrids

When I use the term "fiction-nonfiction hybrid," I mean that the writer has a nonfiction topic in mind, but they embed it into a largely fictional story. For example, they might want to talk about the history of dolls, and to do so, they will personify a doll who'll act as a tour guide and present information. There might even be a narrative framework to this fictional doll and her story, so we're getting an imagined component interspersed with facts.

The difference between this kind of hybrid approach and a picture book biography with fictionalized or narrative elements, is that, with the latter, we are bolstering or embellishing a story about real characters or events, but largely sticking to factual information. In my hypothetical example

---

5. Desdemona McCannon, Sue Thornton, and Yadzia Williams, *The Encyclopedia of Writing and Illustrating Children's Books*, 113.

from the previous paragraph, there is a completely fictional character introduced, and the nonfiction information is presented in the text itself, or in back matter. This is an approach that Jane Yolen takes with *On Gull Beach*, where the main text is a fictional poem, but there's a heavy photo-illustrated article in the last few spreads.

Especially if you are looking to debut as a nonfiction picture book author, and are not Jane Yolen (there can only be one!), I'd strongly urge you to choose a lane. This means you should commit to either doing a narrative fiction picture book, or a nonfiction project, even if it has some narrative elements, but not attempt to blend the two.

It's more common to see nonfiction information supported by a lot of infographics, photographs, figures, or other images, instead of by fiction components. As *The Encyclopedia of Writing and Illustrating Children's Books* explains:

> Writing information books for children requires specialist knowledge. Unlike fiction, most information books are highly illustrated. Such books are often referred to as "integrated"—where words and pictures work together to provide information.[6]

Nonfiction, at its heart, is all about providing information on a certain topic, and every creative choice you make should be in the service of this aim. If you feel compelled to write fiction, or to add fiction to your nonfiction topic, you might want to do a completely fictionalized treatment of it, and express the facts mentioned or used in the story in other ways.

---

6. Ibid., 106.

In fact, no matter what you're writing, whether it's fiction, narrative nonfiction, or a picture book biography or autobiography, you can effectively buttress the narrative, autobiographical, or fictional elements of your story with back matter.

Picture Book Back Matter

Generally, picture books have room for one spread of back matter, which is sometimes also called "after matter." This can include a glossary of terms, an Author's Note, an Illustrator's Note, a Teacher/Parent Guide, or something else relevant to the project. You generally don't want to be totally overbearing with the back matter, because it should be in balance with the nonfiction picture book text itself.

Fiction projects can also have back matter, as long as there's a compelling reason to include it. A recipe could follow a story about baking, for example, though any recipes for the picture book target audience need to be easy and include warnings about safety and adult supervision, especially if they call for the use of knives or heat.

For example, in *I Am Golden* by Eva Chen, illustrated by Sophie Diao, we read the author's family story, including images of her grandparents in the back matter. Caldecott Medal-winning *Thank You, Omu!* has an author's note about the meaning of the word "*omu*" in Igbo, the Nigerian language of the author's ancestors. *Amy Wu and the Warm Welcome* by Kat Zhang, illustrated by Charlene Chua, features a personal note about the author's relationship to her mother tongue, as well as a craft idea. These back matter elements can be creative and imaginative spaces.

It's important to note that back matter isn't required if the project doesn't need it. It's attractive in nonfiction, especially if the bulk of the text is more narrative in nature. But as I outlined in Chapter 7, you won't often get to dictate special formatting requirements for your project. That goes for back matter, too. You can certainly offer an interview you did, that recipe for fried *platanos*, or some personal family history, but this might take a different shape in the final version of the book, or a decision could be made to exclude it.

Sometimes, what you do with your back matter will cause controversy or otherwise overshadow the text itself, as it did with *Love in the Library*[7], written by my MFA program class-mate, Maggie Tokuda-Hall, and illustrated by Yas Imamura.

In your query letter for a nonfiction picture book, make sure to mention the word count for your manuscript, as well as any back matter you're envisioning, with a separate tally for that material.

Credentials for Writing Nonfiction

In many parts of the fiction publishing industry, you don't necessarily need professional credentials to write a book on a certain topic. Sure, "write what you know" is relevant advice, and you might find yourself drawn to stories that dovetail with your educational, work, or life experience. If you're a veterinarian writing adult thriller, your character might run an animal shelter, for example. But fiction is, by definition, made up, and what you don't know, you can always research.

With nonfiction, though, your platform matters more. This means that it's better if you happen to be a researcher, acade-mic, or professional in your topic. A nonfiction picture book about tackling a child's health anxiety is perceived as more expert coming from a doctor, social worker, or therapist, than it would be coming from a civilian with health anxiety, or the

---

7. Here's an article about the uproar: https://www.n-pr.org/2023/04/15/1169848627/scholastic-childrens-book-racism

parent of a child who has dealt with this issue. That's not to say that personal experience is worthless. You could absolutely try to pitch a book on this topic from a lay perspective —but credentials add a sales hook and the sheen of credibility.

A lack of professional experience in your chosen interest area doesn't necessarily hurt you, in that it's a glaring liability that's guaranteed to lock you out of the market, but it's not an asset, either. However, if the project is sound, well-researched, and you're able to overcome your lack of relevant platform by having an expert write your back matter, for example, you might be able to offset any potential concerns.

On a similar note, a lot of writers wonder whether they need writing experience, previous publishing credits, or a creative writing, literature, or English BFA or MFA degree. The short answer is no. That being said, if you studied creative writing or communications, or you've had previous work published, that does indicate that you're serious about learning your craft. If you can't claim any writing experience on your resume, you can attend conferences, take workshops, and otherwise engage with the industry to demonstrate that you're invested. (I talk more about developing yourself as a serious, credible writer in Chapter 18.)

Now that we've done a deeper dive into nonfiction, let's get back to the main purpose of this guide—the discussion of narrative picture books, and the tools we can use to craft compelling stories for young readers.

While you can apply all the following craft elements to concept projects and nonfiction picture books, just as easily as to narrative ideas, it's helpful to have a strong sense of where your particular premise fits in the market.

Making a category decision early on and writing with it in

mind will help you solidify your premise into a compelling, contemporary story for kid audiences.

NINE

CONNECTING THEME TO TOPIC TO CHARACTER

By NOW, you should be well aware that a narrative story stands apart from both concept and nonfiction projects, but can also lend craft principles to both. We've explored the audience for, and basic guidelines of, modern picture books, the publishing market, the kinds of topics you might use, and the possible themes involved. I'd like to think we've learned a lot—and enjoyed some laughs, though that might be my need for validation talking. I'm a writer myself, after all!

With this strong foundation that we've built over the last eight chapters, we can now move forward to crafting a picture book idea from the ground up. Fortunately, I advocate for working smarter, not harder, so I suggest doing this as intentionally as possible—by connecting theme to topic to character.

Building a Story

Many writers start with an idea for a character or plot when they sit down to draft a story. That's fine, too. But if we've learned anything from analyzing those Publishers Market-place deals, which I unpacked in Chapter 6, it's that most picture books have at least a handful of distinct topics, slants, elements, and sales hooks at the premise level.

A character name Silly Sally who likes to eat pickles is … well … not even a topic, slant, or sales hook. In fact, I'd strongly discourage the alliterative name, because this is a common choice in amateur picture book manuscripts and can come across as too cutesy for its own good. It screams that the writer believes picture books have to be juvenile. Yes, picture books are *for* juveniles, but they're not generally juvenile in tone (as discussed in Chapter 14), nature, or content. There's a big difference.

So if you're starting with a character who you made up when telling bedtime stories to your kids, or whatever the case may be, you need more than just a funny name, a favorite food or color, and an attribute or two (Sally is *silly*, obviously). Those things put together might be the start of something, but they aren't enough for a narrative picture book story yet.

Alternatively, you might have an event or two in mind, rather than a character: There's a brine flood at the family pickle factory! Oh no! That's a plot, I suppose. But, in and of itself, it's not enough for a robust narrative picture book, either.

This is why I strongly recommend thinking of your theme and topic(s) before you think of your character(s) and plot. Or even coming up with these ideas simultaneously.

The most important goal here is to make all of these elements cohesive.

Let's go back to Silly Sally and combine her with the terrible flood at Pickles & Co. Sally is silly, and she likes pickles, and she wants to save her family's pickle factory.

…

…

Okay. So what?

Without other elements involved, or a strong sense of theme, this idea, which has *some* narrative ingredients, might not yet have the universal resonance or substance to be a *publishable* story in a very competitive picture book market.

Maybe you think about it and decide to work with a theme of self-acceptance, or the topic of finding one's voice, because both of those are valid and timely. However, at face value, they strike me as a mismatch for the character and plot you've chosen. You can either change the theme and topic, or you can go back to the drawing board on story ingredients.

What if Silly Sally has that nickname (given to her by others), but she's actually an aspiring engineer, rather serious, and decides to step out from under other people's expectations for her by building a dam to save the pickle factory? This pivot can hit notes of self-acceptance and finding one's voice. The inherently comedic tone of the character name and the brine flood might not track with these more earnest identity ideas, but at least now we're thinking of how all the disparate ingredients might fit into a cohesive whole.

However, if you were to start with ideas of self-acceptance and finding one's voice, you might realize that Silly Sally and the unfortunate developments over at Pickles & Co. don't make sense as elements *in the same book*. Maybe your story is, instead, a star vehicle for Silly Sally, who is either rejecting or leaning into her nickname. She'll need more character attributes than just a love of pickles, though. And she'll want a different plot.

Or maybe the pickle factory getting destroyed fires up the town's youngest pickle fan (who is not named Silly Sally because that doesn't fit the down-home Americana tone of the new idea) to rally the community, rebuild the historic pickleworks (is this a thing?), and remind everyone that pickles can be salty, but also sweet. Soft when they want to be, and crunchy and strong when they need to be. Pickles—and the people who love them—contain multitudes. (How's *that* for a theme?)

If you're thinking about theme or topic (or both) first and foremost, it might be easier to see which other elements of your story are a natural fit, and which might want to go back in the drawer and await their turn in a more appropriate project.

Please note: You don't have to put *all* of your ideas in one concept. I see this all the time—writers cramming everything they want to do into one manuscript. Stop it. Fewer *cohesive* elements usually make for a stronger story. Your other ideas can seed other books!

From Theme and Topic

If you're building a picture book project from the ground up with theme and topic as your foundations, it might be easier to create a character who is purpose-built to tell your story most engagingly and effectively, and lead it to a conclusion that resonates with audiences.

For example, if we start the whole pickle story over with "finding one's voice" as a theme, the obvious choice is a protagonist who's having a tough time standing up for themselves. They can be shy by nature, they've been socialized to keep tough feelings inside, or they are usually courageous but struggling to specifically confront one tough issue. The latter two options seem a bit fresher, because the character isn't always quiet (this can be one-note and veer toward carica-ture), they are just quiet sometimes.

If the character is shy by nature, that might be something to accept and celebrate. It would be unclear why, all of a sudden, they would decide to start changing such an innate part of themselves due to one particular situation (see Chapter 11 for more on the question of "Why now?"). It'd also send the possibly unintended message that being shy is bad or wrong or something that needs to be fixed, which doesn't really fit with the market's current desire to validate all kinds of different personalities and ways of existing in the world. Shy/Quiet characters even have their own topic, defined in Chapter 6.

Option one doesn't really do it for me, and it seems too obvious, with unintentional negative implications, so let's choose option three. The character is normally brave, or even if they're not *brave*, per se, they aren't normally shy. They just so happen to feel uneasy or vulnerable about a certain thing. They're not changing a core part of themselves, they're overcoming the discomfort of trying to confront a difficult situation.

The great news is that *you're literally making everything up* when you sit down to write a fiction picture book. If you're passionate about your theme and really want to get a nugget of wisdom or life experience across (without hitting the reader over the head, as discussed in Chapter 5), and you realize that character you've selected, built, or imagined for that purpose doesn't quite work—you can change it! (Remember the "precious" sticker pictured in the introduction?)

You can even change the theme, but in my experience, the theme is usually the foundational idea undergirding everything. If you change the theme, you might want to start over instead of creating some kind of Frankenmanuscript. From there, it's all about reverse engineering the right character and plot to get at that inner marrow of your intended story.

If our character (who needs to summon courage to deal with one difficult situation) doesn't quite do it for you, you can imagine a different character. Maybe it's an eagle—born to be bold and brave, a symbol of courage, actually—who feels like an outcast when it's time to fledge the nest. Flying seems to come so easily to everyone else, and yet our particular eagle struggles. Our eagle is different. And that's a source of conflict and insecurity, until they're able to find their own voice and talent. (This goes back to the first conflict, discussed above, of the character's innate sense of self not fitting with internal or external expectations, and puts a finer point on it. I'll unpack more options for narrative picture book conflicts in Chapter 11.)

Alternately, the character can be too brave, in a way that causes problems. This takes the opposite approach to the same theme. *Acorn Was a Little Wild* by Jen Arena, illustrated by Jessica Gibson, is an example of such a story. The character must either be reeled back from being foolhardy and realize that there are more measured ways to express one of their core traits, or they might be the only one who can solve a plot problem because of an attribute that everyone else has tried to dampen.

In fact, one story can show off multiple shades to the same theme, using secondary characters and subplots—yes, even in picture books!—to explore various layers of an idea. (I'll discuss that more in Chapter 13.) What kind of character is going to help you express your core story theme or nugget in the most interesting way?

It's important to push beyond the first idea you have. The naturally shy character who needs to find their courage is an example of the first idea. Imagine a different cast for your story. "Shy vs. brave" can be a false dichotomy, as we all—including kids—act and feel with great nuance, and our moods and attitudes are not quite so black and white, even in the space of one afternoon.

Imagine the more sophisticated take on your theme. That's the second idea. Now flip it and work with the inverse of your theme. That's the third idea.

It takes courage to go beyond your first idea, and that's where you'll find a unique angle on your particular theme and topic. All themes have been explored before. You're not necessarily trying to do something that has *never* been done. You're trying to do what calls to you, first and foremost, but in a way that's (ideally) fresh, modern, and marketable.

Fleshing Out Character

A big difference between a picture book and a novel is that the former leaves you with a lot less time to establish character and explore the layers of their personality. In a novel, you'll plunge deeply into your main character and explore their unique perspective for 60,000 words (and that's pretty short for a contemporary novel). In a picture book, you only have 1% of that available to you: 600 words. Maximum.[1]

Starting with your theme and choosing a central character attribute to anchor your story is a good approach. We can't possibly get everything we need to know about the character in one picture book. Your character can and should have various layers, which we'll build here, but those ideas should be cohesive and focused. A series character doesn't really yield a wildly nuanced characterization, as we'll discuss in Chapter 10. Those books tend to be more episodic, with the character remaining a constant in a collection of shifting plots and ensemble casts.

---

1. No, but seriously.

That's why I like the theme as an entry point into character development. You can create a personality purpose-built for your specific story. And if that personality type has multiple stories that can naturally extend from their unique foible or quirk—think of Fancy Nancy, who wants everything to be fancy—all the better.

Once you have your one theme-based characteristic, you can then add some *relevant* layers to the character. Let's say we're doing the protagonist who's told she's *too* brave by everyone, only to have her wild, rough-around-the-edges vibe become an asset, rather than a liability, in a specific plot.

One way to brainstorm nuance is to ask questions. These are my questions, and my answers, but you might have you own answers, even given the same theme.

What is the character-driven benefit of courage?

- Leadership. Sometimes, a courageous character will feel compelled to step up, be a leader, inspire others, or be visible.

What is the world-driven benefit or liability of the above?

- Others may start to expect leadership or to put the character in situations she's uncomfortable with. With courage and leadership come expectations. The character may or may not always enjoy this.

What is the character-driven inverse of courage?

- Fear. Shyness. Maybe the character has one irrational fear that her apparent courage has never been able to touch. Write this detail down, even if you might not use it. Let's say she's afraid of saying the wrong thing and being ridiculed.

What is the world-driven benefit or liability of the above?

- Any kind of apparent weakness can really crank up the external (and eventually internal) pressure on a character to lean into their strength (courage) and avoid their vulnerability (fear). This can start out innocently but will eventually look like socialization or conditioning—overt or covert messaging that one way is right, and the other is wrong.

What's the character-driven downside of courage?

- Foolhardiness or short-sightedness. Let's say the character can sometimes act first and think later, which gets her in trouble. (This is also developmentally appropriate for a child, so it's a great attribute to play on for a picture book story, as all kids and families have likely dealt with this kind of scenario.)

What's the world-driven benefit or liability of the above?

- More pigeonholing. If the character's expression of courage is socially acceptable, they are a hero. If they sometimes make the wrong choice or are *too* courageous, or they blurt out what's on their mind, they can earn a reputation as a rebel or troublemaker.

What's the character-driven value system implied by courage?

- What does courage mean to the character and in the character's world? What does it tell them about themselves, about how they see themselves, and how others might see them? Courage can align with proactive action, but also with a character who doesn't know how to "turn off" and be present in the moment. Which does our larger society seem to prize? What about the story's society?

What's the world-driven benefit or liability of the above?

- There are also layers to every attribute and choice. Does the character worry that if they're courageous, they can never ask for help again? That they will be expected to grow up and stay grown up, for example? Is courage the same thing as confidence? Is not having courage the same thing as weakness?

Don't settle for the first few ideas that come to mind when you're thinking about your theme or topic or character. Now, to be clear, you don't need to use all of the ideas or layers that you discover by answering these more pointed questions. Several of the thoughts and dichotomies above could thematically support their own books. Remember: Avoid the pressure of doing everything you want to do, and saying everything you want to say, with one story.

Picture book protagonists will need several dimensions, even if we're playing with a very specific part of their character. I recommend focusing on those characteristics that tie into your theme or topic, first and foremost. Some of your development work will be used to flesh out your story subtly, and some of it will be left on the cutting room floor. That's okay.

By digging more deeply into your character and taking them beyond the surface level of their main personality trait, you are already putting yourself head and shoulders above your competition of aspiring picture book writers.

Character Attributes and Choices

Now that you have some character ideas in mind that come from your understanding of your theme, you'll want to convey this character on the page. We've all heard the old writing adage of "show, don't tell." It generally means that you should be working to convey important character and story elements with action and dialogue, rather than simply explaining them in narration.

Here's a quick example of showing:

> She fidgeted with the straps of her new backpack as the school bus pulled up.

Now, telling:

> She was nervous to start school.

With picture books, you *can* do some telling in order to convey big ideas succinctly and clearly. That means that you can explain or contextualize more in picture book than, say, in a novel.

You might want to try also rendering character attributes via choices and actions, as this is how you'll show what your character stands for, and what they're all about.

Generally, in picture books, the character that changes the most is considered the protagonist, as they go on an emotional (as well as physical) journey. If we're in the world of picture Book 2.0, and the character doesn't need to have a big realization about themselves at the end, the protagonist can also create change in their communities, or for others.

It's important to convey that the protagonist is going through a development arc while actively making choices and taking action. As we'll see in the below examples, the character has something in them that pushes them forward, makes them active, and inspires them to play a role in the story.

All of these are hallmarks of protagonist behavior, and I hope you take them into consideration when creating your picture book main character. As mentioned in Chapter 1, it's unusual for the protagonist to be an adult, though some notable examples are noted elsewhere in this guide. There can sometimes be two main characters, especially in an Odd Friendship structure, per Chapter 12, and they can both experience a mutual growth arc.

A lot of novel writers ask me if their characters *have to* change. I'd say that, in broad terms, they do. Reading a flat character's novel-length story for five hours is not going to be that fulfilling, unless nihilism is the point. In picture books, the character almost invariably has at least one theme-based realization along the way. Otherwise, there's little sense of why the story needs to exist, and why young readers need to read it.

Writing with Pictures: How to Write and Illustrate Children's Books expresses it this way:

> In fact, whatever its subject matter, every story is about *change*. This change must be important to the hero, for if it doesn't matter to him or her, the reader will not care … Sometimes the change is far-reaching and permanent. Other times it is temporary or part of an ongoing natural cycle.[2]

2. Uri Shulevitz, *Writing with Pictures: How to Write and Illustrate Children's Books*, 47-49.

When an imaginary friend gets sick of waiting for his child in *The Adventures of Beekle: The Unimaginary Friend* by Dan Santat,[3] he takes action:

> His mind filled with thoughts of all the amazing
> things that were keeping his friend from imagining him.
> So rather than waiting ... he did the unimaginable.

Rabbit, in *Rabbit & Possum* by Dana Wulfekotte,[4] takes specific action to help Possum get down from the tree:

> But Rabbit refused to give up. She had one more idea.

Even very young characters can be proactive, like Little Man in *Good Night, Little Man,*[5] when he tiptoes out of bed to look for his stuffed animal:

> He searched the bathroom. No, not there.
> He searched the closet under the stairs.
> He looked inside the old guitar.
> "Come out, Sheep-Sheep, wherever you are."

The best way to get a character across on the page in a picture book is to have them push the story forward with actions that declare who they are. These examples demonstrate showing, not telling, even if the writer expresses the reasoning behind the action.

If a character *says* that they have changed, that's one thing. They might not have. If a character *shows* that they have changed, as the wolf does when he starts reading vegetarian cuisine books after meeting—and liking—the sheep at the

---

3. Dan Santat, *The Adventures of Beekle: The Unimaginary Friend*, 8-11.

4. Dana Wulfekotte, *Rabbit & Possum*, 27-28.

5. Daniel Bernstrom, *Good Night, Little Man*, 12-13.

local farm in *Sheepish (Wolf Under Cover)* by Helen Yoon, that's another thing entirely.

Once you know who your character is and what emotional path they're on, think of some choices and actions they can make and take, respectively, to get their character arc across. How do they treat others? How do they treat themselves?

Consider building in a moment at the beginning, middle, and end when you show them making a choice or taking an action that demonstrates where they are in their relationship to the theme at these important touchstone moments.

Anthropomorphism and Personification

If you'd asked me before I did my original research, cited in Chapter 6, whether I thought anthropomorphism (giving human characteristics to animals) and personification (the same, but with objects) were desirable in the picture book market, I would've told you to stick to humans.

I could not have been more wrong.[6]

Animals is the most frequently cited topic in the publishing pipeline of upcoming projects, by a clear margin. Now, this does include books *about* animals, as well as those featuring animal characters, and I wasn't able to get more granular than that from the deal memo descriptions. That distinction is beside the point. The message is obvious.

Anthropomorphic animals are a cornerstone of the picture book market, past and future, and I don't see this changing anytime soon, regardless of my personal feelings on the matter. There are even books currently on shelves and slated for the next few years that feature personified objects, from

---

6. Someone tell my husband that I *can* admit my mistakes.

sticks and stones to sandcastles to sponges. Of the published books I analyzed, *Smitten* by David Gordon, *Lou*, and *Stumpkin* by Lucy Ruth Cummins, are three examples that feature a mitten and sock duo of protagonists, a fire hydrant, and a malformed pumpkin, respectively.

There are some practical reasons this is true. We'll touch upon picture book illustration considerations in Chapter 15, but note that picture book images, especially the character depictions, need to be consistent, and character renderings must be homogenous throughout the project. We can't have Sally looking one way on page 10 and another on page 20, and yet her face can't be entirely static, either. Her expressions and physicality must change ... but still look like the essence of Sally at all times. It's a tall order.

Humans bring an arsenal of tools to our social communication lexicons, from facial expressions (especially eyes and mouths) to tones of voice to body language. Even though picture book children tend to be illustrated in a more cartoony or exaggerated style, without adhering to the same rules of body proportions that are taught in fine art classrooms, characters—and their emotions—still need to be thoroughly consistent, specific, and recognizable.

In short, it's a lot easier to render the facial expressions and body language of, say, a fork or a shape (see *Love, Triangle* by Marcie Colleen, illustrated by Bob Shea) than it is to depict a complex human child. The same can be said of an animal, whether the style is more realistic or abstract. (For more examples, see *Mina* by Matthew Forsythe and *We Found a Hat* by Jon Klassen.) The relative ease of illustration does make for a strong argument to use animals and objects as characters.

There's also the racial diversity issue, which can be controversial. Humans, whether we like it or not, belong to various races that can be visually identifiable. Skin tone, hair color, and eye color, as well as certain features and proportions can be—for better or worse—stereotypically considered as specific to certain racial origins. When a character is Puerto Rican or Nigerian or Mongolian, illustrations tend to depict certain details to suggest heritage. Characters who aren't identified as one race or another in a story can also be illustrated with an eye toward diversity (and they should be, as a homogenous classroom of white students is not only visually boring, but not at all reflective of our world).

That being said, for some creators, the publishing industry's perceived focus on race can be a drawback. They don't want their story worlds to involve race at all. (Whether or not it's a virtue to be "color-blind" is a much wider discussion.) Animals do have species differences, which can play a similar social role to race, but they do not have overt races (though a zoologist would probably disagree!). Some creators opt to use animal or object characters, then, as a way around the sometimes-fraught issue of human racial differences.

Whether your story stars an animal, human, or object, craft each detail of character intentionally, centering on their attributes and how those pertain to your core thematic idea.

Now let's talk about pulling that thread taut between your theme, your newly developed character, and the plot you're about to give them. All of these elements need to be connected, and therefore it makes all the sense in the world to develop them as extensions of your core idea.

TEN

OBJECTIVE, MOTIVATION, STAKES, AND PROACTIVE CHARACTER

WHILE PICTURE BOOKS are nowhere near as complex and layered as novels, you should know by now that executing a good picture book story is no easy feat, especially within the narrative category, which is the largest and most wide-ranging trade segment that you'll find on publishers' lists.

As we've already discussed, a clearly expressed and specific character is the key to pulling off a successful narrative picture book, and even some concept and nonfiction projects, especially those that can also be slotted as narrative nonfiction (see Chapter 8 to unpack these terms).

To continue with our character work, we can borrow concepts from the worlds of novels and memoirs, however. Narrative nonfiction exists in books for teen and adult readers, too. Memoir—sometimes called autobiography, though there is a small distinction—is perhaps the most obvious example of the latter, as it braids together lived experience, a true story plot, a nuanced character, as well as storytelling structure.

Remember this crucial point: No matter their age, readers want, above all, to care about characters and stories, as that's how they will engage with your creation.

The tools we'll discuss here are all in service of this goal, and help to bolster audience connection to your work. Let's define this chapter's concepts, below.

Craft Definitions:

Objective: In the simplest of terms, the objective is what the character wants. This is usually tied to both theme and topic. For example, if you are writing an identity story with a theme of self-acceptance, the character might start out wanting to change who they are in order to fit in. The objective is then either met, subverted by the need, or reversed. In this example, the character might find that people like them for who they are (they don't have to change themselves, and end up maintaining a strong sense of self throughout), or they might discover that changing themselves doesn't make them happy, and they're actually an asset to their community exactly as they are (they realize changing themselves isn't possible or desirable). Sometimes, though, an objective can be as simple as a cookie (*If You Give a Mouse a Cookie* by Laura Numeroff, illustrated by Felicia Bond). The objective helps to add forward momentum and a driving pursuit to the story.

Motivation: This concept works in concert with the objective, and is the character's reason for wanting what they want. Ideally, the motivation is defined, or you've at least considered it, even if it might not appear on the picture book page. With the above example, let's say that the character wants to change the way they look so because they think looks determine personality. Even if they feel they don't fit in, they want to look like they do. This is a more character-driven/emotional motivation. Sometimes, an objective and motivation can be external.

In the *If You Give a Mouse a Cookie* example, the mouse's objective is a cookie, and his motivation is hunger, but getting what he wants opens up an escalating sequence of requests. The child's objective is to pacify the mouse … until it changes to tidying up after the mouse (and keeping his sanity). In novels, motivations can change and shift many times, but in a picture book, we usually see one objective and one motivation driving the story, or two at the most, if a realization or turning point transforms things around the midpoint.

Need: This is not a mandatory ingredient in picture books, though it appears under the surface in most novels and memoirs. I teach it this way: "While the objective is what the character might think they want, on the surface, they discover over the course of the story that they actually have a need that's driving them. This need can be the opposite of the objective and is not fully realized until after the midpoint. For the story to be satisfying, the underlying need must be resolved." In the above example of a character who wants acceptance from others, they might actually need to realize that they should accept themselves instead. Or they change their look, only for their friends to say they miss the character's unique style. The protagonist needs to embrace it, and maybe even ramp it up. In the example of *If You Give a Mouse a Cookie*, which seems to have an extremely surface-level objective and motivation, I'd argue that the mouse needs attention and to be taken care of. Acts of service from the boy might be its love language.[1]

Stakes: The very simple storytelling definition of stakes

---

1. Yes, I really did invoke love languages for the mouse in *If You Give a Mouse a Cookie*. For those who might not know, *The Five Love Languages: How to Express Heartfelt Commitment to Your Mate* by Gary Chapman, is a great framework for understanding people's needs.

is the answer to the question, "Why does it matter?" You've chosen an objective, explained it with a motivation, and even buttressed it with a deeper need that scratches at your theme. But why does it all matter? You also need to define what's at stake for the character— given everything you know about them, their personality, and the theme and topic of your story—if they don't get what they want. There needs to be a reason for them to take a big risk or carry on despite obstacles in pursuit of their desire. In other words: If they don't get their objective, Y will happen. It's a very simple formula. In our example story about self-acceptance, the stakes are both internal and external. Externally, the character will not feel like they have any friends (a big deal for kids in this age group, who are developing a social sense of self). Internally, they will not feel good about themselves. Novels, especially thrillers and mysteries, tend to have life-or-death stakes. So do more literary novels that are about the death of a relationship, or a dream. With picture books, you don't have to go quite that extreme, because you want the story to be relatable to your young readers. In *If You Give a Mouse a Cookie*, the stakes for the mouse are hunger (he will continue to feel more and more melodramatically miserable), and loneliness. The stakes for the boy are never getting rid of the mouse, which will upturn his entire day and/or house. If both characters work together, they can each feel fulfilled.

Proactive Character: A character who drives readers through the story. They take an active part in the plot, pursue a strong objective, and have a clear sense of motivation. A picture book character will not have unlimited freedom, in the sense that they can engage with life as an adult would, because they are expected to be a relatable avatar for a preschool or school-aged child (as discussed in Chapter 3). Therefore, their active drive should feel believable and be within reason. That being said, your character must take action throughout the story in order to try things, make choices (as discussed in Chapter 9), have ideas, allow their actions to convey who they are, realize the theme (see Chapter 4) and moral (see Chapter 5), and otherwise be the hero, rather than a passive participant or observer.

The above explanations go into a lot of detail, but I'll add a few more ideas to the stew of novel techniques as they apply to picture books. First of all, it goes without saying—but I will say it anyway—that if your concept doesn't lend itself to using these storytelling elements, don't use them. It won't hurt to consider them, think about whether they might apply, or put them in your pocket for later. But you don't absolutely, positively have to weave these elements into your manuscript if you don't think they belong.

For example, there is no objective in *Alphabet Boats*. I mean, you could get very pedantic and say that the boats' objective is to get from point A to point B. Their motivation is that they're boats, and that's what they do. The stakes if they don't are that they'll fail at upholding the very essence of their boatdom. (They might also sink.) Applying such high-level character analysis to an ABC concept book would be a bit much.

In stories like *A Funny Little Bird* by Jennifer Yerkes, on the other hand, there are actual life-or-death stakes, when a fox sees the bird and pounces on it. The bird has to hide, and realizes that its perceived flaw (blending in with its surroundings) is actually what's going to keep it—and some of its friends—safe in the big, hungry world. This exemplifies a moment when the character's objective and need are synthesized during a high-stakes situation, and we loop in the themes of identity and self-acceptance.

Synthesis and Wielding

The point of these storytelling elements is to set your picture book character up to learn something—though subtly—by showing them stepping into their own unique power. That's why the synthesis of their objective, motivation, need, and stakes (either at the midpoint or toward the end) makes for such an engaging moment in your story. These underpinnings work in concert to deliver on the promise of your premise and topic, with the character rising to their full potential and, in an aspirational, sneaky way, inspiring readers.

They can then step forward as themselves, into their own glory, and prevail. It's important to note that most picture book characters do achieve their chosen objective, rather than ultimately failing. Even in the novel world, characters might not get what they want, but they usually get what they need. If they don't, then the story can be labeled a tragedy, and it steps outside of the world of mainstream storytelling. We get themes of nihilism, antiheroes, etc. This is a bit dark and hopeless by picture book standards, though.

In picture books, characters can and do fail—in fact, we'll discuss this a lot more in Chapters 11 and 12. But these failures only serve to push them closer to getting their objective or need met by the end, and to uncovering, synthesizing, and wielding the overall theme.

Within reason, picture book characters need to be empowered. Remember, your preschool- or school-aged reader doesn't feel very powerful in their everyday lives, as we first discussed in Chapter 3. As they go through their story, they are made proactive[2] by pursuing a strong objective, which is undergirded by a motivation that makes sense to the reader.

2. More on this idea here: https://kidlit.com/writing-a-proactive-protagonist/

Stakes keep the character moving forward, too, as readers understand that the action of the story matters.

The great thing about picture books—as opposed to novels, with their layers, subplots, twists, and reveals—is that this formula is simple and specific. These ingredients serve a single purpose: to push your character forward, and into readers' minds and hearts.

Their objectives should also be fulfilled, more often than not. Sometimes they might not get exactly what they set out to achieve, but they should get something that's a holistic solution to their initial problem. *Writing with Pictures: How to Write and Illustrate Children's Books* has the following insight:

> When the objectives introduced in stories aren't fully accomplished, when questions raised aren't fully answered, or when problems aren't resolved explicitly, the action remains incomplete for young readers and they are left hanging, frustrated, or unfulfilled. The suspense a story creates must be fully released at the end.[3]

Proactive Character

There's a big, foundational reason that I have chosen to discuss character first and foremost as it relates to picture book craft, rather than starting with plot and structure. In over a decade of working with writers, I have come to understand that some (well, most, anecdotally) come to story through the lens of character, first and foremost. This makes

---

3. Uri Shulevitz, *Writing with Pictures: How to Write and Illustrate Children's Books*, 38.

sense. We are human beings, and we create art to make meaning of our lives. As such, we attach ourselves to characters (or we channel ourselves into our protagonists), and they become the vehicles through which we experience stories.

This makes the writer-reader relationship a symbiotic one, as your reader will also be attaching themselves primarily to your characters, especially in this young age group. Over and over, I see children connect with the character of Fancy Nancy, for example, or Kelp, from the book and, now, TV series, *Not Quite Narwhal* by Jessie Sima, rather than resonating with a specific plot. I'm not sure I could tell you what Fancy Nancy does in any given book (this is especially true in a series). She throws a tea party, surely, but what else? Dresses up? I've read many Fancy Nancy books, but the plots don't jump out nearly as much as the characterizing details that make her relatable. The overall character is the point of contact.

It's important to make your plot an offshoot of your character, instead of the other way around. That's why I'm sequencing my discussion of these tools in an order that flows from theme to character to plot. You'll want to cement what your character wants, why they want it, and what might happen (real or imagined), if they do or don't get it. You can then build your plot on this foundation.

Here's a pro trip: Don't just focus on the stakes of *not* getting something. Sure, it's important to know the worst case scenario for your character, so you can plan compelling conflicts. But sometimes a character gets what they thought they wanted—and discovers an unexpected or unintended ramification. This is often the case as objectives mature and needs emerge. It may be completely irrelevant to your project, but might also be worth thinking about.

All of these craft ideas have a character focus in common, and it's impossible to overstate the importance of a proactive character, even in books for the youngest readers. This idea is defined above, but I want to make sure to meditate on it for a bit longer.

Passive character can be a big issue in novels as well. I can't tell you how many MTS (mystery, thriller, suspense) genre novels, fantasies, sci-fi stories, and Chosen One adventures for middle grade and young adult audiences I've evaluated where the character *doesn't do anything*. Sure, they exist. They have attributes and quirks, as do all characters.

But instead of driving the action forward in a proactive way, they are pushed around by the plot, which eclipses them. A storytelling notion that was popular during the Renaissance championed the idea that your character should be an avatar for any reader or audience member, as a lot of storytelling was done in the medium of live theatre back then. In fact, characters would literally be named Everyman. The idea was to make them so bland and universal, an Average Joe, that anyone could imagine themselves going through the plot. It's not surprising that many of these were morality tales.

This is still how a lot of thrillers or Chosen One stories, for example, function. The writer is so entranced with their plot, or their world-building (in the case of some aspiring fantasy and sci-fi novels), that their protagonist is basically a crash test dummy with a name. Instead of driving the car, they're a passenger, while the car itself is being driven by tracks and pulleys (the plot, in this analogy). The crash test dummy does not steer, and when a big plot point comes along, the dummy merely bounces around in response (because they didn't do anything to make the plot point happen). They're only able to react (unless they go through the windshield entirely), instead of taking action.

Notice: The words "proactive" and "protagonist" share the same root word, "pro-." In fact, "proactive" means, "acting in anticipation of future problems, needs, or changes,"[4] and one of the meanings of "protagonist" is "an active participant in an event."[5]

Long story—full of mixed metaphors—short, your picture book character should make the plot happen through their desires, actions, and choices. In a book this short, you have no margin for error.

Things can certainly happen *to* your character, but that's usually reserved for the very beginning. For example, in *Pine & Boof: The Lucky Leaf* by Ross Burach, a gust of wind blows away Boof's favorite leaf, which he has collected and befriended. Nothing he does (or doesn't do) makes this happen. It's literally a random event.

It's what Boof does after, though (including the choices he makes alongside another character, Pine), that forms the backbone of the story. The gust of wind was incidental. What it unlocked within Boof as a protagonist and hero is anything but.

If you're worried that you've accidentally written a story where your character is not proactive, ask yourself this question: Is the story happening *to* your character, or is your character making the story happen? If your character is merely a crash test dummy, you need to use the tools in this chapter—objective, motivation, need, and stakes—to dig deeper and give your protagonist something to want and, as a result, do. You need to give them logic and reasoning, too. Things should flow in a cause-and-effect way.

---

4. *Merriam-Webster Dictionary*, merriam-webster.com/dictionary/proactive. Accessed November 4, 2023.
5. *Merriam-Webster Dictionary*, merriam-webster.com/dictionary/protago nist. Accessed November 4, 2023.

If you believe that your character is driving the story, you also need to make sure that the story has conflict and structure. At the end of the day, just as theme and topic are inherently tied to character, character is also inherently tied to plot. That's what we'll explore next.

ELEVEN
PICTURE BOOK STORY CONFLICT

Now that we have important character elements percolating in our brains, you might be feeling either very excited to start writing, or completely boggled and overwhelmed. Both are fine and natural. If you find yourself in the latter frame of mind, you don't need to leap onto the page just yet. Give your ideas a little room to breathe.

The next step introduces us to plot, and this is where you will see your ideas take shape—literally. We're talking, of course, about story shape. Plot. Structure. These words are sometimes used interchangeably to mean what *happens* in your story. For our purposes, I'm making a distinction between them.

Craft Definitions:

Conflict: Individual units of tension, struggle, or desire.

Structure: How conflicts come together in a specific cause-and-effect order to tell a story connected by logic, and make an intended thematic and emotional impact on the reader.

Plot: A similar idea to structure, but this term is usually used to refer to the action of the story. "Structure" is a more technical craft term, and "plot" is more likely familiar to lay readers.

We covered concept and nonfiction books earlier, in Chapters 7 and 8, respectively. These types of picture books can have a structure, or they can be more loosely organized according to the needs of the topic.

In the narrative picture book, however, plot is crucial. And so is conflict. I know what you might be thinking: It's a *picture book*, full of fuzzy teddy bears and balloons and rainbows and stuff. *Why* would it possibly have conflict?

I understand this reasoning, but, respectfully, it's completely wrong. Quite simply, conflict is the engine that keeps story moving, and a character's objective and motivation are the gas powering it forward.

Your conflicts in a picture book aren't going to be nearly as big or life-or-death as the conflicts in, say, an international thriller for adult audiences. And that's perfectly fine. They *do* need to feel big and matter to your characters, though (the previously defined idea of stakes). This is a crucial distinction.

Types of Conflict

When I analyzed 90 narrative picture books for this guide (you can find a complete list in Appendix C), I coded them, spread by spread, with a plot label. Sure, sometimes multiple things happened at once, but I committed to identifying one story role or function played by each spread in every picture book. This was my entry into exploring conflict and structure.

As I hoped I would, I started to notice some patterns. Here is a list of potential conflicts I uncovered. These will be the building blocks of your eventual story structure, discussed in the next chapter. Remember, you already know that you need a strong theme and topic, as well as a character who is driven, proactive, and, ideally, pursuing a goal. It's generally better to want something internally as well as externally, as you will see below.

Simply coveting a toy isn't really enough to provide conflict in modern picture books, and I'm about to unpack why. That toy should represent something bigger, something more personal. Wanting a toy is low stakes, besides, even though it feels extremely high stakes to a child in the moment, especially *my* child, when a sibling starts playing with *that specific LEGO set*, but that's a different issue entirely. Freaking out over a toy feels very real and valid to the individual child, but it's also a type of melodrama—as every parent knows—and is therefore not true conflict.

Let's dig deeper into some conflict types that I identified in my analysis. To be clear, stories have conflict, but they also have structure. Both combine into plot. Most effective picture book stories will have conflict (and often more than one type of conflict) *and* structure (and sometimes more than one type of structure).

Let's unpack those conflict types, which will help to illustrate your options:

Character vs. Character: This kind of conflict is not as straightforward as it seems, in that one character is wrong while the other is right. In picture books, there are often two different sides to every coin. As you will see in the following chapter, the Odd Pairing structure is one where both characters are right, they just go about life in different ways. This is important to note. For stories where there is an overt bad guy, that's a Character vs. Antagonist conflict, defined below. Here are some Character vs. Character variations from the shelves:

- Two characters in rivalry with one another, as seen in *Confiscated* by Suzanne Kaufman, though the two brothers do team up at the midpoint. In *Say Hello to Zorro!*, the rival dogs also find common ground through a surprising revelation.
- Sometimes you can have a group of people against one person, and yet both sets of characters are relatable. *Maxwell's Magic Mix-Up* is a great example of this, because you think the story is about the partygoers vs. the magician (who flubbed a magic trick and turned the birthday girl into a rock), but the author is able to create sympathy for the magician by giving him accountability in the form of a more powerful nephew who has to come bail him out. If anything, this is a Midpoint Shift structure (discussed in the next chapter) with partygoers vs. magician and then magician vs. nephew (or magician and nephew vs. the malfunctioning magic trick).
- In *The Worst Teddy Ever* by Marcelo Verdad, there is a perceived conflict between the child and their teddy bear. Teddy is always tired, and the child just wants to play. However, both characters are sympathetic because the child wants to engage with their favorite toy (understandable) and we learn that Teddy is only tired because he's been keeping monsters away from his child all night. There's a gentle reminder here that not everything is as it seems, and everyone has a story that, once we learn it, can explain an apparent interpersonal conflict.
- The delightful *A Spoonful of Frogs* by Casey Lyall, illustrated by Vera Brosgol, is another example of an individual vs. a group. The cooking show host witch

(!) needs to catch frogs for her soup recipe ... but they don't want to be caught. She's redeemed and relatable, so she's more of a protagonist than an antagonist, though I'll unpack this more when discussing the Villain Redeemed structure.

- The rather dark (by picture book standards) *Sugar Would Not Eat It* by Emily Jenkins, illustrated by Giselle Potter, is a battle of wills between a boy and a cat he finds. It also deals, subtly, with the universal childhood topic of picky eating.

- In *Rabbit & Possum*, we have two friend characters who see the world differently and are afraid of different things. After a mishap, they have to come together and trust one another. They don't agree, and nobody changes their essential selves, but that doesn't make anyone the bad guy.

- In *More Than Fluff*, the character has several conflicts. At first, it looks like she has individual conflicts with different characters who try to hug her when she wants to establish body boundaries. This book also deals with a Character vs. Society's Expectations conflict, defined below, because the larger community thinks that chicks are cute and fluffy and should all be hugged. Finally, this book also has a Character vs. Emotion conflict, because the chick doesn't deal very well with people coming at her and asking for hugs, and she learns to temper her own big feelings.

- *Nerp!* by Sarah Lynne Reul features the conflict of the well-meaning parents preparing meal after meal for the picky eater character to eat—a universal parenting topic. But this is not an antagonist relationship because the parents are well-meaning, and the conflict is resolved with a clever twist that leverages the child's own agency.

- The big trucks in *The Digger and the Flower* by Joseph Kuefler are in conflict because they have differing values. In the vein of the classic *The Story of Ferdinand* by Munro Leaf, illustrated by Robert Lawson, the tough digger falls in love with a flower, but his construction truck colleagues crush it to make room for a building. The story doesn't point fingers too much, though—they're just doing their jobs. This is also a Character vs. Society's Expectations type of conflict.

- *Found* by Salina Yoon has several interesting things going on. Bear finds a stuffed bunny and wants to keep it. Of course, Bear tries to do the right thing first —puts up fliers, etc.—but when no owner materializes, Bear thinks that the bunny is his. However, Moose recognizes the bunny … and readers think it's all over. Moose will take it back. But Moose says that "special toys are meant to be passed on to someone special,"[1] and Bear and the bunny, who we learn is named Floppy, are reunited, this time, for good. Here, the character conflict between Bear and Moose is implied (Moose will take the toy that Bear fell in love with) but a change of heart prevents it.

- Similar to the above, *Swim! Swim!* by Lerch (a pen name for James Proimos) features a lonely fish who is rejected (or that's how he interprets it) by pebbles and bubbles in his tank. (He tries to make friends with both and gets no response.) The pebbles and the bubbles are characters that introduce conflict, but they are not, of course, enemies. He's projecting his loneliness upon them. The cat that comes on the scene later is positioned as an antagonist, for obvious

---

1. Salina Yoon, *Found*, 34-35.

reasons, but there's a twist, and the cat actually ends up finding the perfect friend for our hero.

- A favorite in my house, because we are all fans of Oliver Jeffers's work, is *This Moose Belongs to Me*, which I didn't technically analyze for this guide, but know well. The titular moose in this story does whatever the heck he wants, much to the frustration of the boy who thinks he owns him. Then it turns out that everyone in this slightly weird world has a different relationship with the moose. The boy has to deal with his own feelings of betrayal and envy (Character vs. Emotion), before accepting that the moose is his own creature and doesn't belong to anyone. However, this doesn't preclude them from being friends, except maybe on a more equal playing field.

Character vs. Problem: This is a very straightforward conflict, where there is an actual problem, and one character (or group) tries to solve it. The problem can result in negative motivation—avoiding something bad. Or the problem can result in positive motivation—wanting to overcome the issue and achieve a goal. Here's how it plays out on shelves:

- *Bubble Trouble* by Margaret Mahy, illustrated by Polly Dunbar, could not be more straightforward as a Character vs. Problem conflict. I'll quote directly from the book here. The problem is that "Mabel blew a bubble and it caused a lot of trouble[2]" by encapsulating her baby brother and wafting him away. Then the entire town bands together to get the baby down safely (with one notable exception, which you'll hear about later in this chapter).

2. Margaret Mahy, *Bubble Trouble*, 6-7.

- In *A Little Ferry Tale* by Chad Otis, there is a fire on an island, and the boats have to work together and save the stranded animals. It's pretty clear-cut. Sometimes this type of conflict is layered on top of a different conflict, just to give it more juice. This is also an example of a Character vs. Own Expectations story, because the ferry has to realize that her unique characteristics, which she mistook as flaws, will actually save the day. (This switch from self-as-liability to self-as-asset is a very common device in picture books, especially those with a Had It All Along structure, detailed in the next chapter.)

- *Kitten's First Full Moon* by Kevin Henkes has a very straightforward conflict—the kitten can't seem to reach the big bowl of milk he sees. But this is only enough to justify a book because of a great twist. The "bowl of milk" is actually the moon. This story features a mounting sequence of tries to solve the problem and reach the milk/moon, which is an Escalating Attempts structure.

- In *Good Night, Little Man*, the surface-level conflict is a missing bedtime stuffed animal, but there's also a Character vs. Character issue in that the father is unreasonably frustrated by the boy sneaking out of bed (though this is redeemed by an apology, so there's no bad guy).

- Sometimes there are different teams of characters in a story, and the conflict configuration depends on which team's perspective you take. In the excellent *Click, Clack, Moo: Cows That Type*, the cows and chickens in the barn are cold and want electric blankets, so they try to solve the problem by negotiating with the farmer. The conflict erupts into Character (Farmer Brown) vs. Problem when the animals decide to strike. The farmer isn't a bad guy, he simply wants his cows and hens to go back to making milk and eggs. This could also be a Character vs. Character story, because each party's proposed solutions to the conflict are at odds.

- In *Smitten*, the overt conflict is that a mate-less mitten and a mate-less sock are having a tough time living in the real world (getting dirty in the street, shrinking in the laundry, unraveling, etc.). Only through an unlikely friendship can they survive the conflicts of the larger world together. This is also an Odd Friendship structure.

- In *Amy Wu and the Warm Welcome*, the surface conflict is a language barrier between a second-generation Chinese immigrant and a student who has newly arrived. But there's also a Character vs. Own Expectations conflict, because the protagonist doubts that their welcome will be enough, or well received. (This is, of course, not the case, and a friendship forms.)

- In *Imogene's Antlers*, the problem (or "problem," if you're Imogene) is that a girl wakes up with antlers. Some people in her household—and Imogene herself —think it's great. Others, not so much. This can also be a Character vs. Society's Expectations conflict, as there's an inherent disagreement over what's socially acceptable.

- In *On Account of the Gum* by Adam Rex, we are presented with a simple problem—a kid with gum in their hair—that gets more and more ridiculous with each proposed "solution" from a wide-ranging cast of characters. This is also an Escalating Attempts structure.

- *Duck Soup* by Jackie Urbanovic has two concentric problems, one inside the other, which could be considered either a Nesting Stories or Three Act structure, which I'll describe in detail in Chapter 12. First, Max, a duck, decides that he wants to make his very own soup recipe. He's cooked everyone else's recipes, and his objective is to create something new. He engages in the conflict of trying to figure out what the soup needs and realizes he wants some herbs from the garden. While he's gone, his friends come in, can't find him, and become convinced that he has fallen into his own soup pot. They then try to solve the problem of rescuing Max by pouring the soup out, only for Max to return. This book falls a bit flat to me, personally, because Max's conflict is not resolved. In fact, his friends ruined his soup. They did it for a good reason, which prevents them from being antagonists, but they hand-wave his disappointment away by saying, "At least you're not duck soup,[3]" which, while technically true, leaves poor Max no closer to his goal.

- In *Pine & Boof: The Lucky Leaf*, the loss of Boof's favorite leaf is the problem that kicks off the story. It's important to note here that the conflict of Character vs. Problem can be inherently tied to the character's goal, meaning that Boof's objective at the outset is to recover his lost leaf. Max's goal above, in *Duck Soup* is to perfect a soup. But this initial tension is merely a springboard for a larger conflict—the story usually escalates from that opening gambit.

- With the contest mechanic plot of *Grimelda and the Spooktacular Pet Show* by Diana Murray, illustrated by Heather Ross, we have a positive motivation story where Grimelda wants to win a spooky pet competition (she's a witch, so it's quite a compliment to have the spookiest pet). Except she decides that her

---

3. Jackie Urbanovic, *Duck Soup*, 36-37.

cat isn't "spooktacular enough.[4]" She tries to find another pet to enter into the competition, but this is the wrong way of solving the problem. I'd also argue that this is a Character vs. Own Expectations conflict, because part of the issue is Grimelda's opinion of what's spooktacular and what isn't. Where did she get her idea of whether her cat is "enough" or not? To solve the problem, she needs to change her preconceived notions.

Character vs. Antagonist: It should be clear by now that most picture books refuse to unilaterally name a bad guy. Even the youngest readers should be treated with respect, and most already know that a simplistic "good guy vs. bad guy" plot is straightforward and boring. (The monster in *Eat Pete!* by Michael Rex is having a Character vs. Emotion conflict, surprisingly, not a child vs. monster conflict! In fact, the child is incredibly game to play with the monster, if only the monster can curb his temptation to eat him.) There are, however, some books with a relatively straightforward antagonist, or villain. Having a classic bad guy gives a picture book some stakes and adds a frisson of potential danger. It can also make the hero seem more heroic, by contrast. Let's comb through our published stories for some examples:

- *Room on the Broom* by Julia Donaldson, illustrated by Axel Scheffler, features a classic antagonist whose only role is to threaten the main character and have her come together with the allies she met earlier in her journey. The menacing dragon, when threatened by a creature who appears to be higher on the monstrous pecking order of the bog (but is actually the friends in disguise), folds like a greeting card. But

---

4. Diana Murray, *Grimelda and the Spooktacular Pet Show*, 8-9.

the story is also about small acts of kindness building into something bigger, and about inclusivity (except when it comes to the dragon, of course).

- *Extra Yarn* by Mac Barnett, illustrated by Jon Klassen, has a classic antagonist who comes into the story late … and gets dispatched very quickly. His greed is his own downfall—that's important to note. The main character does not retaliate in any way, shape, or form, as that would make the protagonist morally gray. The antagonist's choices are his undoing. This particular antagonist does not have a redemption arc.

- A character in *Bubble Trouble*, discussed above, actively works to make the problem of the floating baby worse by bursting the bubble. This character is a classic antagonist, with no redemption, though the other characters are able to save the baby, which keeps the antagonist from endangering an innocent and becoming a total monster.

- It's more common to see antagonists somewhat redeemed, even though the reader is primed to side with the protagonist. Three examples would be *Clovis Keeps His Cool* by Kate Aronson, illustrated by Eve Farb, *Oddbird* by Derek Desierto, and *The Proudest Blue* by Ibtihaj Muhammad with S.K. Ali, illustrated by Hatem Aly. In all of these cases, we have a group of bullies who make things tough for the protagonist. However, it's important to note that the antagonizing forces spurn the character to grow or realize something, so there's payoff to the struggle. (*Clovis Keeps His Cool* is notable in that the bullies trigger Clovis's anger, which adds a Character vs. Emotion layer of conflict to the story, but they also make him realize that he can control himself.) The former two books feature sets of antagonists who are redeemed in the end, and all the characters pull together. The bullies in *The Proudest Blue* are quickly forgotten and the book goes in a different direction halfway through, with a Midpoint Shift structure.

- There's an apparent antagonist in *Iggy Peck, Architect* by Andrea Beaty, illustrated by David Roberts—the teacher—but we're given her backstory (unusual for an adult character in a picture book), which explains why she diminishes Iggy Peck's architecture passion. After the midpoint, she has a breakdown (which we are sympathetic to because of the backstory), and a Character vs. Problem conflict arises (a bridge collapse), which Iggy Peck solves (with engineering). The teacher ends up coming around and is redeemed.

- In the hilarious *The Three Canadian Pigs* by Jocelyn Watkinson, illustrated by Marcus Cutler, the mean-spirited wolf wants to settle his quarrel with the three pigs "the Canadian way[5]," which obviously means a game of hockey. But the wolf cheats because he's very hungry, and none too noble. In a surprise twist, the pigs invite him over for dinner to bury the hatchet (and eat poutine and watch more hockey, of course), and the wolf apologizes. Not only is the antagonist redeemed, but the protagonists look even better by comparison for their squeaky-clean behavior.

- *I Want My Hat Back* by Jon Klassen is an interesting antagonist case study for the character of Rabbit, because it pulls the protagonist into a revenge plot. The protagonist, Bear, is sympathetic because he has been wronged by Rabbit, who stole his hat. Rabbit is not sympathetic. Unlike some of the above examples, though, Bear does not emerge from their face-off morally pure. There's a very strong suggestion that Bear kills Rabbit (off the page), but this book is

---

5. Jocelyn Watkinson, *The Three Canadian Pigs*, 10-12.

somehow a delightful read, regardless. The author/illustrator's fame has allowed him to pull this off. I'm not sure implied murder would work from a debut.

Character vs. Society's Expectations: This type of conflict usually loops in the SEL idea of the child being wonderful, just as they are, and society needing to change. In fact, there's an entire story structure with this dynamic (Get On My Level, described in the following chapter). An overarching theme of this conflict is that the child is doing something right, and society is doing something wrong, and there needs to be a collective "step into the light" moment for those characters who have unrealistic or unfair expectations. Here are examples from shelves:

- In *Puddle Pug* by Kim Norman, illustrated by Keika Yamaguchi, a pug is in love with puddles and is always looking for the perfect one. Percy finds his ideal puddle—a pig wallow—but, unfortunately, the pigs don't want to include him. They put up a sign that says *Pigs Only*, which points to a division by species within their society. But when the pigs need help and Percy gladly offers it, despite having previously been rejected, there's a reckoning that brings pigs and pug together.
- As discussed above, *Imogene's Antlers* is a great example of a Character vs. Society's Expectations conflict, because a few people in Imogene's household actually think the antlers are delightful. It's some of the stuffier adults—the principal, doctor, and Imogene's long-suffering mother—who try to fix her "shameful" condition.
- In *The Adventures of Beekle: The Unimaginary Friend*, the imaginary friend character journeys into the human

world and is very confused by modern society, where nobody seems to be having any fun. So a character's expectations of society can also create this conflict, especially when society doesn't measure up, in this instance, and it's implied that societal improvements could yield a better quality of life.

- *Martha Speaks* is a very fun classic picture book in which Martha, the dog, eats alphabet soup and starts talking. And talking. And talking. To be clear, she has done nothing wrong, but her family gets frustrated. At one point, they wish that she had never learned to talk at all. Is Martha at fault here? No. The conflict of Character vs. Society's Expectations is that the family didn't seem prepared for what she had to say. They thought it was great at first and encouraged her. But when someone is unapologetically themselves, you can't only take the good. That the family wasn't prepared to accept her wholeheartedly is their problem, not hers. She ends up saving the day, a repair is made, and she even learns a *little* bit of self-restraint.

- *Moo Moo & Mr. Quackers Present What's Cooking Moo Moo?* by Tim Miller has a Character vs. Character conflict initially, because Moo Moo and Mr. Quackers disagree about what to do with Mr. Quackers' life savings, which Moo Moo steals to open a restaurant. However, the primary conflict is Characters vs. Society's Expectations because the animals go on to whip up their favorite foods, only for their crowd of human customers to find them disgusting—because the secret ingredient in Mr. Quackers's pasta sauce is worms. But since readers are aligned with the animal characters, we are on their team, and therefore society (and its dislike of worm-based food) is wrong.

- *Uni the Unicorn* by Amy Krouse Rosenthal, illustrated by Brigette Barrager, features parallel protagonists, a little girl and a unicorn, who are "othered" by their friends and families for their belief in unicorns and little girls, respectively.
- *Lou* is a fabulous story where Lou, a fire hydrant, struggles with being … well … a loo (hence his name). He believes he's inherently capable of greatness, and yet society (represented by a never-ending stream of dogs and their, ahem, streams) has brought him down. It's not until a fire breaks out that Lou discovers his true purpose (with the help of some firefighters).
- In *The Princess and the Pony* by Kate Beaton, our main character wants to be a warrior brute, but everyone—much to her frustration—sees her as an adorable little princess. By leveraging her cuteness, and with the help of a misguided present from her parents (a dysfunctional pony who is decidedly not the powerful steed she asked for), she unlocks the cuddly desires of the actual warrior brutes in the kingdom, and everyone embraces both their badass and their snuggly sides together.
- A girl power STEM-inflected fairy tale retelling, *Interstellar Cinderella*, not only pits Cinderella against the usual conflict of her unreasonable family, but against society's idea that a girl can't be a spaceship mechanic.
- *Wutaryoo* by Nilah Magruder shows a character exploring society's label for him. He's not an identifiable species, so everyone's always asking, "What are you?" (Hence the title.) This is an analogy for racial identity. He goes on to discover himself and decide whether labels matter or not.

- This is also the basic gist of *Mr. Tiger Goes Wild*, except Mr. Tiger's personal quest for freedom ends up liberating his Victorian-style society, too.
- In one of the first picture books that I sold as an agent, *Buglette: The Messy Sleeper* by Bethanie Deeney Murguia, Buglette hears the message, over and over again, that she shouldn't thrash around so much in her sleep. This questionable "talent" of hers ends up saving the day.
- Finally, in *Not Quite Narwhal*, we see Kelp embraced by the narwhals who raised him in the sea, only to discover he's actually a unicorn. The character never questions *who* he is but does grapple with society's labels and ideas about *what* he is, and what that might mean.

Character vs. Own Expectations or Change: There are a few layers to this one. First, Character vs. Change is easy to understand. Sometimes things change and it's hard to deal. There's an entire Growth/Change topic discussed in Chapter 6. And other times, a character has valid feelings or expectations that aren't met. This can be a hard adjustment. Sometimes, though, those expectations, while well-meaning, need to change. The character must realize the error in their thinking, and grow. I toyed with calling the latter instance of this type of conflict "Character vs. Reality," but that's a bit of an adult understanding. Let's go to the shelves:

- *Toby Is a Big Boy* by Lou Peacock, illustrated by Stephanie Christine Pym, features a Character vs. Change conflict, which is projected at Mom, who Toby feels has been distant ever since the baby came. But, really, the issue is that Toby is growing older, and sometimes that means doing hard things by himself. The lovely thing about this book is that it provides a gentle reframe for the double-edged sword of wanting to grow up, but also needing a safe place to be a kid.

- The wonderful *Sheepish (Wolf Under Cover)* tackles the wolf's prevalent notion that wolves and sheep can't be friends. When he gets to know the sheep he was trying to eat, he realizes he can no longer see them as food. His expectations need a tune-up.

- *Owl Moon* by Jane Yolen, illustrated by John Schoenherr, deals with the implied expectations of the father for the child—that they stay quiet and brave enough to venture into the dark forest to see an owl, because they are now old enough to join him on this adventure. But it also tackles the child's expectations for themselves—that they stay quiet and are brave enough, up to their own standards. There's also some gentle tempering of expectations, as an owl sighting is not guaranteed.

- In *The Princess and the Pony*, initially described, above, in the Character vs. Society's Expectations section, we also come to realize that Princess Pinecone has some mistaken ideas about what it means to be a warrior. She believes, wrongly, that she needs a certain kind of horse to make herself a brute, only to realize that there's no right or wrong way to be fierce. She can still be formidable on her little demented pony, all while wearing an adorable sweater.

- In *Children Make Terrible Pets* by Peter Brown, Lucille, a bear, is so convinced that she can keep a child as a pet (echoing every child who has begged for a furry friend to call their own) that she disregards Mom's sage advice that "children make terrible pets.[6]" In this case, her expectations are her own undoing and she

---

6.   Peter Brown, *Children Make Terrible Pets*, 12-13.

realizes her folly … sort of. (In the endpapers, she tries to bring an elephant home.)

- In the lovely *Mel Fell* by Corey R. Tabor, Mel gamely leaps out of the nest, expecting to fly, only to fall. And fall. And fall. (As suggested by the title.) There's a little bit of fear of change here, a parallel for fledging from the nest into the unknown, but Mel's indomitable spirit helps him rise above (literally).

- A book that resonates with me very deeply because of my heritage and my family's immigrant history, *The Boy Who Tried to Shrink His Name* by Sandhya Parappukkaran, illustrated by Michelle Pereira, introduces readers to a boy named Zimdalamashk-ersmishkada, who feels self-conscious about his name and wants to shrink it. He believes that it will make him more approachable at school. I didn't mention this book in the Character vs. Society's Expectations section because the core conflict is really the boy's *own* perception of his name. Sure, someone in his classroom struggles to say it correctly, but Zimdalamashkersmishkada's self-consciousness is the painful issue that he must grapple with.

- *We Don't Eat Our Classmates* by Ryan T. Higgins could easily be a Character vs. Character conflict, because Penelope, a dinosaur, keeps eating her delicious human kindergarten classmates. However, the true issue is that she doesn't understand what getting eaten is like until the class goldfish chomps on her finger. Then she realizes that her own behavior was causing great strife to those around her, and she gains perspective that will allow her to succeed in a mixed-species classroom. This is also a Character vs. Emotion conflict, because she learns some self-control (eventually).

Character vs. Emotion: This is a very common conflict in picture books because kids are prone to being overwhelmed by their big feelings, whether they're fear or anger or grief. (Kids can also be overwhelmed by positive emotions, with happiness tipping over into hyperactivity, but I haven't come across many stories that tackle this particular SEL issue.) The resolution to this conflict isn't generally to shove one's feelings down or make them more socially acceptable, because, remember, picture book characters are generally inherently good, even when their behaviors or choices aren't. The solution to this conflict usually comes from working through certain feelings alone or in community with others, and getting perspective on them. Some books will introduce self-regulation strategies, either modeled in the story or discussed in back matter. This plays out on shelves in the following ways:

- In *Dragon Night*, by my former client J.R. Krause (I did not sell this book when I was agenting, but we did collaborate on an early draft, and I sold his debut *Poco Loco*, co-authored with Maria Chua, which came out from Two Lions in 2013), Georgie and Dragon are both afraid of various things. By coming together and thinking creatively, they are able to transcend their individual fears.
- *Courage Hats* is very similar, and also features two characters who buttress one another through an anxious time.
- The amazing *Finn Throws a Fit!* by David Elliott, illustrated by Timothy Basil Ering, which I'll discuss in more detail in Chapter 13, is quite literally the conflict of Finn working his way through an epic fit, which is portrayed in very visual terms. It also underscores the idea that big feelings can come suddenly and go suddenly, too.

- *The Heart and the Bottle* by Oliver Jeffers is unusual in that it shows a picture book character aging from childhood (when her grandfather dies) into adulthood. To deal with her grief, she has locked her heart away in a bottle, which keeps her safe from feeling her strife, but also keeps her from feeling all of the other emotions—including the good ones—of life. A child helps her reawaken to her feelings, and to a fuller existence. The conflict isn't solved, per se, as most of these Character vs. Emotion issues are never truly resolved for good, but readers are left with the sense that she's now on the right track.

- In a similar vein, *The Rough Patch* is the beautiful and heartbreaking story of a farmer whose beloved dog dies. He reacts to his grief by slashing his prize-winning garden. "But a good place can't stay empty for long,"[7] and by tending to the plants that insist on growing, he nurses his broken heart. He will never stop loving his late dog, but he can also continue to live.

- The *Food Group* series, which began with *The Bad Seed* by Jory John, illustrated by Pete Oswald, features a character who grapples with various behavior issues, sometimes being a Bad Seed (or a Sour Grape or a Good Egg … you get the point). The characters aren't all good or all bad, and they all have things they're working on about their personalities and behaviors. (I do take issue with the relatively straightforward expository tone of these books. Each installment features a character simply explaining themselves directly to the reader.)

- *Eat Pete!*, mentioned above, features a boy and a monster in an Odd Friendship structure (discussed in

---

7. Brian Lies, *The Rough Patch*, 18-19.

Chapter 12). The monster is not an antagonist character—but the monster's appetite is. The boy just wants to play, and the monster tries so hard not to eat him, but eventually succumbs to temptation, which is why I've chosen Character vs. Emotion as the true conflict here. Of course, a reversal comes when the monster realizes that life is worse without his friend … and spits him back out.

- *Gator, Gator, Gator* by Daniel Bernstrom, illustrated by Frann Preston-Gannon, isn't necessarily a conflict between a girl and the gator who lives in the bayou, but with the character's own courage as she goes exploring.

- Finally, *Meow!* is a semi-wordless story (for the majority of the book, the only words on the page are iterations of "meow") of a cat who just wants his family to play with him, but they're busy. He gets frustrated and loses his cool—Character vs. Emotion—and gets everyone's attention, all right, but in all the wrong ways. By getting a handle on his anger, he's able to make a repair and get what he wanted all along.

There are many available types of conflict. By using the above broad conflict categories, you will be armed with tremendous ideas for building your plot into something larger than its parts.

Summarizing Conflict

Whenever I read any story, whether for kids, teenagers, or adults, I am always wondering a few things about the conflicts involved. Remember, conflict is the engine of story. (Even if it's cute or funny conflict, which abounds in picture books, like *On Account of the Gum* or *Dragons Love Tacos* by Adam Rubin, illustrated Daniel Salmieri.)

When you add conflict to your story, or decide what kind of conflicts your story should have, ask yourself a few basic questions:

- **Chronic or Acute**: The conflict in your story can be a new development (like the fire in *A Little Ferry Tale*) or an ongoing situation that comes to some kind of head (Lou's role in society in *Lou*). You can have a chronic conflict that's exacerbated by something acute as well.
- **Internal or External**: Is the conflict in your story going to be largely internal or external? This can be a trick question, as internal conflict (the character grappling within themselves) and external conflict (an event or situation that acts upon your character from the outside) are often symbiotic. Most stories, even at the picture book level, have both kinds of conflict, but it can be helpful to break your sources of tension down into these two categories in order to better analyze them.
- **Why today?**: Especially if you have a chronic internal conflict (the grief in *The Heart and the Bottle*, for example), you'll want to preempt the question of, "Why does this particular story happen to this particular character today, of all days?" There should always be a specific reason to start your story with a concrete where and when, even if that reason is quite straightforward (in *Mel Fell*, Mel decides to fledge from his nest because that's just what birds do at a certain point in their development). Even if this question isn't answered anywhere in the text of your story itself, it's something you should know. Otherwise, there's no strong reason for your story to

be structured the way it is, and that could indicate or trigger some larger issues.

But wait, you might be thinking, *does absolutely every single picture book need conflict?* Well, there is actually an industry label you'll sometimes hear in picture book publishing: "the quiet book." What is this, and what's the prognosis if you think you might've written one?

Quiet Books

Sometimes a book is very specifically marked by the absence of conflict, though this is rare. Some examples are *Monster & Son*, *Grandfather Twilight*, and *Beaver is Lost*. When I first started in children's books in 2009, as an intern at Chronicle Books in San Francisco, a "quiet book" was not a compliment. This often meant that a narrative project didn't contain enough:

- Story
- Character development
- Conflicts
- Sales hooks

This is, indeed, a liability if you're missing all four of these elements. You could theoretically get away with missing one or two of them, but you'll usually want something to balance an apparent lack of conflict or character growth (especially in a fiction project, where these ingredients are expected).

Monster & Son is loosely structured around a day between various monsters and their sons, and the appeal of the monster characters is a sales hook. There's also a bedtime angle, and a Mommy/Daddy/Baby topic, as the tone is very Sweet/Positive. I like how this contrasts with the monsters, sort of a "softer side" exposé, which makes for an appealing reversal.

Grandfather Twilight is a very straightforward story, though it does offer a lovely modern origin myth for the moon. There's a peaceful tone for bedtime, and lovely art (it's an author/illustrator project), but notice that it was published in 1985. Without one of the other factors that sometimes affect book sales and acquisitions detailed in Chapter 6, such as a notable author, I'm not sure this one would be picked up today. I definitely don't think this would sell as a text-only project, either, because much of the appeal is in the gorgeous, symbiotic illustrations.

Beaver Is Lost is an almost wordless picture book that shows Beaver's journey—getting swept up on a logging truck and taken to Chicago, then having to find his way home again via the waterways—without a lot of chatter. Notice that this is also an author/illustrator project. If it wasn't almost wordless (there are four total words, and you know three of them from the title), I'm not entirely sure it would be that interesting or marketable. It almost goes without saying, but it wouldn't sell as a text-only manuscript from a separate creator—the art makes it.

Ironically, there's even a picture book, which I did not analyze, that is called *The Quiet Book* by Deborah Underwood, illustrated by Renata Liwska, though in classic Deborah Underwood fashion, it flips the idea of a quiet book on its head by demonstrating the power of quiet. (This came out in 2010 and felt almost like a knowing wink to the publishing industry, because so many conferences, presentations, and aspiring writers were concerned with having a "quiet book" around this time.)

If you fear that you have a quiet book on your hands—one which lacks the four broad strokes narrative elements defined above—and you don't happen to be an author-illustrator, you might want to pay careful attention to the following chapter and make some interesting structural choices to offset the relative lack of tension. Or you might want to add some characters, tighten up your theme, and dig deeper into what your protagonist wants. Think about stakes. Remember, conflict doesn't have to be overt or negative in order to add energy to a story.

By this point, we've established almost all of our key narrative picture book ingredients, from theme to topic to character to conflict. What else could there possibly be to talk about? Well, structure is the key to bringing everything together at long last. Read on to learn how to give all of these crucial storytelling elements some shape.

TWELVE
PICTURE BOOK STORY STRUCTURE

EVERY TYPE of story has a structure, whether it originates naturally and implicitly (like the flow of the seasons or the familiar cadence of the ABCs in a concept book, or the chronology of a lifetime in a nonfiction picture book biography) or whether it is applied in the service of storytelling (as it is in most narrative projects). Some concept and nonfiction picture books don't have structures, per se, though you should always think about how to organize your information.

Narrative picture books, for the most part, do have to be heavily and robustly structured, so that's what we will discuss in this chapter. First, we'll have to get on the same page about the broad strokes of story structure—the beginning, middle, and end of picture books—and then I'll detail the types of structures that I codified in my analysis.

Plot Ingredients: Beginnings

In the beginning, there was … the beginning. I know, right? These are the kinds of groundbreaking insights that I've built my career on. You're welcome. Okay, okay, but seriously, beginnings are important to every narrative picture book story because they have a big job to do. They must communicate:

- Who the protagonist is (in some cases, there are multiple equally important characters, like those in an Odd Friendship structure);
- Where the story is set (illustrations can also play a big role in world-building);
- When the story is set (if the time setting matters, like in a historical project);
- What the character's objective is (this is often one of the first things established in the beginning of a story, soon after we meet the character);
- What the conflict is (also crucial, as the story isn't going anywhere without one);
- What kind of tone the story will have (this is largely a writing and voice distinction, which we'll talk about in Chapter 14); and
- What the rhyming pattern will be, if the story is written in rhyme (which we'll discuss in Chapter 14 as well).

Whew! That's *asking a lot* of a few pages or spreads. But before you get overwhelmed, imagine doing this for a novel, where you have hundreds of moving parts. If you ever find yourself in a Character vs. Emotion conflict with your picture book beginning, just go ask a novelist how they feel about first pages or first chapters. Don't be surprised if they start to cry (a Character vs. Emotion conflict, in and of itself, as well as Character vs. Own Expectations).

But don't get too smug, because you will still need to pull off the above to have a compelling narrative picture book beginning. Also, there are a few very clear don'ts to keep in mind. Here's one to permanently remove from your idea bucket:

Once upon a time ...

Mentioning this one might sound like a joke, but it's done, over, and we're all immune to it. (You can use a "Once upon a time" opening line for a picture book ironically, or if you plan to twist or subvert this obvious fairy tale framework, but don't do it earnestly. You will get eaten alive.)

Then there's this one:

Hello! My name is Jenny and I'm five years old and I like ice cream and OH BOY do I love my puppy dog!

This first sentence—and the millions of iterations of picture book opening lines just like it—is fine for a first draft, but it should never see the light of day. First, it's boring. Second, it beats the reader over the head with demographic information that they don't need, presented in an obvious way. Third, it's too cutesy. Fourth, what a character likes and doesn't like is low stakes and doesn't matter, in the grand scheme of things (unless something is going to happen to this puppy dog in the plot, though I wouldn't advise endangering cute animals unless you're Jon Klassen). And finally, there's no objective or conflict presented, which means that this long sentence doesn't actually start any kind of story. As we've learned, objective is key to a proactive character, and conflict is crucial to plunging them into action.

In my analysis, I evaluated every spread of 90 narrative picture book manuscripts. I color coded it all into a spreadsheet. I literally lost sleep over this. (I have no social life, and I never got tired of doing book reports in school, so don't cry for me, Argentina, I actually had a great time putting this together.)

Because of the various formatting considerations of picture books, page counts, and bindings (which we will talk about in Chapter 16), the exact starting page numbers for picture book stories vary. But I can tell you with 100% absolute certainty (and I have the spreadsheets to prove it) that every picture book I analyzed starts with either:

- An introduction to an initial conflict or the larger story conflict (28%);
- An introduction to a character, who is often already *"in medias res,"*[1] or in the middle of an action, and doing something other than explaining their name and age and favorite ice cream flavor (45%);
- An introduction to the character's objective (13%); and
- An introduction that establishes the story world (13%).

Now, please keep in mind that the opening page or spread often introduces *more than one* story element. You can't start a story with a character's objective without also having the character on the page, for example. And yes, all stories take place in a story world, even if an introduction to the world is not the primary focus of the opening pages. You can't have much of a conflict without character, either.

For the purposes of this exercise, though, I had to pick the *primary* focus on the opening page or spread. Alas, I could not color code a single cell in a spreadsheet as more than one thing, so I had to choose. (It's actually perfectly possible to indicate multiple variables in one cell, but I had to pull myself out of the rabbit hole somehow, or I would've ended up in a different kind of cell … a padded one.)

---

1. *Merriam-Webster Dictionary*, merriam-webster.com / dictionary / in%20me-dias%20res. Accessed November 4, 2023.

By the third spread, 100% of the narrative picture books I analyzed had introduced a character *and* at least one conflict. In stories where strong objectives were identified (in 42% of the books I analyzed), 100% of those were also introduced by the third spread.

What does this tell me? Character and conflict need to be introduced ASAP in a narrative picture book, and objectives are important. By the third spread, you'd do well to have all of these ingredients established. No long warm-ups. No besotted character sketches that take up pages and pages and pages (and if you're not even thinking of your picture book in terms of pages yet, I'll disabuse you of this notion in Chapter 16).

Picture books aren't long, that much is already clear. So there's no time to waste.

Now, what do you do with the rest of the story? This is where it gets fun. Or stressful, depending on how you feel about plotting.

Plot Ingredients: Middles

Picture book story middles are tricky to summarize, because all kinds of stuff can—and does—happen. Fortunes rise and fall, conflict escalates and de-escalates, the midpoint is often hugely impactful, and your character is ideally driving all of that dynamic momentum forward with their own choices and actions.

Middles are also where the story lives or dies. If you are dreading your own narrative picture book story middle, just ask your novelist friends how they feel about *their* books' middles (and watch all the light drain from their eyes).

When I did my analysis, the following elements that tended to be present in the middle of narrative picture books. A specific tally of elements is beyond reason, and one concrete pattern is also impossible to name—that's why I'll identify eleven of them later in this chapter. Narrative picture book middles (pretty much all of the material after the first three spreads and before the final three spreads) tend to contain some or all of the following:

Conflict Escalation: Any story point where the conflict gets worse.

- This can happen either early on, after an unsuccessful attempt at solving the problem, or all the way up to the climax (if the story has one).

Character Clash: Characters are the key to conflict, as discussed in the next chapter.

- Even if two characters are friends (*especially* if they're friends), they can still have interpersonal conflict in picture books.
- Pages with this element tend to feature two or more characters taking different approaches to solving a conflict, or having a disagreement that's character- and personality-based, rather than plot-based.

Idea: This is any spread that is primarily about a character (or multiple characters) getting an idea.

- The idea can spell victory, or it can spell failure.
- If it happens toward the beginning, the latter is generally true.
- If it comes toward the end, odds are higher that it will lead to success.

Turning Point: I've used this label to indicate any moment when the story substantially changes.

- This can happen anywhere in the narrative as well.
- This can be a character-based change or a plot-based change. The midpoint is a very popular spot for a turning point, as you will see with the Midpoint Shift story structure.
- Or a story can have multiple turning points, as you'll see in the classic Three Act structure.

Resolution Attempt(s): The character (or a group) attempts to solve the conflict.

- They are generally not successful until the end, especially if there's a twist or reversal.
- The classic picture book writing advice is to include three attempts to solve the conflict, with only the last one ending up successful. However, this did not bear out in my analysis to the extent you'd think, given how popular this talking point is. (I've literally given entire conference keynotes that hinged on this advice, but that was before I decided to dig a little deeper.)
- Every story is different, but the "three attempts" rubric seems to really have fallen by the wayside, especially by Picture Book 2.0. I call it Escalating Attempts in my discussion of structures, later in this chapter. (If you want a really cute call-and-response version of the classic "three attempts," check out *Toad on the Road: Mama and Me* by Stephen Shaskan. There's nothing cuter or more life-affirming than a toddler chiming in with a refrain of "Hip, hip, hooray!")

Fun and Games: Sometimes you'll hear people refer to this section as the "promise of the premise," and it's an excuse to show off the concept and world you've created, and let your characters have fun or take a breather.

- This concept and nomenclature are borrowed from *Save the Cat! The Last Book on Screenwriting You'll Ever Need* by Blake Snyder and *Save the Cat! Writes a Novel: The Last Book on Novel Writing You'll Ever Need* by Jessica Brody, who adapted Blake's original teachings from screenwriting to fiction writing.

- It might seem odd to showcase "fun and games" when I've gone blue in the face telling you that picture book stories run on conflict instead of fun. Am I talking out both sides of my mouth? Sort of. As it turns out, narrative picture books often strike a delicate balance between conflict, character struggle and realization, escalation, de-escalation, failure, and victory.

- At certain points, even in seemingly serious stories like *Owl Moon*, we want to build in room to have a bit of fun and showcase the story world.

- If the Fun and Games sequence comes at the beginning of the story, that's a strong signal that something is about to change, and this ideal situation is going to be taken away, as it is in *Iggy Peck: Architect*.

- If it comes before a midpoint Turning Point, same thing. The false victory picnic in *Found* is a great example. Sometimes, though, the Fun and Games section comes at the end, as a bit of a reward, which happens in *Acorn Was a Little Wild* (though there's a pretty long Fun and Games section at the beginning of that book, too).

- Here, you really fulfill the picture book's core topic or idea, whether you glory in the world a little bit and show off your protagonist doing something they can only do in a book with your setting or plot or cast of characters, like Mortimer getting ready for the ball in *Zombie in Love* by Kelly DiPuccio, illustrated by

Scott Campbell. It's a little aspirational wish fulfillment for your audience, and meets the reader expectations that were generated by your pitch, title, and cover.

Struggle: This is more of an emotional development, where the character gets in their feelings about whatever is going on in the plot.

- Sometimes this can escalate a situation or be used for de-escalation purposes, as the character takes a break from the plot action to think or make a different decision.
- Certain pauses and lulls are built into picture book stories, which we'll discuss in Chapter 15 when we talk about page turns.

Failure/Dark Night of the Soul: This is familiar to novel writers as the scene before the climax, and it usually goes hand-in-hand with the Synthesis/Wielding dynamic described in Chapter 10.

- This usually happens at the midpoint (with certain structures) or before the victory (in other structures) and is the "all is lost" moment when the character believes they're never going to solve their conflict or achieve their objective.
- In novels, though, the climactic action tends to be a big sequence, and the protagonist's character is really forged in this battle.
- In narrative picture books, the failure generally swings upward into victory pretty quickly because, remember, the character's sense of self is more or less already established—they just need to solve a specific problem by harnessing their unique attributes.

Coming Apart: Sometimes this low point can be interpersonal, and I've labeled this Coming Apart.

- This is a different plot point from a failure that is plot-based, like when the character tries to achieve their goal and doesn't succeed.
- This is also distinct from a failure that's a Struggle or Dark Night of the Soul, when the character really grapples within themselves in light of an Identity Crisis (see Chapter 6) brought on by the story.
- Relationships are the key focus with this plot development.
- Coming Apart is higher stakes than Character Clash, defined above, and feels like it might end a friendship or parent/child relationship for good (it won't, of course, because this is a picture book).

Coming Together: As opposed to Coming Apart, Coming Together is all about, well, characters coming together.

- This can happen at the beginning of a story, like it does in *Eat Pete!*, but this placement often means that there will be some conflict in the relationship later.
- It can happen at the midpoint of a story, like it does in *Benny's True Colors* by Norene Paulson, illustrated by Anne Passchier, which shores up the character's allies (and own sense of resolve) before a midpoint struggle. It often happens at the end, also, especially if interpersonal conflict was present throughout the story.

Victory: Pretty self-explanatory.

- For the love of all things good, let your protagonist lead and proactively achieve this, rather than having it come from adult actions or with overbearing guidance.

Lesson Learned: Sometimes, a book is not complete without a lesson learned.

- As you can probably guess from my rant in Chapter 5, I dislike this plot point.
- If this lesson happens early on in the story, the character development can play off of it.
- It can also happen around the midpoint, and then the story continues toward a new realization, as it does in *We Don't Eat Our Classmates*.
- It also happens at the end, of course, as it does in *Mighty Red Riding Hood: A Fairly Queer Tale* by Wallace West. Options for a picture book resolution will be discussed in the next section.

De-escalation: This is a quiet moment, similar to the Dark Night of the Soul, but with a more peaceful or contemplative tone. It can involve only the protagonist, or a group of characters.

- This plot point also happens at the end of some stories, but it's interesting to note when it happens in the middle.
- In *Sugar Would Not Eat It*, there is a de-escalation beat pretty much smack dab at the midpoint, as the characters retreat to their corners after a long day of trying to force a kitten to eat chocolate cake. Everyone is exhausted and emotionally spent.
- The same thing happens in *Meow!* (What is it with these cat books?) It's a good moment for some synthesis.

As you can tell, there are many possible ingredients that can populate the middle of any narrative picture book story, including some fun ones and some not-so-fun ones. How they're arranged depends on the type of plot you're working with. The more straightforward button that comes at the denouement of a narrative picture book story is the ending, and I'll present some options for that before we explore how to sequence these elements into a structure.

Plot Ingredients: Endings

The great news is you probably already know how you want your picture book story to end. In fact, as we discussed in Chapter 5, some writers only have their ending in mind because they want to impart wisdom upon the youths. But that's an unenlightened approach. Good narrative picture book endings, luckily, tend to be a little more complex and nuanced.

Here are some plot options for bringing your narrative picture book in for a satisfying and elegant landing:

Resolution: This is the most generic type of ending available, and the catch-all category where I filed most of the endings that didn't offer anything else of note.

- With this ending, the conflict is solved, characters come together, there's a hug here and there, and we're left with the idea that the protagonist is going to be just fine, or even better off than they were before.
- This is the generic takeaway in most narrative picture books. It obviously hits by the last page or spread (depending on the layout, as sometimes a picture book will end on a spread, but more often ends on a single page), but can be drawn out for longer.

- Sometimes, this kind of peaceful resolution also appears one or two spreads before the actual end of the story, in case the book needs a page or two for a Reversal, Twist, or Joke, all of which are detailed below. A classic example of a more leisurely Resolution is what you'll find in *Llama, Llama Red Pajama*, where Llama and Mama are reunited, and Llama falls peacefully asleep.

Coming Together: You'll recognize this point from the discussion of middles, in the previous section, but it takes on special significance when it happens at the end of a story.

- When characters come together after the bulk of the story, it usually brings a narrative of interpersonal conflict to a close. It is very commonly seen in the penultimate spread, too.
- A lot of stories end like this. *Acorn Was a Little Wild*, *Good Night, Little Man*, *Sheepish (Wolf Under Cover)*, *Tea with Oliver* by Mika Song, and the resplendent *Nell Plants a Tree* by Anne Wynter, illustrated by Daniel Miyares, all finish with a Coming Together beat, either on the last page or the spread before it.

Reversal or Full Circle: With a Reversal or Full Circle button, there is a surprise at the end, which is less jarring than a Twist (described below), but which delights because it harkens back to the beginning of the story, or plays with an element established in the middle. Here's where endings start to get fun.

- Take, for example, *Sheepish (Wolf Under Cover)*. This story starts with the wolf infiltrating the farm in a sheep disguise. It ends with the sheep coming to Wolf's house wearing wolf costumes. This is both a Full Circle *and* a Reversal.

- The title page of *Confiscated* features Mom saying that a toy will be confiscated if the brothers don't play nice. Of course, they don't. During the last two pages, we see Mom again, and the boys are afraid that she will dole out the promised punishment, even though the brothers have figured out a way to play together. Mom bookends the beginning and end of the story, bringing it Full Circle.
- *Duck! Rabbit!* starts with the characters arguing whether an animal is a duck or a rabbit. At the end, they see a creature that could either be a brachiosaurus or an anteater, and the reader imagines the whole exercise repeating.
- Sometimes a Full Circle is indicated by language. The line "You'll be looking out your window when something wonderful comes your way"[2] kicks off *Your Alien*, and appears again at the end, but has taken on a different meaning in the interim.
- The entirety of *You Be Mommy* by Karla Clark, illustrated by Zoe Persico, is a role Reversal, where a tired Mom asks the child to do all the bedtime things she usually does. In the process, though, the child gets tired, and there's a Reversal at the end, because Mom assumes the mom role, after all. This is only a Reversal, of course, because they started outside their usual roles. (A reversal on a reversal, if you will.)

Twist: A twist is unexpected, by nature, whereas a Full Circle or Reversal beat has been foreshadowed or seeded either at the beginning of the story, or somewhere in the middle.

- Twists aren't just for the end of a narrative picture

---

2. Tammi Sauer, *Your Alien*, 2-3 and 30-31.

book story, but when they happen in the beginning or middle, I've labeled them a Turning Point (see above).

- At the end of a story, a Twist adds a jolt to an otherwise straightforward resolution, often with the aim of sneaking in some humor. *Click, Clack, Moo: Cows That Type* ends on a Twist because a new element, introduced in the middle, the duck, goes from being a neutral party in negotiations between Farmer Brown and the cows and hens to writing up demands on behalf of the ducks. The major conflict of this story involves the farmer fighting the animals in a tense negotiation. But once duck starts asking for stuff, the farmer gives in immediately.

- There's a Twist at the end of *A Spoonful of Frogs*, too, where the witch sits down to share a vegetarian version of her planned frog soup with the very frogs she spent the whole book chasing.

Joke: Sometimes, the final moment of a story is given to a joke that enhances our understanding of what we just read.

- As we'll discuss more in Chapter 14, humor is generally a welcome addition in narrative picture books that have a lighter tone.

- The boy in *Sugar Would Not Eat It* spends the plot trying to force Sugar, the kitten, to eat chocolate cake until he gives up (and not a moment too soon). He then has another great, "cat-friendly" idea for Sugar —a bath.

- After being treated to the magic show of a lifetime in *Maxwell's Magic Mix-Up*, the main character admits that he would rather have a clown for his birthday (intentionally funny because he's probably too scared to have a magician after seeing his sister turned into a rock, but also ironic because children tend to either like clowns or be terrified of them).

- Mr. Quackers starts off *Moo Moo & Mr. Quackers Present What's Cooking Moo Moo?* upset at Moo Moo for squandering his savings on a restaurant, because he was hoping to travel. The restaurant doesn't go according to plan, so they sell it and book a trip. The final page is a visual joke, depicting our characters arduously hiking up a mountain toward a hotel, unaware that they're about to encounter a *No Vacancy* sign.

I'm specifically not offering examples of narrative picture books that end on an overt message, because I want you to avoid this route. See if you can craft a story that conveys the lesson without stating it outright. However, these types of picture books do exist. I'd encourage you to check out *Dragonboy, The Little Ferry Tale, Oddbird, Walter Does His Best!* by Eva Pilgrim, illustrated by Jessica Gibson (a celebrity project), and *Hattie Harmony: Worry Detective* by Elizabeth Olsen and Robbie Arnett, illustrated by Marissa Valdez (another celebrity project) for examples of (*cough cough*) what *not* to do.

It's also very important to remember that you will want to give your character their objective (or fulfill the need underlying their stated objective, if the two things are not the same). I cannot tell you how often I read a story (not just a picture book, either) where the ending resolves a problem … that isn't introduced at the beginning.

For example, the end of a book shows our character in the park, surrounded by new friends. Great! But the initial framing of the objective and problem had to do with the character losing their dog. They went to the park to look, made friends … and that's all fine and good, but what about the dog? To me, this story isn't about friendship or loneliness, it's about the child-pet relationship. By ending on a final image or feeling that's not seeded as a problem or want or need earlier in the story, you really don't close the loop in a satisfying way.

Writing with Pictures: How to Write and Illustrate Children's Books has this to say on the topic, about an imagined story scenario where a character wants to go on a picnic:

> In *Picnic* the action is complete not simply because the actor arrives at the picnic, but because his *desire* has been fulfilled. The reader experiences the completion of the action only when the actor fulfills his desire at the end of the story.[3]

Beginnings and endings have a tight relationship, where one informs the other. If yours do not align, and more importantly, do not connect in the form of a satisfying resolution, you might want to do some work on either how you set up the story, or how you finish it.

Types of Story Structure

For avoidance of doubt, there are more than eleven narrative picture book structures in the world. And not every instance of these eleven structures looks the same on the page (that would be very boring). Not every story that's identified as having one of these structures follows the parameters perfectly—especially because I'm developing and applying the parameters retroactively. And a single story can fit

---

3. Uri Shulevitz, *Writing with Pictures: How to Write and Illustrate Children's Books*, 33.

multiple structures, just like one book can involve several topics, as we saw in Chapter 6.

Some structures are driven by the shape of the story, known as the plot arc, while other structures are more concerned with the character arc(s). All structures obviously involve both plot and character elements.

That being said, I have identified eleven pretty prominent story patterns during my close reading analysis of 90 narrative picture books (some older, a lot published since 2017). Some structures are pretty common. Others are less common. I'm presenting them here in no particular order:

Midpoint Shift, aka The Problem Isn't What You Think: This is by far one of the most prominent structure types I noticed, and I like it because it's beautifully balanced, because the story changes trajectories at the midpoint. In a 40-page picture book, we generally have about 18 usable spreads, a first half that's approximately seven spreads, then a turning point spread that hits around pages 20-21, and then another seven spreads to the resolution. In a 32-page picture book, the balance is a little different, where we still have about seven spreads that bring us to the (apparently magic) 20-21-page mark, and then a shorter resolution. (Remember, the number of available pages you have to work with depends heavily on whether the book is self-ended or separate-ended, which you'll see very concretely in Chapter 16). A Midpoint Shift type of story is more common with 40-page layouts because you have more room to grow the initial conflict and then the *real* conflict, which hits after the middle. Here are some examples:

- In *Your Alien*, the boy finds an alien and thinks it's the coolest thing ever … until he realizes the alien misses his family. Then he starts working on sending him home.

- With *Found,* Bear tries to find Floppy's owner, only to be successful—and learn he doesn't have to part with the bunny, after all.
- At the beginning of *The Princess and the Pony,* we think the story is going to be about getting the best, toughest, and fiercest horse. Then it emerges that the story is actually about modulating the character's preconceived notions of what it means to be tough.
- Nowhere is the Midpoint Shift more apparent than in *Mel Fell,* which asks readers to literally flip the book upside down on pages 24-25 of 40, a very clever interactive format that likely helped this project get a Caldecott Honor.

Wrong Way Right Way: This structure is similar to the Midpoint Shift, though with one very important distinction. In a Midpoint Shift, the story itself changes around the midpoint, as the character realizes that they've perhaps been pursuing the wrong conflict or objective (as in *Your Alien*) or an external twist upsets the direction of the story (as in *Found*). In Wrong Way Right Way, the character is the one who experiences a change or realization because they try to solve their problem the wrong way first, and when that doesn't work, they finally change tactics and discover the right way to achieve their objective. It's demonstrated in the following stories:

- *Grimelda and the Spooktacular Pet Show* is a great example of this because Grimelda is convinced that her cat won't win the spooktacular pet contest, so she tries to buy or find another pet. The second part of the story isn't possible until she snaps out of her false belief and joins forces with her existing cat.
- *Meow!* shows the cat trying to get his family to play with him by being inflexible and impatient. It's not

until his feelings boil over around the midpoint that the whole family can come together.

- *Clovis Keeps His Cool* sees Clovis, a former hothead, responding to bullying with anger. After a blow-up, he not only recaptures his peace, but spreads it to his former bullies (and future friends).
- *The Heart and the Bottle* follows a misguided approach to grief that ends up doing more harm than good, until the character realizes she needs a course correction.
- In *The Boy Who Tried to Shrink His Name*, Zimdalamashkersmishkada acknowledges that he can't shrink or change his name by the midpoint (so this is also a Midpoint Shift). He then goes about accepting it, sharing it, and standing up to American society's standards for what a palatable name looks and sounds like.

Escalating Attempts, aka Struggle Showcase: This is perhaps the closest structure model to the Three Attempts plot that I discussed in Chapter 11. However, as I mentioned, I'm not seeing the "magic number" of three tries to solve a problem in some of these stories. Here's how it plays out on shelves:

- Sometimes the attempts to resolve the conflict happen at the beginning, as they do in *Room on the Broom*. The witch loses three things and makes three new friends, yes, but that's not the end of the story. There's a Midpoint Shift structure here as well, as the dragon's appearance changes the entire plot trajectory.
- *Maxwell's Magic Mix-Up* seems like it will be all about fixing the magic-trick-gone-wrong at the party, but the magician is only active in the first half. He calls for reinforcements in the second half.

- Sometimes, Escalating Attempts occur for part of a story, as with the above examples. Other times, the structure is more concerned with maximizing the character's struggles.
- This structure is often done for comedic effect (as in the case of *Lou*), and sometimes for tragic effect that makes the inevitable resolution all the sweeter (as in the case of *Kitten's First Full Moon* and *Bubble Trouble*).

Three Acts: This is a very simple structure where there is a lovely balance between a beginning, middle, and end, usually with turning points (plot or character or both) between each act. Here are some published examples:

- *Interstellar Cinderella* is a great example of this, which the rather classic plot makes sense, because it's a fairy tale adaptation. First, we establish Cinderella's character, skill for fixing robots, and desire to go to the ball. In the middle, she gets her chance to meet the prince. At the end, he identifies her as the girl who fixed his ship and proposes.
- *The Worst Teddy Ever* features a beginning and end from the child's perspective, with the middle showing Teddy's adventure.
- *Lots of Cats* by E. Dee Taylor introduces readers to a witch who casts a spell to fix her loneliness, but summons a huge army of cats by mistake. She gets sick of the cats in the second act, because they're all-consuming. By the third act, she gets lonely again and wants them back.
- *Amy Wu and the Warm Welcome* shows us a girl who wants to make a new student feel welcome at school, only to feel insecure about her Chinese language skills when he doesn't respond. Then she sees him in his own element, and it makes her brave enough to

invite him over for a dumpling party. They come together in the third act.

- *Coqui in the City* by Nomar Perez features a boy leaving Puerto Rico (and his favorite coqui frog) behind to move to New York City. He then struggles to find anything familiar in the city, until he stumbles onto a neighborhood pond full of frogs.

- In *Lost and Found* by Oliver Jeffers, the boy tries to find the stray penguin's owner in the first act, then decides to return Penguin to the South Pole in the second act. He realizes: "The penguin hadn't been lost. It had just been lonely"[4] in the third act, and they go back home together.

- With *Sarah Rising* by Ty Chapman, illustrated by Deann Wiley, the Black character spends time in her safe space, with her family, goes to a Black Lives Matter protest, and gains new perspective on social action and law enforcement.

- Finally, *The Snow Fox* by Rosemary Shojaie is a lovely wintertime forest tale about a fox who enjoys playing with friends in the fall, but gets lonely when winter comes. He builds a fox out of snow in the second act and they engage in Fun and Games. Then he meets a real Arctic fox in the third act, and is no longer lonely (and can celebrate the things winter brings, not just mourn what it takes away).

Nesting Stories: This is an interesting structural designation because it can overlap with some other categories. What I mean here is that we are telling multiple stories in one picture book. Sometimes this takes on a story-within-a-story shape, and this neatly fits with Three Act structure as well. Here are examples:

---

4. Oliver Jeffers, *Lost and Found*, 24-25.

- *The Worst Teddy Ever* starts and ends with the kid's POV (point of view) but spends the middle in Teddy's perspective, to explain why Teddy is so tired all day.
- *Duck Soup* starts and ends as Max's story, then removes Max for the middle and follows his knucklehead friends.
- *Violet and Victor Write the Most Fabulous Fairy Tale* is literally a metanarrative story within a story (well, several stories) as twin siblings fight over the "right" way to tell a fairy tale.
- But perhaps my favorite example of this is *Nell Plants a Tree*, which seamlessly weaves together the present and historical timelines of one family on alternating spreads. It traces the story of a grandmother who, as a young child, planted a tree from a seed. That narrative is intercut with scenes of her grandchildren enjoying the now-mature tree. It also comes Full Circle as her granddaughter plants a seed at the end.

Reframe: This structure type will remind you of my discussion of the Full Circle and Reversal ending elements, because it is mostly concerned with building up to the ending. There, we either revisit the beginning with new perspective, or reframe a common idea in the story with new meaning. Ideally, it's done in such a way that the message isn't heavy-handed (unlike my heavy-handed reminders to not make the message heavy-handed). In published works, it looks like this:

- *Toby Is a Big Boy* examines both the excitement and responsibility of growing up. First, Toby is forced to be a big boy (as Mom is too busy with the baby to help him). Then he acts too adult for his age by running away. Finally, he's able to admit to wanting Mom's attention as her first baby, after all.

- *Where the Wild Things Are* is a classic example of this structure, as it starts and ends in the same location. (It also has elements of a Three Act structure, Nested Stories, and Dig Down Deep.)
- *The Adventures of Beekle: The Unimaginary Friend* comes full circle and works with either a Three Act structure or Nested Stories, depending on what you consider as the portal fantasy world: the imaginary world (where the story starts and ends), or the real world (which we get in the middle).
- *The Rough Patch* is, emotionally, a Wrong Way Right Way, structurally a Midpoint Shift, and also comes Full Circle, because it begins and ends with a dog.

Get On My Level: If you were paying attention in Chapter 1, you know that Picture Book 2.0+ is all about characters who already know that they have a special spark, and aren't afraid to use it. They are in possession of an attribute or inherent trait that makes the story come together. These are notable instances:

- In *Buglette the Messy Sleeper*, Buglette's quirky habit of making a big mess in her sleep ends up helping her community. It's true that she doesn't consciously defeat the crow (the antagonist) but what she does while asleep is informed by her big dreams, and inspires the solution. The rest of her family and community then realize that they should stop giving her a hard time. Her messy sleeping isn't hurting anyone, and it's actually an asset.
- In *Extra Yarn*, the character knits and knits and knits. Her teacher doesn't understand her, but she's not knitting for him. She just keeps right on doing what she wants to do (knitting), and rebuffs a pretty classic villain by the end.

- *Puddle Pug* gives us a protagonist who keeps copious notes about puddles. This quirk ends up saving the day and winning him the friendship (and puddle access) he desires.
- *Mr. Tiger Goes Wild* is a classic example. The character in a Get On My Level structure doesn't change—they generally show society that it needs to adjust, rather than bending themselves to the will of public opinion.

Had It All Along: Now, you might be thinking that Had It All Along sounds a lot like Get On My Level. In both structures, the character is who they are, and they don't change. But with Had It All Along, they only realize their quirk is an asset at the end of the story. Consider these examples:

- In *Tea with Oliver*, both characters are able to come together despite struggling to connect. Neither character changes—both could be called shy and retiring—but by forging a friendship, they're able to enjoy their quiet lives more.
- *A Little Ferry Tale* features a boat that is slow and steady, but that's what it takes to come to the rescue. Her perceived liability is reframed as an asset by the end.
- Perhaps my favorite example is *I Don't Want to Be a Frog* by Dev Petty, illustrated by Mike Boldt. The titular frog doesn't want to be a frog—he's too wet, slimy, he doesn't like eating bugs, etc. He wants to be a cat or a pig or an owl instead, because those seem cooler. Then a wolf comes along and reveals that he loves eating cats and pigs and owls, but never frogs, "because they are too wet and slimy and full of bugs."[5] Everything the frog dislikes about himself is

---

5. Dev Petty, *I Don't Want to Be a Frog*, 20-21.

actually saving his life. It's important to note that this lesson, realized by the frog, doesn't make the wolf into a villain, either. The frog can acknowledge that, "I guess we can't fight nature. We are what we are."[6]

Dig Down Deep: This type of story almost always accompanies a Midpoint Shift and either a Get On My Level or Had It All Along structure. Here, however, the Midpoint Shift is largely internal, and it involves a recommitment to solving the conflict or achieving the objective when the going gets tough. Here are two examples:

- *Owl Moon* presents a great version of this structure. The character is scared out in the woods and doesn't know whether they will see an owl, but by leveraging their own expectations for themselves and Dad's expectations for this new, more grown-up activity, they are able to persevere despite the cold and silence.
- In *Your Alien*, the character thinks it's very cool to have a pet alien but realizes that the alien is homesick. The boy goes from making a selfish choice to a selfless one, because he discovers his empathy and sends the alien home.

Odd Friendship: This structure type is all about two characters who are different, but instead of anybody changing, they learn how to navigate life by being unapologetically themselves. You'll see a lot of titles that feature character names (and a lot of ampersands!) with this type of structure. These stand out:

- *Pine & Boof, Moo Moo & Mr. Quackers, Rabbit & Possum* are examples that could also accommodate a series

---

6. Ibid., 22-23.

treatment, with multiple adventures for these same characters.

- They key point to remember is that neither character is wrong. They can be in conflict about approaches to life, values, or solutions to problems they face. But on a deeper level, the friendship works simply because all parties are unique, wonderful, and sure of themselves. They find a way to navigate life together.
- I love *This Moose Belongs to Me* because the boy and the moose aren't really friends—who knows what they are or where the moose's true loyalties lie—but that doesn't stop them from trundling around in the wilderness as companions.

Villain Redemption: This structure type is pretty self-explanatory. A villain was making a bad choice and, by seeing the demonstrated virtue of the other characters, decides to make a better choice or take a better action. Let's go to the shelves:

- *The Three Canadian Pigs* and *Eat Pete!* are obvious examples of overt villains finding the right path.
- *A Spoonful of Frogs* belongs here, too, which is interesting because the character who changes the most is the witch—she really gives the frogs a run for their money but ends up making a vegetarian version of the soup to share with them at the end. She's our protagonist, but also the story's antagonist, if we see things from the frogs' perspective. And it's not like she *wants* to change. I fully believe that she would've cooked the frogs if they hadn't evaded her. However, she's able to pull herself together and get off of her murderous rampage (bet you didn't think you'd see those words in a picture book guide).

- It's not clear if these tentative new friendships will last, but for the purposes of this structure, that's beside the point.
- Fulfilling the reader's emotional expectations is key with this type of story, and a villain redeemed is satisfying.

It's impossible to codify all of the available conflict and structure options for a narrative picture book, and doing so would be a fruitless exercise. But mentor texts can help us organize our ideas, and it's always good to know what other creators are doing, which is why I began this guide with the advice, in Chapter 2, to read before you even bother sitting down to write.

Ideally, you now not only have picture book ideas, but a strong sense of how to sequence them to see your story take shape. Remember, the goal of your project is to have a specific and intentional effect on young readers, whether it's enlightenment or entertainment, or a little bit of both. Theme, topic, character, conflict, and structure allow you to do this.

Once you have the main skeleton in place, there are other elements—the muscles and organs that flesh out the story—to consider.

THIRTEEN
SECONDARY CHARACTERS, SETTING, AND STORY WORLD

SOMETIMES, a story really can be as simple as one character following their objective (and sailing on the winds of a strong motivation) until they reach their goal. This is a very basic structure, and even some of the more nuanced plots discussed in Chapter 12 can be boiled down to these essentials.

Books like *Take a Ride by My Side* and *Dragonboy* could not be more straightforward, as they are simply the stories of an adventure, and go from beginning, to middle, to end. *Race!* tracks a car race, though this one also has a Nesting Stories or Three Act structure, since we first inhabit the boy's perspective, then the car's, as if it's in a real race, and then we rejoin the boy's story to realize that he's imagining the whole thing as he plays with toys.

However, at a very high level, stories can seem too small or one-note if they don't also bring in other characters, settings, and world-building elements. These are optional, but worth learning about, as they can add depth and richness to a picture book.

Secondary Characters

When we talk about story, we often think about conflict (Chapter 11) and structure (Chapter 12). But if we go back to the well of novel storytelling wisdom, we will find that most conflict actually arises from characters and their relationships.

The recipe for a successful novel scene is widely accepted to be:

(Character A's objective x Character A's motivation) / (Character B's objective x Character B's motivation) = Conflict

---

This means that if Character A enters a scene wanting Character B to be their friend, and Character B has actually been nursing a secret grudge against Character A and wants to be left alone, the friendship ain't happening. Nobody's objective is met. Character A doesn't get a relationship, and Character B is unable to shake their frenemy.

In fact, Character A might be so upset and surprised to hear about the resentment, that the two might fight and end up in a worse relationship than before. Maybe the source of the resentment was a misunderstanding. Or maybe Character A is actually a very bad friend and in denial, and Character B is wise to avoid them. Alternately, Character B could be unfairly punishing Character A, and is actually in the wrong.

No matter what the underlying issue is, we generate conflict between the two characters by bringing them together in scene. It is invariably more conflict than we would've had if we were following either Character A (oblivious and wanting to make friends) or Character B (simmering in their own sour feelings) on their own. We do want to give readers a sense of each character's inner life and perspective, but it's only when they interact and start driving toward their objectives, which are diametrically opposed, that we get tension and plot.

When you introduce secondary characters to your story stew, odds are that you can make everyone frustrated, blocked, or unfulfilled—and that's a good thing!

There's often less obviously explosive scenework expected in picture books than in novels, of course, but don't neglect developing a cast of supporting characters for your story. Secondary characters generally play one of several roles:

- Friend or ally
- Family member
- Wise supporter
- Antagonist

In terms of cast size for a picture book, I would suggest a maximum of three named characters, or characters who readers will need to follow throughout the story. The protagonist is obviously one of these, but we can also have a friend/ally and a wise supporter teacher, for example, in a classroom story. An antagonist character, if you're using one, should have the spotlight, too.

There are some books like *Thank You, Omu!*, *Hattie Harmony: Worry Detective*, and *We Don't Eat Our Classmates*, which name multiple children over the course of the story because there's a community or school setting involved. In these cases, it's okay to have many characters shown (some as set dressing), but it's also important to note that we don't receive the entire roll call of Penelope Rex's classroom, for example. The children also don't play an active role in the story—they are merely the recipients of various interactions by the protagonist.

Trying to meaningfully follow a large group of characters—four siblings in a family, for example—might mean you're sacrificing depth for breadth, and you should have a very specific reason for doing so[1].

Sometimes multiple characters in a story act out variations on a theme. In *Dragon Night*, we see two characters grappling with fear. Georgie, the boy, is afraid of the night. That's fair, and universally relatable to kid readers. Then he meets a storybook dragon—a representation of courage! Except Dragon is afraid of the knight in the book where he lives, so there's an unexpected twist. We see another shade of fear, too. Georgie's fear of the night is abstract, but Dragon fears the knight because he's mean and always trying to slay him.

Both can be seen as fantasy scenarios, or the products of over-active imaginations, but they're very real concerns for the characters.

The great thing here is that two types of kids (the scaredy cats and the tough guys) can see themselves on the page and interface with the story and its themes in different ways. By offering two characters who have different relationships with the topic and with one another, the story really ratchets up its universal thematic appeal.

Character Relationships

Think of the types of people who normally inhabit a preschooler's life. The close nucleus of their existence likely contains their family members, from parents to siblings to pets, with potential roles for grandparents, cousins, and other relatives. It's important to note that these people can either be allies or antagonists in a story, and can sometimes both (ha!).

---

1. That you grew up with three siblings isn't usually a good storytelling reason, unless you're writing autobiography, of course.

For example, one would be tempted to think that the brothers in *Confiscated* are enemies. They fight over every single toy in their household until Mom confiscates them all. This, by the way, is a wonderful premise for a picture book because it rings so universal. What kid has never had a toy taken away because they couldn't share? What parent doesn't immediately recognize their family in this story?

However, the conflict here is not Character vs. Character. The brothers start at opposite poles, because their initial desires are opposed, but it isn't long before they come together. When I analyzed the structure of this book, I was surprised to find that they actually unite on pages 14-15 to solve the problem of their toys being confiscated, and then their conflict goes from Character vs. Character to Character vs. Problem (getting their toys back) or even Character vs. Emotion (overcoming competitiveness and sibling rivalry).

They recognize that, to beat their boredom and resolve their toy-less existence, they need to work together. This book has a Midpoint Shift structure or Wrong Way, Right Way, because their initial issue (or what they think is their initial issue) isn't actually the issue, and the ending highlights that.

A similar book is the low-word-count *Meow!* This is an author/illustrator project, so a lot of the heavy storytelling lifting is accomplished in the pictures. The unnamed cat character wants his family to play with him, but everyone's busy. One would imagine that the conflict is Character vs. Character, especially since the family doesn't truly come together until the end.

But the actual conflict is Character vs. Emotion, because the main character's frustration with his family is expressed in such a way that he alienates everyone. To be clear, the family does reprimand him for his tantrum around the midpoint (pages 16-17). But then he has to Dig Down Deep, realize that he has contributed to his own bad day, and they're able to resolve things together. This is also Wrong Way Right Way conflict.

In *Toby Is a Big Boy*, we might see a Character vs. Character conflict between Toby and his mom, who is busy with the baby. Or maybe a Character vs. Character conflict with his new sister. But it's actually Character vs. Change and Character vs. Emotion, because Toby is really struggling internally with his changing role as "big boy" in a family with a younger sibling. It's about his sense of betrayal when something he used to enjoy—being treated like the precious baby of the family—is no longer offered.

Similarly, it's easy to say that *Good Night, Little Man* is all about Dad and Little Man's power struggle over bedtime (as Little Man keeps getting out of bed to look for his sheep). But I'd actually say that the character who changes is Dad, as he apologizes for letting his frustrations get the better of him. It's Character vs. Emotion, but on the part of the adult.

As you can see, a lot of these conflicts, which may at first glance seem like interpersonal issues, work in concert with an internal struggle on the protagonist's part. The secondary characters add texture, layers, and new angles on a theme. The protagonist bounces off other people and makes choices that show who they all are.

There's also a growing trend of showcasing a child's "found family," especially if the topic of the book deals with a problematic nuclear family dynamic. For example, the child may have a mentor or a group of friends or a kind neighbor in the apartment building who plays a parental role. A published example is *Benny's True Colors*, as the butterflies become significant supporters (even though his mother is also wonderful). My research of future deals has turned up several projects that deliberately mention "found family," so if your character has no positive nuclear family to speak of, unrelated supporters are also an option.

We then expand a preschooler's or elementary student's world into school or the community, and we get friends/allies, antagonists (the bully is a classic example), and wise supporters (teachers, counselors, coaches). This is where stereotypes can really come into the picture, and I sincerely hope you can avoid painting the bully as all bad or the teacher as all-knowing good, for example. Remember, the wise supporter or family member also shouldn't be the one expressing the moral of the story, or you will veer into preachy territory. (Hey! I rhymed! More on rhyming picture books in Chapter 14.) These choices sound like the first idea to me, and you will want to push yourself beyond them.

In a school setting, your job is to explore the increasingly complex nature of social relationships. Kids have been learning about themselves and their place in the world with their families, and things will shift when they interface with a larger community as their proving ground. Here, the conflicts are also layered, consisting of internal and external problems.

Who should your character be? Will people like the identity they've developed so far? What happens when two children clash? Or when enemies agree? What happens when the bully is unexpectedly nice or troubled in a way that inspires empathy? Not only do people change over the course of a school year, but they can act differently from day to day, and even hour to hour. Avoid giving your characters—even supporting players—only one label or attribute. As discussed in Chapter 9, some characters, including series protagonists, can be somewhat static, but they shouldn't be one-note.

Clover Kitty Goes to Kittygarten by Laura Purdie Salas, illustrated by Hiroe Nakata, which I did not analyze, is a great example of a cat character, Clover, with an implied sensory processing disorder, who is easily overwhelmed when she starts kittygarden (kindergarten). There's a universal topic hook here—parents are always looking for books to ease big life transitions, especially parents with kids who may be overwhelmed or more sensitive to stimuli, whether they're diagnosed with anything officially or not.

In this story, the cat decides to stay home from kittygarden after trying it for one day. She does, however, make a friend before she retreats. When the friend comes to check on her, she rejects him and stays in her safe space. The friend is undeterred but not pushy. When Clover is ready to give kittygarden another try, the friend is a patient, steadying presence who accepts her for who she is, and is part of the reason she decides to return. To be clear, it's not the mother, teacher, or friend who bring this change about—the choice is hers, but everyone's unconditional acceptance, especially her ally's, helps.

Antagonist Characters

The antagonist relationship is an interesting one in picture books. Sometimes, the antagonizing force comes from a sudden event that's unpredictable and messes with the character's normal. I'll once again reference the gust of wind in *Pine & Boof: The Lucky Leaf*. However, some picture books do have a more classic antagonist who works to block the character or cause havoc. Sometimes they are "on screen," meaning that we see and interact with them.

There's an active "on screen" antagonist in the classic *Room on the Broom*. It's a dragon who comes to menace a witch who has been busy dropping things from her broom and collecting friends in the bog. Various animals find the scatterbrained witch's objects, and she invites them to ride along. But the broom gets too heavy, and they suffer a crash landing near a dragon's den. The dragon is very dangerous, coming into the story at the 18-19-page mark, but the new friends reward the witch for making "room on the broom" for them by chasing off the villain (this refrain does, indeed, appear three times in this story, which really takes the "rule of threes" from Chapter 12 to heart). They are reunited and bonded forever by pages 24-25.

It would be easy to say that the conflict in this story is Character vs. Character (witch vs. dragon), but I actually think the underlying conflict is Character vs. Emotion (loneliness), as each of the animals (and the witch herself) are looking to build community, even in the small microcosm of a broom flying through the air. Though this story has an overt antagonist character, there is a lot more going on below the surface.

We're a big Peter Brown household, and the argument could be made that the teacher in *My Teacher Is a Monster! (No, I Am Not.)* by Peter Brown is, in fact, a monster. She's certainly drawn that way for the first half of the book, because she *really* doesn't like the protagonist's rowdy behavior in the classroom. (She also has something to say about his perception of her, as you can tell from the title.) Yet this is a story of Character vs. Own Expectations, because they both realize, by the end (as shown in the illustrations of the teacher and by her behavior toward the protagonist) that they've judged one another unfairly.

They work their conflict out by going on an unexpected adventure, where the boy can be rowdy all he wants outdoors, and the teacher lets her metaphorical hair down. They do return to the classroom and snap (somewhat) back into their usual roles, but with a new attitude toward one another. This is very subtly done, and in clumsier hands, it could've easily fallen flat.

Sometimes the antagonist is off-screen, like the idea of the mean knight who menaces Dragon in *Dragon Night*. The knight is referenced, and Dragon is afraid, while the kid, Georgie, is afraid of the "night" (the dark). This leads to an unexpected kinship—and some fun misunderstandings about homophones—and both characters are able to jointly solve one another's problems. But we don't really see the knight—we just hear about him. (Because the knight lives in the storybook that the dragon came from, Georgie draws a new, friendlier book for him to live in. More on fantasy settings, below.)

As is the case with *Room on the Broom*, the conflict here isn't just Character vs. Character with dragon vs. knight and Georgie vs. night, which are beautifully braided together. The conflict is Character vs. Emotion as well. The child not only becomes brave for himself, but he becomes brave on the dragon's behalf in a way that also helps to creatively solve Dragon's problem.

Oftentimes, the antagonist isn't internal or epitomized by one character. The conflict can come from a societal or world issue, as discussed in Chapter 11. *Mr. Tiger Goes Wild* is a lovely example of a character escaping (and then changing) societal expectations for his behavior and appearance by being his true self.

Setting and Story World

No matter what you choose for your story's setting, you need to keep one key thing in mind: Setting should ideally affect both character and plot. If there's no overt connection that makes these elements cohesive, then you might not need to pursue a certain setting.

Picture books are generally very setting-driven, which also gives them a neat, holistic feeling. The farm animals live on a farm, the forest world generally has either a complete universe of forest/woodland creatures, as you see in *Acorn Was a Little Wild*, or takes the approach of putting a human in nature, as either a friend or someone on the outside, looking in. A lovely young picture book that shows children interfacing with the natural world and its animals is *Little Bitty Friends*.

The world of your story can be absurd and funny, and we're invited into just such a universe in *Moo Moo & Mr. Quackers Present What's Cooking, Moo Moo?*. It can be soft and lovely and a little bit fantastical, like the world in *So Many Days*, though I would caution you against creating randomly fantastical worlds for no reason, as I discuss in the following section about fantasy- and imagination-based books.

That being said, I would think of some visual metaphors to work into your setting to make it concrete and enhance your illustration potential (we will discuss "thinking in pictures" more in Chapter 15). The home or school environment can be seen as "boring," but remember, this is a big part of your reader's (and, by extension, your character's) world when they are young. If possible, make the home a place where the character can have fun in a way that's relevant to the story.

I am thinking here of *Imogene's Antlers*, where Imogene's new antlers (a fantasy complication that's never explained) get caught up in the chandelier of her stately manor house. This is a very rich family, because they have a milliner on speed dial, a grand piano, and a fainting couch for Mom, who hits the deck a few times in a comedic refrain. The cooks and laundrywomen add a lot of Fun and Games to the setting by decorating Imogene's antlers with donuts and sending her outside to feed the birds.

One of my personal favorite young picture books, *Finn Throws a Fit!*, uses a home environment in a fresh way. I love this book not only because my four-year-old son (at the time of this writing), also named Finn, throws legendary fits. I especially love it because Finn throws a fit for no good reason (he decided he doesn't want peaches for a snack). His fit then becomes a character in the story, and as the fit grows and grows, weather events happen inside and outside the house, menacing his parents and sending the family's adorable little dog to seek shelter.

Storms swirl in the kitchen, a blizzard blows in the bathroom, an "earthquake shakes the world."[2] The fit itself is personified. Then it stops (also for no reason, because that's a very universal and relatable thing about tantrums), and the flood waters recede. The home is put somewhat back to normal, if maybe a bit worse for wear. Finn, on the other hand, is fine, grinning cheekily up at his disheveled family, and "he'd like those peaches now. Please."[3] The "boring" domestic setting serves as a backdrop and visual metaphor for big emotions.

Sure, sometimes a house or school or backyard is just a house or school or backyard. And that's fine. But remember that picture books are intended to be illustrated, and as a result, you will want to make sure that yours will have enough visual interest. If two characters are talking in their living room—*Tea with Oliver* is set completely within one character's apartment, for example—you could easily get into the problem of redundant illustrations. A conversation in one setting is a big challenge for an illustrator because there're only so many ways to execute picture after picture of "talking heads" and make it fresh.

You might want to dream up several locations or several rooms in the house for your characters to use in order to add visual interest. An example of a book that is also confined to

---

2. David Elliott, *Finn Throws a Fit!*, 16-17.

3. Ibid., 30-31.

one apartment, yet manages to be visually rich, is *Three Little Monkeys* by Quentin Blake, illustrated by Emma Chichester Clark, because the monkeys move their mayhem from room to room in a beautifully ornate Parisian apartment, which adds a lot of charm and atmosphere.

Time Period

If you are writing nonfiction or narrative nonfiction, it's pretty easy to define your time period. Pegging the story to a specific era is expected in these categories, as the main objective is to teach. For example, in *Hidden Figures: The True Story of Four Black Women and the Space Race*, we need to first understand that the word "computer" didn't always mean what it does in the present day. So we get the following explanation early in the story:

Today we think of computers as machines, but in the 1940s, computers were actual people like Dorothy, Mary, Katherine, and Christine. Their job was to do math.[4]

If a nonfiction book is set in a specific time period, it will usually tell you. If you are writing a narrative picture book that takes place in a different era, you can put that in the text. Use historical settings only if they're relevant and necessary to the story. Even though "nostalgia marketing" is a thing these days, a time period setting should be an intentional choice, not just used as an autobiographical detail from your own childhood memories.

If you're not looking to hammer home a time period setting in

---

4. Margot Lee Shetterly, *Hidden Figures: The True Story of Four Black Women and the Space Race*, 8-9.

the text itself, you can always include subtle time period details in the illustrations (or the illustration notes, which we'll talk about in Chapter 15). For example, *The Adventures of Beekle: The Unimaginary Friend* is very clearly set in modern New York City for a large part of the story. There's a historical setting visually implied in *Extra Yarn*, but there's also some overlap with a kingdom/fairy tale setting, because the villain sails across the sea to reach our character. It's "old time-y," but not precise.

In fact, a lot of picture books seem to exist in a bit of a time-less space that's sort of vintage, or at least doesn't have overt trappings of modern life. This is probably intentional because a lot of parents are trying to raise their kids without a dependence on screens or other contemporary distractions. So in certain picture book worlds, the characters don't have phones or access to TV (and are sometimes bored about it, as in *Badger Is Bored!* by Moritz Petz, illustrated by Amelie Jackowski). They exist almost outside of any chronology. Examples that come to mind of a "simpler time" setting in a picture book are *Sugar Would Not Eat It*, *Nell Plants a Tree*, and *Eat Pete!*.

Unless it's absolutely critical to inhabit a specific year or era in, say, a nonfiction picture book biography, you can indicate time period with a lighter hand, or leave it up to your illustrator.

Story World-building

Some story worlds are very straightforward. Others have elements of magic or imagination. If you go the latter route, make sure there's a very clear story- and theme-based reason for this world existing with your particular character in it (or about to visit it), and that the fantasy setting has a clearly defined set of rules. These choices must serve the story.

A great example of using a science fiction world to underscore and support a narrative is found in *Interstellar Cinderella*. It is, as you can imagine from the title, a STEM- and girl-power-fueled retelling of Cinderella from the perspective of a young servant who has a burning interest in engineering. She wants to be a spaceship mechanic, if only her terrible step-family would let her.

Throughout the story, which is drawn in rich jewel tones against a fantasy space background, she's fiddling with various whimsical machines in her home. It's not until she's able to fix the prince's ship (and leaves her wrench, rather than a shoe, behind) that she's proposed to.

However, in true girl-power fashion, she declares that she's "too young for marriage"[5] but will be his chief mechanic instead. It's important to note that the child is suggested to be a bit older. Though she's drawn as a six-or-seven-year-old, she's obviously meant to represent a teenager who uses tools and goes into the world on her own. This is an attempt to bridge her up to the age of Cinderella, a maiden running around all night and going to balls.

I wouldn't recommend making your picture book character quite so independent in your story, unless there's a strong reason for that choice. Here, the fairy tale adaptation explains this decision and also helps to ground readers in the fantasy world, as a familiar story superimposed on something unfamiliar helps audiences enjoy the innovative setting.

Craft Definition:

Fairy Tale Adaptations: In the concept book discussion in Chapter 7, we talked a bit about using a familiar song

---

5. Deborah Underwood, *Interstellar Cinderella*, 34-35.

or structure to underpin your work. A classic example is "The Wheels on the Bus Go Round and Round." In my house, we have at least five books that use this song as a structure, for example, *The Wheels on the Fire Truck* by Jeffrey Burton, illustrated by Alison Brown. If you are planning to adapt something familiar in your own story, you need to add a lot of value. *Interstellar Cinderella* is a great example because not only does it add a new setting (with timely STEM-inflected interests for Cinderella that make it contemporary), but it reverses the ending. Cinderella turns down the prince's proposal, which makes the story seem fresh. Simply putting a word-for-word version of the Cinderella fairy tale into space would not have had the same delightful effect. When you choose to adapt something, you need to contribute and "earn your keep." Use the original as a springboard. Otherwise, you will not be innovating enough in today's crowded market. *Mighty Red Riding Hood: A Fairly Queer Tale* is another example. It features a gender-nonconforming character in the title role, and regardless of what you think about the politics of gender identity, it found a timely foothold in the market for its inclusion-forward message.

Setting can do a lot for picture book, so be sure that you're mindful of yours and how it interfaces with and adds layers to your project. There is an additional caveat that I'll give about fantasy or imagination-based settings, below.

Flight of Imagination

There's a specific type of attempted picture book manuscript that I see quite often, which I call the Flight of Imagination. This story isn't usually set in reality, or it uses a portal fantasy or frame narrative structure (beginning and ending in our world, like *Where the Wild Things Are*, but going elsewhere in the middle). It features a character entering either a dream or imagination-based world where they interface with their creativity or are visited by fantasy creatures.

The adventure is a big part of the story, and the theme usually has to do with self-expression. Most of these projects feature the protagonist learning from a wise, otherworldly guide (who can represent the child's own inner voice or intuition).

I'd like to share a word of caution about these types of stories. There's a reason that agents and acquisitions editors at publishing houses don't generally prefer novels that begin with a dream. Dreams *seem* high stakes, larger than life, and fully immersive, but when the character wakes up after the prologue and readers realize, "Oh, it was just a dream," all of the conflict and emotion evaporate. What happened in the dream is therefore less impactful, and what's introduced during the flight of imagination might not matter as much to the character's real life as readers were initially led to believe. The whole experience can feel a bit like a bait and switch.

For example, the urban human story world of *What If…* is enhanced by what the character imagines. The power of imagination becomes almost another character in the story. However, this book is not *just* a showcase of the author and illustrator's imaginations. Its theme and topic are creativity, and it's also the child's manifesto that she will "always create,"[6] no matter what, even if all of the physical means of creation are taken from her.

We're not simply treated to the *product* of her imagination, we're following the *process* of creativity, and the illustrations give readers a reminder that everyone is creative in their own

---

6. Samantha Berger, *What If…*, 30-31.

ways. This book works on multiple levels, as a result, and the fantasy elements are perfectly superimposed onto the real world.

Dreams and daydreams are fanciful. They lend themselves well to all kinds of fabulous illustrations. But they also need to have logic, rules, and bearing on the character's real life. Avoid crafting a story where the character is merely going on a tour of a really cool fantasy landscape.

It's not objectively bad to place a character into a dream, an imagination space, or a portal fantasy. After all, this is basically the structure of *Where the Wild Things Are*. However, there's also an emotional arc to Max's adventure in the land of the Wild Things, and the story is about him owning his moods and needs, and deciding to come home, after all.

The takeaway here, with a fantasy or imagination story, is that it also needs structure and theme and to be "about" something, on a foundational level. We can't just do a flyover tour through a child's imagination and call it a picture book.

Ultimately, the world of your picture book is up to you, whether the story is grounded in reality or floating out in the stratosphere. When you're layering in secondary characters, time periods, or settings, the choices you make must feel cohesive and complimentary with the rest of the project and its intention.

Now we're done with defining the main components of most narrative picture book stories. This brings us to the most granular—yet crucial—picture book storytelling element: the voice and writing itself.

FOURTEEN
PICTURE BOOK VOICE AND WRITING STYLE

WHEN YOU THINK about the gatekeeper conversation in Chapter 3, we remember that picture books have more than one potential audience. This means that the adults reading the story aloud should have a good time, not just your child listeners (or the kids who flip through the book focusing mostly on the illustrations because they're not yet reading independently).

Picture book voice and writing style are especially important, because you are targeting the youngest readers. To be clear, nowhere in this guide will I suggest that you "dumb down" your picture book ideas, concepts, topics, themes, characters, conflicts, settings, or story structures. Even young kids are capable of understanding complex or even nebulous ideas (like self-esteem and creativity), as long as they're packaged cohesively with character and story.

However, adult readers, young listeners, and kids learning to read for the first time will absolutely get tripped up by needlessly complex language and syntax.

Simple writing is actually very difficult to pull off convincingly, so you will not be sacrificing any artistic integrity or

Serious Writer Credibility by making your picture book manuscript clean, succinct, and easy to read. Discard the notion now that you have to twist your prose into complex sentence pretzels in order to be A Real Writer. The urge to overwrite and to overcomplicate is, in my experience, often a symptom of insecurity.

This is not a bad thing. We all grapple with it, as creatives. I often joke with clients that I'm not a licensed therapist, even though some of my consultation and coaching sessions do turn into a beautiful mix of creative encouragement, life advice, and holistic writer-as-human discussion.

But rest assured that you do not have to write "fancy" in order to create picture books. In fact, you shouldn't. Children's books are incredibly segmented, with rules and guidelines for each age of audience category, from board books all the way to middle grade. Early readers, briefly discussed in Chapter 1, are the most regimented, in fact, because their job is to keep an eye on Lexile scores (and many other similar frameworks), as newly independent readers use these books to climb the skills ladder.

I didn't have time to write a short letter, so I wrote a long one instead.

MARK TWAIN

Now, I am less of a stickler about Gunning Fog, Flesch-Kincaid, and other readability formulas[1] when it comes to picture book texts. I once did a picture book edit where the

---

1. Please see Appendix B for a link to the free readability formula checker that I use.

client was shocked—open-mouth shocked—that I didn't provide a precise dissection of her Lexile score. This isn't neglect on my part. In fact, I will do a readability framework analysis for some clients, but only when I want to objectively demonstrate that the prose is too wordy, verbose, or syntactically complex, and reads at a much higher grade or age level than they intended. If your SMOG Index says you've churned out eleventh-grade writing, your manuscript is not going to be compatible with the picture book market.

That being said, while these readability scales can be incredibly important, especially for those early readers, you can take your eye off the dial more with picture books. There's a little bit of freedom, since adults are translating the text for kid listeners. You are welcome to include some fun, fanciful language and "reach" words, where your target audience might not know the meaning but can guess it from context clues.

You would still do well to exercise caution and only use fanciful language if your specific story calls for it. After all, *Fancy Nancy*—along with the fifty, yes, *fifty* (as of this writing) books in that series—has been teaching vocabulary and French to preschoolers for years, but that comes with the territory of being fancy. (Although the *Fancy Nancy*-branded early readers do have to adhere to stricter language and syntax guidelines.)

Unless you have logical and compelling story reasons to do so, avoid going overboard or making your text too complex. Simplicity is still key here.

Word Choice and Syntax

Let's unpack what I mean by simple word choice and syntax. Your lines and sentences should be short. In verse, which we discuss in more detail later in this chapter, you don't want to go longer than, say, 18 syllables per line. Sometimes poetry sentences run over one line (called "enjambment"), and a sentence is an entire couplet, or 36 syllables.

More often, though, I see lines hovering closer to 12 syllables, or 24 syllables for a couplet. Don't get me wrong, I don't necessarily want you to sit there, counting out syllabic counts for your prose. (You should absolutely do this if you're writing rhyme, however.)

I say this more to give you an idea of appropriate sentence length for prose picture book text. If you're using mostly one- and two-syllable words (three syllables and above tend to be more complex words, which I would use very intentionally), that means that your sentences should be shorter than 24 words.

The first sentence of the previous paragraph is 18 words, for example, and I almost had to stop and take a breath to read the whole thing aloud. Picture book sentences should also be very straightforward. The second sentence of this paragraph, on the other hand, is a 35-word nightmare with a parenthetical aside and multiple clauses. It's a great example of what not to do in your picture book manuscript, as you want to aim for declarative sentences that don't branch off or try to cover too much ground.

Here's a great example of simple preschool-appropriate language from *Toby Is a Big Boy*:[2]

> Being a big boy, thought Toby, was exciting. He was also bigger than his little sister, Iris. Iris was very, very small. And because Iris was so small, Mama was very busy. Sometimes it felt like Toby had to do everything all by himself. Even the hard things.

2. Lou Peacock, *Toby Is a Big Boy*, 9-10.

The sentences are 8 words, 9 words, 5 words, 10 words, 12 words, and 4 words, respectively. You can't get much simpler than this. To some writers, this seems boring. The declarative sentences are also full of telling (see the discussion of "show, don't tell" in Chapter 9). Toby is excited, but he struggles with being left alone to do the hard things. The voice is very much centered in Toby's experience, which reads quite straightforward.

But this story is about the ups and downs of getting a new sibling and grappling with what it means to be a big boy (while still being and feeling small), so the emotions are presented in a way that's very easy to unpack and understand.

Simple, declarative sentences are also the backbone of *Small in the City* by Sydney Smith.[3] The protagonist is speaking to an unseen character (assumed to be another child, but there's a wonderful twist toward the end) using second-person direct address, which adds some interest to the text:

> The streets are always busy. It can make your brain
> feel like there's too much stuff in it. But I know you. You'll
> be all right. If you want, I can give you some advice.

As was the case with Toby, above, this child narrator is sharing their emotions and experiences, though perhaps in a more imaginative and evocative way ("It can make your brain feel like there's too much stuff in it"). The protagonist's encouragement of the listener breaks the fourth wall and speaks directly to the audience. The narrator is technically addressing another character, of course, but this "giving advice" dynamic transcends the bounds of the book and

---

3. Sydney Smith, *Small In the City*, 14-15.

offers courage to kid readers as well, as a nice secondary layer of meaning.

Direct statements aren't the only way to evoke emotions, though. You can absolutely make your work more image-forward, as we see in *Platanos Go with Everything*.[4] The book starts with this image:

> Platanos are like golden slices of this afternoon's sun
> on our dinner plates.

The food continues to represent the complex emotions of a family grappling with immigration and their version of the American dream. Notice that we see the adults and their objectives through the eyes of the child, without going into any grown-up POVs (as discussed in Chapter 1). However, he is aware that the entire family unit is coming to terms with their new lives, so he shares about the adults, too (within reason):[5]

> Sweet slices of maduros frying in the pan remind me
> of Mami's dream of owning a house with a garden.
> Crispy, salt-sprinkled tostones are like symbols of Papi's
> hope for a quiet office to write his poetry.

These descriptions are a bit wordier—the sentences are 20 and 17 words long, respectively. However, we don't add any complex clauses, and the phrasing is still quite straightforward. It's important to note that this book has a 702 word count, which is on the longer side for current market trends. In part, there is more vivid, detailed language. Some of these descriptions could be offset by illustrations, as discussed in

---

4. Lisette Norman, *Platanos Go with Everything*, 2-3.
5. Ibid., 14-15.

Chapter 15, but then we would lose the imagery in the writing itself.

If you want to see an example of effective picture book voice from a "fancier" (Nancy would be proud) or more literary[6] book, look no further than *Owl Moon*. We are treated to some beautiful images of the woods at night:[7]

> The moon was high above us. It seemed to fit exactly over the center of the clearing, and the snow below it was whiter than the milk in a cereal bowl.

At first, they make several owl calls without answer. Then:[8]

> I listened and looked so hard my ears hurt and my eyes got cloudy with the cold ... an echo came threading its way through the trees.

And, finally, there's the big climax of the story:[9]

> The owl's call came closer, from high up in the trees ... Nothing in the meadow moved. All of a sudden an owl shadow ... lifted off and flew right over us. We watched silently with heat in our mouths, the heat of all those words we had not spoken. The shadow hooted again.

We see the owl as part of the shadowy night forest, and we also get the very interesting emotional image of the "heat in our mouths, the heat of all those words we had not spoken."

---

6. In publishing, this term is generally used for books that are less focused on plot and more focused on character development and the use of imagery and carefully crafted, intentional language.

7. Jane Yolen, *Owl Moon*, 18-19.

8. Ibid., 20-21.

9. Ibid., 24-25.

This is a mysterious and evocative way of talking about the character, who wrestles with their own courage in the dark woods, as well as the companionable silence between the inexperienced child (whose siblings have all gone owling before, when the narrator was too little to try it) and the father (who is strict, though not unkind, about them staying silent).

The sentences are longer, the voice, more haunting, and the total word count is on the long side, at 770. (But Jane Yolen can pretty much do whatever she wants at this point in her decades-long picture book career, so I wouldn't take this as license to write long, beautiful descriptions for a debut project, unless this style very much fits the overall story.)

An interesting case study in terms of word choice is *Nerp!* The topic of this book is picky eating, and the plot showcases the great lengths parents sometimes go to feed their children, who refuse whatever's on the table. Of course, there's a nice reversal in the story structure itself, when the child and dog switch bowls and are perfectly happy. More significantly, there are no words in this book that we would recognize as English, except "Slurp!" (Kids will also get a kick out of listening to their parents trying to pronounce the gibberish.) The author/illustrator has created a unique language, and yet the book is very easy to understand and enjoy.

A similar story is *Meow!*, which I've discussed at least six thousand times in this guide, because I love it. The only text in that book is the word "meow" (except for the last word, which is "purr"). But the tone and use of the word "meow" changes from page to page, and audiences are invited to add their own emotional context to the reading. It's very clear and easy to understand what the cats mean, even though they are technically all saying the same exact thing.

The takeaway here? As long as you have a great story already in place, you can dress it up or down in whatever language is appropriate, as long as it fits the concept, isn't unnecessarily complicated or ostentatious, and is easy to read.

Read-aloud Potential

Always read your work aloud when you're writing picture book manuscripts. Even as you're composing your first draft of the text. This is, after all, how picture books are going to be consumed, at least in the parent/adult use case (as opposed to being read by newly independent readers).

Too few writers do this, and I understand why. You'll see this advice in this guide, and out in the larger writing and publishing worlds, and you will be tempted to think, *Great idea, I'll be sure to try it*. But then you might not follow through. Do not file this advice away into your writing toolbox and let it sit there, unused.

Read your work aloud. If you're self-conscious, get over it. Growth hurts. Stretching yourself hurts. You need to take the good with the bad, the brave with the vulnerable. If you're worried about your loved ones thinking you're crazy for talking to yourself, you *are* crazy. You want to get involved with the fickle publishing industry, after all. (I'm crazy, too. You have to be somewhat cracked to hitch your wagon to publishing, and I've been in this business for over a decade.)

Even better, have someone read your work aloud to you. Sit on your hands. Put a wooden spoon between your teeth and bite down hard, if you have to. There's no better way to realize that all of your beautiful prose isn't coming across exactly as intended. When we read our work in our heads, or even aloud to ourselves, we tend to read it how we *meant* it to sound.

Give it to a total stranger and watch all of those good intentions and preconceived notions crumble. This is a good thing. It will help you arrive at clarity, which is so important in picture book writing. This additional layer of insight will guide you toward fixing the issues you encounter.

Note where your reader stumbles or flubs their words. Go back and smooth out those sentences. It's important to have your draft pretty well hammered out before taking this step, because you want to do this exercise mostly once you believe the project is finished. Add this step to your revision process, which we'll discuss in Chapter 17. If the reader is already familiar with the manuscript, they may give it the same biased interpretation that you're capable of, and this experience will be less effective.

Now that you've committed to both reading the work aloud and having it read aloud to you, let me also explain the term "read-aloud potential," as it applies to picture books. You may have heard this description bandied about, or you might even be tempted to use it as a sales hook in your query letter (which is explored at length in Chapter 18).

First and foremost, though, let's define what this industry term means.

Craft Definition:

Read-aloud Potential: This designation doesn't just refer to the fact that picture books are read aloud. In that sense, every picture book manuscript has "read-aloud potential." What this description means, more specifically, is that a picture book has some engaging element that makes it *more* fun to read aloud, like rhyme, onomatopoeia, dialogue, or a combination of these. *Rhyming Dust Bunnies* is a great example, and the premise is described in Chapter 7. It works especially well because it invites children and adults to guess what the end rhyme might be. Jan Thomas, by the way, is a great writer to study for humor, which we'll discuss a bit later on.

The darkly hilarious *I Want My Hat Back* also has great read-aloud potential because it prompts readers to do the various voices of the animals that Bear encounters as he searches for his hat. There are ridiculous animals, including one who doesn't know what a hat is, as well as the very nervous Rabbit, who denies stealing the hat. He is, of course, wearing the hat as he does so. The Rabbit's words are then parroted by Bear later in the story, but with an entirely new meaning, as he denies killing Rabbit.

Duck! Rabbit! presents readers with an argument between two characters, where the different voices can take on a more conversational dynamic. This is always a fun one to read aloud. Dialogue adds this layer, and this book is almost all dialogue. *Don't Let the Pigeon Drive the Bus* by Mo Willems begins with a bus driver enlisting the audience's help in keeping the pigeon from driving the bus, as the title suggests. Then the listener has to deal with the pigeon passionately pleading his case in various ways[10]. This potential for interactivity adds to the franchise's appeal.

Finally, read-aloud potential can be as simple as a book with a lot of onomatopoeia and wordplay. Onomatopoeia, is, of course, when a word sounds like the intended noise that's being described, like "buzz" for what a bee does. In the

---

10. Each argument is also a masterclass in "beats," a craft idea that's too granular for most picture books, but refers to individual attempts a character makes to reach their objective. Notice how often the pigeon changes tactics.

rollicking *Wheels*, readers are treated to a lot of really fun language. For example, the fire truck is depicted as having:[11]

> Zoomy wheels, vroomy wheels, racing-to-a-fire wheels!

The words "zoom" and "vroom" are onomatopoeia and frequently associated with wheels and motion, so these choices are perfectly suited to this particular book. This story also has a very engaging "call and response" mechanic, where children learn a line and are prompted to repeat it. This allows them to feel active and engaged, and almost like independent readers.

If you want to claim "read-aloud potential" as a sales hook, considering using dialogue, different voices, a call-and-response structure, and onomatopoeia to enhance the text.

Now, let's move on to two somewhat controversial picture book writing elements, but ones that can also enhance the reading experience (or send you right into the reject pile): rhyme and rhythm.

Rhyme and Rhythm

If you've already tried to submit a rhyming picture book manuscript to agents and publishers, you might've been surprised to see how many submission guidelines specifically *discourage* rhyming projects. This is why I say that rhyming picture books are somewhat controversial in the contemporary publishing industry.

Before I unpack this, let me say that wonderful rhyme is classic. It is engaging. It allows children to memorize a story more

---

11. Sally Sutton, *Wheels*, 16-17.

quickly, because it establishes patterns and a familiar flow. Publishers issue rhyming picture books every season, and literary agents represent them. You are not wrong to want to write a rhyming picture book, and you are not wrong to point to all of the many, many published rhyming picture books on shelves as evidence to support your desire.

However, you won't find a lot of industry love or encouragement for rhyming manuscripts from debut writers. This seems like such a frustrating catch-22.

Why is that?

Well, the behind-the-scenes truth that few publishing professionals are willing to admit (at least not publicly or in print) is that most rhyming projects from new writers … suck.

They absolutely suck.

I can validate this opinion. I edit picture book manuscripts every single week that don't have what it takes to be competitive in today's market. (To my lovely picture book clients who probably think I'm talking about you, especially if I've given you notes about rhyme and rhythm—it's not just you. In a big-picture sense, I really do see profound issues in aspiring rhyming manuscripts every single week.)

Why is there such a raft of truly uninspired rhyming picture book writing out there?

I'm so glad you asked.

First, if someone is writing a picture book manuscript in rhyme, they might be doing it because they remember picture books in rhyme from their own childhoods. Cute, right? Well, it could also mean that they haven't read any picture books since their childhoods, which means that they are not clued into what's going on in today's industry. If you paid attention to the first part of this guide, you know that picture book publishing is a complex, modern, and very competitive landscape. You can't just dash off 600 words of "sun" and "fun" rhymes and expect to be ushered into print. Before you sit down to write a rhyming picture book, do your homework and read widely, both rhyme and prose.

Second, there are a lot of cliché rhymes that writers reach for because they don't know any better, or because they think they can scrape by with the low-hanging fruit of "cat" and "hat" (for the avoidance of doubt, this particular rhyme might as well be copyrighted by Dr. Seuss because that's all anyone imagines when it's invoked) or "sad" and "bad."

This makes me think of all the agents and acquiring editors who've told me that they judge alphabet books almost entirely by how creative the writer gets with letters like Q and X. It's fabulously easy to pick A for apple, B for ball, and all that. But when you get to the dregs of the alphabet, your choices will absolutely make or break you.

The same wisdom applies to rhyme. If your end rhymes (or internal rhymes, more on that in a moment) are expected and basic, then you aren't going to get past any gatekeepers. If your text is full of the first rhymes that come to mind, then discard it and challenge yourself. Remember, growth hurts. Stretching is hard. But agents and editors maintain a very high bar for rhyming projects, so you need to *go there*. (Without getting too weird, though. It's often a balance.)

Third, most aspiring rhyming manuscripts suffer from a lack of rhythm, or are written with needless complexity, or both. Writers become absolutely fixated on end rhyme, so they twist themselves into awkward, inverted, Victorian-sounding sentence pretzels to get where they believe they need to go.

Here's an example I wrote, and it might seem ridiculous or exaggerated, but I see rhymes in this vein, and worse, every week:

> The falling rain, it made her sad, *(8)*
> Causing feelings that were very bad. *(9)*

Not only is the end rhyme uninspired, but I really went far out of my way to say "causing feelings that were very bad," when the more straightforward "bad feelings" is simpler, more streamlined, and easier to read. It doesn't rhyme with "sad," though, so I've had to contort my sentence, and the end result is stilted. (Here's a pro tip: Whenever you find yourself trying to force something, that's a strong intuitive signal that it's not working.) I've also reached for "causing," which is an overly formal word that I wish every aspiring writer would strike from their creative writing vocabularies forever, especially for picture books.

The rhythm on the couplet isn't bad, with the first line at 8 syllables and the second line at 9 (which I've indicated in parentheses), but the "very" trips up the flow.

Here's another example:

> Upon the bench, the teddy bear sat, *(9)*
> Wondering what he could do about that *(10)*
> Which troubled him and made him mad. *(8)*

In this example, I ended on an obvious slant rhyme (inexact or imperfect rhyme), which we'll discuss later, but aside from "sat," "that," and "mad" not lining up as exact rhymes, this stanza (if we can call it that) is also unbalanced in terms of overall syllabic counts. We have a sentence interrupted by a line break without any syntactical cue (called "enjambment" in prosody) and some very clunky language with "do about that / which troubled him." I wouldn't want to read this kind of dry language in an adult novel, let alone a children's book.

The more I talk about bad examples of poetry, the closer I get to the fourth reason that many agents and editors are seemingly allergic to rhyming manuscripts: Poetry is *hard*. There's a lot that goes into it. I still remember buying the third edition of *The Norton Anthology of Modern and Contemporary Poetry* in college. It was 1,100 pages long. The current edition of *The Norton Anthology of Poetry*, which, as of this writing, is the sixth, is 2,384 pages long.

Poetry is not quick or easy to learn. Sure, a lot of unstructured things can be called "poetry" (and many "blank verse" or "free verse" poets take this liberty), but that's not all there is to it. Poetry is an eternal art form, with a long history, and so many different intricacies, that if you haven't really studied the art or applied the principles to your own work, you are going to be in over your head writing rhyming picture books.

I'm absolutely not gatekeeping poetry here, or saying that only those who've studied the masters and write in iambic pentameter can do it. Not at all. Alternative poetry is alive and well. There's a bleeding experimental edge to rhyming or rhythmic writing, and there always has been.

But.

Before you break the rules (unintentionally), you have to know there *are* rules operating below the surface of poetry. And once you learn that poetry is incredibly complex, you might be tempted to go "off road" and get away from the whole messy business of it altogether. Well, instead of ignoring the rules (intentionally), you have to internalize, learn, and practice them.

When I read some aspiring rhyming picture book manuscripts, it's very clear to me that some writers are completely unaware that anything else is involved in poetry aside from end rhyme. Those writers haven't learned about rhythm, they don't know about meter, and it shows.

As I said earlier in this guide, you very well *can* write a 500-page picture book. But having one traditionally published, or *successfully* self-published (I'll discuss this more in Appendix A) is another matter. The same goes for rhyming picture books.

You can, technically, do whatever you want. And who am I to squelch your creativity and tame your wild artistic spirit? But before you wade neck-deep into the very complex waters of prosody, you need to be aware that you're going for a swim.

A general ignorance of the poetic form is why a lot of aspiring rhyming picture book writers never get off the ground. Of course, this guide is not intended as a complete poetic forms and tools primer. The aforementioned Norton guide would be a fun read (or doorstopper) for anyone truly interested in getting into the weeds.

The fifth and final reason a lot of verse projects are unsuccessful is that most writers seem unaware that *rhythm* is also a crucial component of rhyme.

I've mentioned counting out syllables already, but that's only one part of it. You can then get deeper into poetic feet, stressed and unstressed syllables (all of these patterns have specific names), and how you sequence these "feet" across the lines of your poem. Not only do we have rhyming pattern to worry about, but you have to consider the number of lines per stanza, the overall arrangement of the poem, and almost countless other craft elements that come together into the study of prosody.

Defining all of them is well beyond the scope of this guide, but there's one thing I want to make crystal clear: End rhyme isn't everything. It might not even be the most important component of poetry.

Let's get back to word choice and pull in a few rhythm elements as well, with examples from shelves. Ideally, this will inspire you to do some of your own self-education.

In rhyming stories, you can get away with more elegant or complex word usage, syntax, and wordplay. One of my favorite lines in a rhyming story comes from *Iggy Peck, Architect*:

> "Gothic or Romanesque, I couldn't care less (11)
> About buildings, ancient or new," (8)
> She said in her lecture about architecture (12)
> That it had no place in grade two.[12] (8)

Imagine using the term "Romanesque" in a picture book! Here, however, it works because the topic is architecture, though the story is very much about self-confidence and identity as well. If you were to try and describe a Romanesque building in a picture book text that didn't have anything to do with architecture, I would be less enthusiastic.

I do have a small quibble with the second sentence, enjambment, and rhythm, but the cleverness of the internal rhyme overshadows it. Notice the rhymes of "Romanesque" and care less," and "lecture" and "architecture." These are subtle opportunities to integrate rhyme that writers miss if they're focused solely on end rhyme. I've also counted out the syllables for each line and added them in parentheses, just to show that this is a pretty balanced stanza, with those eight-syllable lines anchoring it.

Bubble Trouble is an absolute masterclass in rhyme (end and internal), though it's an older title. As you'll see in the sections reproduced below, it does use some more complex

---

12. Andrea Beaty, *Iggy Peck, Architect*, 16-17.

language ("nefarious intentions") and even invents a word, Shakespeare-like, for a specific purpose ("catchwork").

Here's a section where the conflict escalates because of Abel, the antagonist:

> But Abel, though a treble, was a rascal and a
>   rebel, (15)
> Fond of getting into trouble when he didn't
>   have to sing. (15)
> Pushing quickly through the people, Abel clam-
>   bered up the steeple (16)
> With nefarious intentions and a pebble in his
>   sling.[13] (15)

And here's how the conflict is resolved:

> Oh what calculated catchwork! Baby bounced
>   into the patchwork, (16)
> Where his grizzles turned to giggles and to
>   wriggles of delight. (15)
> And the people stared dumbfounded as he
>   bobbled and rebounded, (16)
> 'til the baby boy was grounded and his mother
>   held him tight.[14] (15)

As you can tell, Margaret Mahy continues with the rhythm of 15- and 16-syllable lines throughout, and it is *tight*. Poetry is, at its very core, a pattern of rhyme and rhythm. As such, it expects restraint and focus from the writer.

A book teaches us how to read it, and if you jump in with a specific rhyming pattern, number of lines per stanza, syllabic

---

13. Margaret Mahy, *Bubble Trouble*, 24-25.
14. Ibid., 34-35.

count, or meter, you are giving readers the following information: This is how the story will go.

An obvious example of how this pattern breaks can be found in *Giraffes Can't Dance* by Giles Andreae, illustrated by Guy Parker-Rees. The entire story is written in rhyming ABCB pattern stanzas, which means that the second and fourth lines rhyme, while the first and third don't have to. Here's an example from the middle:

> Then he found a little clearing, (8)
> and he looked up at the sky. (7)
> "The moon can be so beautiful," (8)
> he whispered with a sigh.[15] (6)

You'll notice that "sky" and "sigh" are exact rhymes. But then, when a cricket helps Giraffe solve his problem of not knowing how to dance "right" by providing him with different music, we get this:

> With that, the cricket smiled (7)
> and picked up his violin. (7)
> Then Gerald felt his body (7)
> do the most amazing thing.[16] (7)

I don't make this point to disparage *Giraffes Can't Dance*. The slant rhyme of "violin" and "thing" hasn't stopped it from selling millions of copies. It's actually impressive that the writer reached for "violin" as an end rhyme in the first place! The rhythm is also spot on, especially in this second example. But this demonstrates that established patterns are embedded with instructions to the reader. With every other rhyme in this book, we are implicitly primed to expect exact rhymes. Then

---

15. Giles Andreae, *Giraffes Can't Dance*, 15-16.
16. Ibid., 19-20.

that "promise" is broken in one instance, and it really sticks out.

For some writers, the strict framework of poetry is freeing and challenging, in a good way. They find themselves thriving within the confines of a set expectation. Other writers chafe within these restrictions, knocking painfully against the rules they've set for themselves (whether they were aware of them or not).

If you're writing rhyming picture book, ask yourself why. Because you believe all picture books rhyme? Because that's what you remember from childhood? These are bad reasons.

If you're writing because rules and patterns make your story come alive, good.

But if you constantly find that you're breaking out of the pattern or forcing your sentences into convoluted knots for the sake of pulling off a rhyming couplet—I give you permission to stop. You don't have to do this, because the end result will not be good.

Too often, I see writers lock themselves into rhyme for the wrong reasons, only to lose sight of the story. Their end rhymes dictate all of their choices. Is the character's "dress a light blue" because the writer was grasping for something that rhymes with "do"? Is the character named "Lunday" because nothing else easily rhymes with "Monday"?

Stop it.

Prioritize substance (the story) over style (poetry). If you rip the rhyme out of your manuscript and you don't quite know what's left, then you don't have a good story for a picture book to begin with. That might sound harsh, but I see this issue every week.

If the choice to write in rhyme is backing you into corners that don't serve your meaning, rewrite your idea in prose. Make sure it works as a story, and that you are making intentional choices from the first word to the last. Then, and only then, should you try to express the story in rhyme. You might find that the pattern inherent in rhyme is acting as a prison that has clouded your thinking. Or you might find yourself thriving as you express your idea in poetry, with all of its attendant rules.

Proceed with a rhyming picture book only if the latter applies. Otherwise, prose is just fine, and will probably increase your odds of successfully submitting your idea, because your execution will be smoother and more organic.

Humor and Tone

Humor is a key component of many picture books. Even stories that are heartfelt or sweet can have funny moments, while some are overtly funny, first and foremost. Humor can be tricky, because you need to decide what your sensibility is and how it might align with your target audience. For example, *You Be Mommy* seems somewhat geared toward parents, as it is a grateful nod to all the things they do. The parent and child can have a fun time imagining what it'd be like if the kid was tasked with everything that's on Mom's plate.

Jan Thomas is a preschool humor expert. I've mentioned *Rhyming Dust Bunnies* several times, but I also love *The Doghouse* and *A Birthday for Cow* and other books from the appropriately named *Giggle Gang* series. The *Elephant & Piggie* early readers by Mo Willems—most of Mo Willems' work, actually—are a masterclass in humor with kid appeal (and some of his bibliography has adult appeal as well, which you'll find in *Knuffle Bunny Too: A Case of Mistaken Identity*, when Trixie wakes her parents in the middle of the night).

While humor can be an incredible picture book selling point, I'd also caution you against predicating an entire book concept on the reveal of a pun or a joke. Wordplay works well, but if the whole idea of your picture book is to pull off one punchline at the end, it might fall flat, as it somewhat does in *Duck Soup*. (That story has other things going on, but there is a joke at the end that attempts to make the resolution satisfying.)

The risk with a joke or pun being "the point" of a story is that some readers (especially younger ones) might not fully understand it. Or they might understand it, metabolize it, and find the entire story much less exciting, now that they get it. This might immediately make the whole book old news. When the story hinges on one joke or reveal, positioned at the end, it might not invite rereading, because once a kid experiences it, they want to move on to something else. The fix would be to build in escalating moments of humor, then try for a different joke or twist as the last image.

Humor can come from:

- Language
- Premise
- Character
- Plot
- Theme
- Setting
- A mix of some or all of the above!

Certain stories with an Escalating Attempts structure lend themselves well to humor, because the events get funnier and funnier, and you can start creating inside jokes with your audience as the story rolls on. *Maxwell's Magic Mix-Up* is a great example, especially when the dad keeps appearing in broom form (just read it!) to punctuate the action. Sometimes the set-up is so good, that all the writer needs to do is deliver on the "promise of the premise" (discussed in Chapter 12), as with *Boss Baby, Dragons Love Tacos,* and *The Day the Crayons Quit.*

Tone is an idea adjacent to humor, but it can also refer to serious works. We first encountered an explanation of tone in Chapter 6, where I presented picture book topics. There, we learned about tones like Funny, Poignant, Sweet/Positive, and Quirky.

Some authors write stories on a whole range of subjects, featuring different characters, but they keep a specific tone as their authorial signature. For example, Oliver Jeffers, Peter Brown, and Jon Klassen have an offbeat illustration style, with a bit of a subversive, weird, or quirky element to their storytelling (and choice of stories, to begin with) that make them unique.

But Peter Brown leans silly, Jon Klassen leans a bit dark and strange, and Oliver Jeffers can be incredibly poignant, with deep themes operating close to or below the surface.

Basically, what you say, how you say it, the words you use, the presence or absence of overt jokes, wordplay, and other read-aloud elements, and the theme you're exploring all inform humor and tone. As you develop your picture book storytelling and writing craft, you will discover and fine-tune these features of your work.

You can also change your tone or explore shades of humor or something more heartfelt across various projects. Not all writers get pigeonholed into doing a specific style of book—but even if you do, you can always choose a pen name and work on something new and off-brand compared to your existing bibliography.

There are two last quick consideration of picture book writing, and these are simple decisions you can make before you begin your project, or fine-tune later in the drafting and revision process.

Tense and POV

There is no set rule for tense and POV in picture books, which means you can experiment. For POV, which stands for "point of view," your options are generally:

- **First Person**: Very common, and puts us firmly into one character's experience. An example is *Platanos Go with Everything*.
- **Close Third Person**: The most common POV in narrative picture books, which follows the protagonist and even dips into their heads, but does not have access to any other characters. An example is *Toby Is a Big Boy*. This can also be called "limited third."
- **Omniscient Third Person**: The narrator floats above the action and relays it without necessarily bringing readers into the minds of specific characters. Access to more than one POV is incredibly unusual in picture books, except with Split Person, below, so I'd avoid what's called "head-hopping." *Bubble Trouble* is an example of a classic omniscient.
- **Split Person**: This is generally not a recognized literary POV but I did notice that some books, especially those with a Nested Stories or Odd Friendship structure, like *Tea with Oliver*, tended to split the POV focus between (usually two) characters.
- **Second Person**: This POV is also sometimes called "second person direct address," as it breaks the fourth wall and speaks directly to the reader. It's a less

common choice for fiction, and more common in nonfiction, especially in prescriptive titles like *Alphabreaths*. *Your Alien* is a good example on the fiction side, as is *Gator, Gator, Gator*.

Because I love my data, I analyzed the 154 books in this guide for tense. Here are the occurrences of each tense in each category:

First Person:

- Narrative instances: 10
- Concept instances: 11
- Nonfiction instances: 2
- Narrative nonfiction instances: 7

As you can see, narrative books, concept books, and narrative nonfiction books (obviously, since a lot of these are autobiographies) generally use first person POV.

Close Third Person:

- Narrative instances: 41
- Concept instances: 7
- Nonfiction instances: 1
- Narrative nonfiction instances: 2

The obvious winner is close third person for most narrative picture books. I was shocked to do the numbers and find out that first person lagged behind close third by such a wide margin. I expected them to be more even.

Omniscient third person:

- Narrative instances: 13
- Concept instances: 13
- Nonfiction instances: 2

- Narrative nonfiction instances: 1

The relative lack of omniscient is not a surprise at all, as closer access to individual characters—which you'll find in first person and third—is more marketable right now.

Split Person:

- Narrative instances: 15
- Concept instances: 2
- Nonfiction instances: 0
- Narrative nonfiction instances: 0

These findings make a lot of sense because we usually only follow multiple characters in a fiction piece.

Second Person:

- Narrative instances: 6
- Concept instances: 18
- Nonfiction instances: 2
- Narrative nonfiction instances: 1

I was also surprised by how many second person concept books there were in the analyzed sample. I guess I shouldn't have been, because a lot of concept books apparently speak directly to the reader, but here we are. There's always something to learn.

For tense, we have two main options, and two that can be used to curious effect. These tenses can be paired with any of the above POVs, though I have chosen first person for my examples. Available tenses are:

- **Present Tense**: This tense feels very immediate, and usually plunges readers right into the action—"I write a picture book guide and sip my coffee."

- **Past Tense**: This is considered a more classic tense— "I wrote a picture book guide and sipped my coffee."
- **Future Tense**: An oddball choice, but it works well for some projects, like *Your Alien*, which has taken a more experimental approach with both POV and tense. Another example is *So Many Days*, which is a concept book. This tense refers to something that will happen in the future—"I will finish my writing session and reward myself with another coffee."
- **Dialogue Only**: This is not technically a tense, either, but I did notice some books that only used dialogue, without narration (like *Duck! Rabbit!*), and therefore removed the project from traditional tense considerations.

Here we go again with the data, broken down as before.

Present Tense:

- Narrative instances: 29
- Concept instances: 36
- Nonfiction instances: 5
- Narrative nonfiction instances: 4

This is definitely a contender for most popular tense for narrative and concept projects, because it's very immersive, as mentioned above. It makes sense for concept projects because those often exist outside a sense of time.

Past Tense:

- Narrative instances: 55
- Concept instances: 14
- Nonfiction instances: 2
- Narrative nonfiction instances: 7

But there's clearly no unseating the OG—past tense is a classic for a reason, especially for narrative projects.

Future Tense:

- Narrative instances: 1
- Concept instances: 1
- Nonfiction instances: 0
- Narrative nonfiction instances: 0

This is clearly a very niche choice, so make sure you have a great reason for using it.

Dialogue Only:

- Narrative instances: 2
- Concept instances: 1
- Nonfiction instances: 0
- Narrative nonfiction instances: 0

Same with the dialogue-only approach. If you don't use any (or much) narration, you can go heavy on dialogue. (Minimizing narrative description can be a good idea, anyway, as we'll see in the next chapter.)

And that's it! As simple and as complex as all that.

But wait, there's more …

In fact, this entire guide up to now has largely avoided two of the most important components of a picture book project. You might not be responsible for these elements, but you need to consider them all the same: the layout and illustrations.

FIFTEEN

LEAVING ROOM FOR ILLUSTRATIONS AND FORMATTING THE MANUSCRIPT

WHETHER OR NOT YOU'RE an illustrator—heck, whether or not you can draw a straight line—you will want to start thinking in pictures if you want to level up your picture book writing game. I've alluded to this idea a few times, and now we'll unpack it in detail. I'll even offer some original resources that you can use to get started.

Picture books are inherently incomplete without illustrations. *Writing with Pictures: How to Write and Illustrate Children's Books* offers us this lovely reminder:

The main function if illustrations is to illuminate text, to thrown light on words. In fact, illustration in medieval books is called *illumination* and the term *illustration* derives from the Latin verb meaning "to light up," to "illuminate."[1]

---

1. Uri Shulevitz, *Writing with Pictures: How to Write and Illustrate Children's Books*, 120.

Even if you're not an illustrator, you need to plan for the visual accompaniments that might one day illuminate your words.

What does it mean to "think in pictures"? Well, when you write a picture book, the premise and text are merely half of the equation. They're an important part, to be sure, but they will not stand alone without illustrations, at least if you want the final project to have pictures, which 99.999999999% of picture books do.[2] If you don't want to share glory with an illustrator, write a novel.

For your picture book to be a *picture* book, you will need to either hire an independent illustrator (if you're planning on self-publishing), learn to illustrate yourself (incredibly difficult to go from zero to sixty on developing *competitive* illustration skills with the downright geniuses working in today's market), or get out of the way of your own story and leave room for a professional to come in after a publisher acquires the manuscript.

To be perfectly clear: If traditional publication is your goal, and you are not a professional illustrator, **you do not need to pay to have your book illustrated before submission**. A traditional publisher harbors the cost of illustrations as part of acquiring and producing a picture book. They also, however, get to choose the illustrator.

You might be tempted to commission an illustrator yourself, especially if you can't stomach the idea of ceding any creative control over the future illustrations. You might be tempted to get your graphic designer cousin to do it. You might even be curious about learning how to draw yourself.

---

2. *The Book with No Pictures* by B.J. Novak is an obvious exception. Sort of.

Do not do any of these things unless you are 100% sure of your skills and strategy.

Odds are you're not a fine artist. Even if you *are* a fine artist in another medium, or for another audience, you might not be a picture book specialist. Odds are your cousin isn't a competitive picture book illustrator, either. Odds are also good that you're not an art director, who is professionally trained in telling an illustrator what to do.

So even if you hire an expensive professional illustrator—and the professional ones are incredibly, eye-wateringly expensive, as they should be—you might not make the most of their skills and talents because you likely won't know how to instruct them properly.

It is totally fine to be "just" a picture book writer with "just" a picture book manuscript as you approach submission to literary agents and traditional publishers. Picture book texts are acquired every day, with the publisher then choosing an illustrator from their network of artists.

But when you start to research agents and publishers, which we will cover in Chapter 18, you might find that a lot of them are looking for author/illustrators only, and you might start to freak out. Let's get that conversation out of the way first.

Author/Illustrator Projects

As the term suggests, an author/illustrator is a person who does both the writing and the illustration on a single picture book. You can also call it an author/illustrator project if a separate a writer and an illustrator have worked together so beautifully and seamlessly that the book is pitched to a publisher as a package deal. (I'll discuss the partnership route toward the end of this chapter.)

It is worth noting that 64 of our analyzed books from the shelves, or 42%, have a single creator who did both the text and art[3]. This is not an insignificant number. Author/illustrator packages tend to be very appealing to agents and publishers because the same person dreamed up both the text and illustrations, and if both are well done, then they often play in concert beautifully. The gatekeeper has to work with only one individual, and the project can be presented in a more complete format before the book deal is struck, giving everyone a very clear sense of the vision.

How do you know if you're an author/illustrator? You'll know, because you have likely started out as an illustrator first, and you are learning how to write solid picture book stories in the service of your art. Even though writing is hard, most of the author/illustrators I represented (when I was agenting) or known personally started out illustrating, then came to writing and storytelling later. Writing a picture book is not what I'd call *easy*, but it's easier than successfully illustrating one.

Should you try and become an illustrator because you think that author/illustrators have higher odds at getting a literary agent and publishing deal?

No. Please don't.

Chances are, your illustrations aren't going to be competitive, especially if you're just starting out. **Remember, it's okay to be a picture book writer, instead of an author/illustrator**.

As we discussed in Chapter 1, picture book creators with certain kinds of lived experience (race, heritage, gender identity or expression, sexuality, etc.) are somewhat more desirable in today's publishing landscape. If you are not Black, it is

---

3. Alas, it's impossible to know how many projects with a separate author and illustrator were assembled *before* submission, if any.

not going to be an asset to try and write from a Black perspective. You cannot change your own demographic profile. You should not try.

Similarly, you are either a high-performing illustrator, or you're not. Of course, artistic talent and skill aren't the same thing as cultural identity or race. You can theoretically change the former, but not the latter. However, it is incredibly difficult to go from "not illustrator" to "illustrator," especially at the high-performing level required for today's picture books. If you are only doing it to try and make yourself more marketable, I'd strongly encourage you to work on your writing and storytelling instead.

Skills can be learned. Talents are more difficult to cultivate, if there's no natural affinity already in place. Some people can become talented illustrators if they work very hard and spend years of dedicated effort on it. Some people can never become talented illustrators, no matter what. You can absolutely draw and paint and design to your heart's content. Human creativity is boundless. But I don't believe that everyone can become a commercial Big Five-publisher-quality illustrator in one lifetime.

My mother is literally a fine art painter, represented by galleries across the nation. I am theoretically genetically predisposed to make art. And yet I am hopeless at visual self-expression. I have zero natural talent for anything to do with art and graphic design, even with tools like Canva, which helps most people look good. I have tried. I know my limits. I would rather work smarter, not harder, and find my own creative expression. (Which I've done, joyfully, with writing. This advice doesn't come from a sense of sour grapes or stunted artistic desire.)

I once had a novelist ask me the following question: "If I want to get a book deal for a novel, should I try and publish a short story in *The New Yorker* to get attention?"

Well, sure!

However, there are writers who spend *their entire lives* trying to figure out what makes a good *New Yorker* story, crack the code, write one, and get it published in that specific magazine. There are people for whom getting a short story into *The New Yorker* is their entire life's purpose.

It doesn't make a lot of sense, to me, to try and get published in *The New Yorker* as a stepping stone to selling a novel, though. Will a story in a top-shelf literary journal help you get noticed by the literary community? You bet. Doors will open. Would it be simpler, more straightforward, and potentially much more effective to put your time and effort into learning how to write a good novel—instead of a good *New Yorker* story—if your goal is to sell a novel?

Also yes.

So if you want to be an illustrator (rather than simply trying to label yourself an author/illustrator because you think it'll make your picture books more saleable), then you should put your time and effort toward learning illustration. You are an aspiring illustrator who will probably want to learn how to write picture books at some point, but the writing is not your main focus.

If you see picture book illustration as a means to a different end—writing a picture book and getting it published—then devote yourself wholeheartedly to crafting the best picture book premise and text that you can, and let a different professional handle the illustrations. The option of a separate illustrator exists. Writers and publishers use it every day.

Keeping this in mind, let's talk about what you can do with

your picture book idea and text to make it as attractive as possible to a future illustrator.

Making Room for Illustrations

If you're writing a text with the goal of having it illustrated one day (whether by you, by an illustrator you hire, or by an illustrator that a publisher furnishes), you should write in a way that leaves the door open for illustrations.

A lot of picture book texts I see are incredibly overbearing. They describe all of the visual elements that the writer imagined in their heads when they first dreamed up the story: the character's exact looks, down to the color and pattern of their clothes; the setting and scenery; the colors of buildings and cars; the patterns of clouds in the sky; the expression on Mom's face; the exact type of dog and what it's currently doing with its body, like raising its left leg to scratch its ear, etc.

What do these elements all have in common? They're visual.

What would you think if I told you to remove *all visual elements* from your picture book text? It's not "an autumnal forest of maples with leaves fading from vermilion to burnt sienna." It's a … (get ready) … "forest."

Some writers will be ready to throw this guide (or their ereader) out the window. What the heck is the writer supposed to be adding to the product if they can't do elaborate, descriptive *writing*? It's right there in the job description of "writer." Have I never met a writer before? Do I not understand what they do?

Well, sure. But a picture book is a partnership between words and pictures, the writer and illustrator. Both are professionals in their own right, even though I understand that writers feel more possessive of a story because they came up with the premise.

Your potential future illustrator is not just a hired hand who comes in to serve and enhance the writer's brilliance. Writers and illustrators are collaborators and equals. They're paid equally and share royalties equally. The illustrator is a partner in creating a picture book. (In most cases, by most publishers, unless they're a famous illustrator paired with a debut writer, or vice versa. The more prominent creator might then receive a favorable split.)

As such, the artist needs something to do. To add. They get to make choices. And those choices might include the types of trees in the forest and what color the leaves are. (Obviously, the story will dictate whether the setting is Vermont or the Costa Rican cloud forest, and all of the relevant climate and animal species there.) So if the writer says "forest" and we know the story is set in Vermont, then the illustrator gets to have ownership over how individual details are depicted.

The same goes for a character's appearance. The writer often has strong feelings about what their protagonist looks like— often the fictional person is an avatar for the writer, or a favorite grandchild (though they'll never admit it publicly). That's all fine and good. You can, indeed, offer *some* guidance to the illustrator. We'll talk about illustration notes in a moment.

But if you find yourself defining exact hair length, eye color, and sock pattern for your plucky heroine, you're being overbearing, and an illustrator will not appreciate it. (Neither will an agent or acquiring editor who is evaluating your text, in part, for how well you leave room for illustrations.)

I recommend removing all visual cues and descriptions from your text.

I'm serious.

This does two things. It leaves room for illustrations, but it also tells you whether or not you have enough story in your picture book manuscript. Some texts are *all* description, and no character or story. If you pare back all of the literary writing in a project like this, you're left with a blank page. This writer needs to go back to the (pun fully intended) drawing board and add more story, character, conflict, and structure.

If your work is *all* beautiful language and no substance, you're navel-gazing. It can also be insecurity talking. As I mentioned in Chapter 14, writers often overwrite because they feel they need to prove they are A Real Writer with a Capital W. Save it for your therapist, write confidently, and shake the gnawing urge to prove yourself on every page. As we've discussed, clean, simple writing is actually difficult to pull off.

Once you've shaved your visual cues back, you can add in some spare descriptions, but deliberately. You don't need that much literary or imagery-driven language in a picture book. Even books like *Owl Moon* and *Platanos Go with Everything*, which I cited for lovely writing, are more plot driven, on the whole.

The same goes for descriptions of action and emotion. The dog scratching behind one ear with its left foot, used as an example above, fits this rubric. If the dog needs to be scratching for *plot reasons*, put that in an illustration note. Otherwise, it doesn't matter, in 99.99% of stories, which individual limb does what in the illustrations, and we certainly don't need to get that specific in the text.

Illustrations are also great at conveying action and body language, so "Mom crossed her arms" is unnecessary if Mom's frustration is built into the story. Illustrators can choose this specific body language to create emotion, or they can depict something else that sends the same message.

Similarly, facial expressions almost never need to be written out. If your story contains the rise and fall of emotions, brought on by conflicts and resolutions, escalations and de-escalations, then illustrators will be able to translate those emotions into your characters' visual appearances. "She scrunched her face in concentration" isn't necessary to say in the text, because the story will be about the character making an effort, and illustrators will know how to get that across.

Finally, if you want extra credit, consider making room for a story that's rendered in the illustrations only, or a second layer of storytelling that depends heavily on the images. For example, the mouse in *Goodnight Moon* is mentioned in the text, but mostly because "mouse" rhymes with "house" so well. What's not mentioned, however, is that the mouse appears on every page. Kids routinely enjoy a fun secondary activity—finding where the mouse is hidden—while listening to this book. Whether this was built into the story originally by the author or introduced by the illustrator, I don't know, but it adds an element that's primarily visual.

The Encyclopedia of Writing and Illustrating Children's Books makes the following point:

> Sometimes, the illustrations may even tell a different story. This tension between what is said and what is shown makes picture books a unique and exciting form of graphic expression.[4]

---

4. Desdemona McCannon, Sue Thornton, and Yadzia Williams, *The Encyclopedia of Writing and Illustrating Children's Books*, 10.

Similarly, you can build a story element into your text that's *only* communicated visually. For example, the dangling vines in *Pine & Boof: The Lucky Leaf* are obviously snakes. When Pine suggests they "swing from the vines,"[5] readers are in on the joke before the characters are, creating dramatic irony. The snakes react poorly to having characters dangling from them, so this visual joke bears fruit in the plot itself. This series is great about adding illustration-only elements that allow readers to be smarter than our heroes (and kids love to outsmart books, as long as this is set up intentionally), because it makes the comedic characters even more ridiculous.

In the second installment of these adventures, *Pine & Boof: Blast Off!*, the characters find an egg that obviously fell from a nest, but they decide it came from outer space (a natural assumption for imaginative characters in this age group). They build a spaceship that launches … down the hill and into a cave full of fireflies. Readers know the rocket went down, instead of up, but the characters are so disoriented, and the inside of the cave looks so otherworldly, that they truly believe they went to space. Nowhere is this actually explained in the text.

We already know not to overdo our illustration instructions, but what happens when we desperately need to communicate something to a potential future illustrator and won't take "no" for an answer? How do we go about that? I'm so glad that I—pretending to be you, the curious reader—asked!

Illustration Notes

If you've gone through the above section and removed all unnecessary description, pared down the micromanagement,

---

5. Ross Burach, *Pine & Boof: The Lucky Leaf*, 27-28.

axed your imagery, and thought of creative ways to add visual-only elements to your project, congratulations. You are now ahead of about 90% of aspiring picture book writers.

But sometimes—deep sigh—it's necessary to talk directly to the potential future illustrator in the text itself. This is especially true if you're working on something like *Pine & Boof: Blast Off!*, mentioned above, where an integral part of the story is not explained anywhere in the text itself. (That project is by one author/illustrator creator, who probably didn't write illustration notes to himself, but it's such a good example of an idea where notes would absolutely be appropriate.)

Another great instance of the entire story changing context because of an illustration-only piece of information is the end of *The Rough Patch*, where we learn that the protagonist is willing to give a new puppy a chance, while still honoring the dog who passed away.

Finally, *Sam and Dave Dig a Hole* by Mac Barnett, illustrated by Jon Klassen, would be an incredibly boring manuscript to read without the illustrations, which basically make the story. Nowhere are the diamonds mentioned in the text, nor is the suggestion of an alternate universe stated anywhere.

When you're writing and you want to convey something about how you see the page illustrated, you include illustration notes, usually in parentheses. Here's the suggested format:

(Illo Note: The content of the note you want to give.)

"Illo" stands for "illustration" in the publishing industry. Speaking of the industry, you can't spend any time around the picture book community without hearing some *strong* opinions about illustration notes themselves. Some gatekeepers say they're a no-no, and others insist that you can use them, but sparingly. I'm in the middle of the debate on this one. The reason so many people advise against them is because too many writers use illustration notes to micromanage, and we already know that micromanaging the illustrator —a brilliant creator in their own right—is the wrong approach.

For example, you'll see illustration notes like:

> (Illo Note: Sally has brown hair, glasses, and a blue skirt. She skips down the street with a red backpack in one hand, a lunch sack in the other, by a house with a green mailbox, while her braid swings to the left.)

Or the writer will include an illustration note for every page. The list of illustration note misuses goes on and on. My least favorite illustration notes do the following:

> Sally skipped down the street, giddy to be going to Maya's house.
> (Illo Note: Sally is skipping down the street toward a house, looking happy.)

One should hope that some measure of reading comprehension is required in publishing (though sometimes I wonder). In the above example, the illustrator will read the actual text and glean the exact same information that appears in the illustration note without any help. If you find these types of redundant illustration notes in your own project, delete them all, and knock it off.

The point of an illustration note isn't to jot down every single thing that you see in your imagination. The point of an illustration note is to convey something to the children's book manuscript reader or evaluator (and eventual illustrator) that isn't obvious from the text. They're more common in text submissions. If you're submitting an illustrated mock-up, you might still want to include some, as the manuscript could be plucked from the slush pile and reviewed before the illustrations are.

Only use illustration notes in your picture book manuscript if there is something integral to the plot that you want the illustrations to convey, but it's not described or alluded to anywhere in the text. In other words, if I will be oblivious to something from simply reading the text, use illustration notes to describe it, but really do keep these simple, and few in number. Ideally, you'd have between zero and two, tops.

An example of an effective picture book illustration note is:

> I am writing a picture book story.
> I think it's very fun.
> (Illo Note: Mary typing, blithely unaware that a monster is sneaking up behind her, claws bared.)

Here, we get information in the illustration note that we wouldn't otherwise have. The gatekeeper evaluating the project can then interpret your intentions. This is the purpose of the illustration note. Next, let's get clear on what a picture book manuscript actually looks like on the page.

Picture Book Manuscript Format

Picture book manuscript formatting doesn't need to be intimidating. Also, remember that you will likely be submitting your picture book manuscript copied and pasted into an email or submission form, so a lot of your very intentional formatting might be lost during the evaluation phase. Don't expect it to look like a perfect approximation of your Word document. That said, I strongly encourage all aspiring picture book writers to follow industry-standard formatting guidelines in their Word or Google Doc files.

Presenting your manuscript professionally from the very beginning, even if you're the only person looking at it, sets a polished tone for the entire creation experience and makes potential future submissions easier. (I'll talk about email-specific manuscript formatting in more detail in Chapter 18.)

Let's deal with the manuscript file itself first.

There are some intrepid writers who submit their picture book projects as Word docs that have 32 or 40 individual pages and giant font size in an attempt to reproduce picture book layout. This is not industry standard manuscript formatting, but at least they're trying to think about page turns, which I'll cover later in this chapter.

Instead of doing *that*, learn proper manuscript formatting once, and use it forever.

First, the basics: Your margins should be 1" all around, with indents going out to .5" for each new line for prose, and no indents for rhyme. Use a 12-point font like Times New Roman, which is considered industry standard. You can choose to double-space your prose, but use single-spaced lines for rhyme. (Double-spacing doesn't easily translate to email submissions, but if a gatekeeper asks for a document version, one should be available.)

You can communicate page turns using parentheses. Indicating page turns is optional—I'll give one example with and one example without, below—but you should absolutely think about page turns as part of your writing process. The manuscript continues as formatted in the following examples until the story is over. There's no need to put "The End," or similar.

When you begin your manuscript, you can choose to use a header, and appropriate content for one is:

- Manuscript title
- Your last name
- Word count
- Total umber of pages

Use your word processor to automatically insert the header and the number of pages. (You can Google instructional videos that pertain to your specific program.) That said, a header and the page count might be overkill to include if your picture book manuscript only spans one page.

Then the official content of the manuscript begins!

At the top of your first page, you will want your contact information. Then the title, byline, and word count, centered. There's no need to say "picture book for young readers" or any otherwise overbearing explanation. Any manuscript submission will be accompanied by a query letter (which I'll discuss in Chapter 18), so by the time an agent or acquiring editor reaches the manuscript material, they'll know what they're reading.

Below that, add one extra line, and begin the manuscript. Here's an example of proper formatting, including a line that's meant to represent a header at the top:

———

Manuscript Title / Kole / # Words / Page 1 of X

Mary Kole
123 Main St.

Town, State, ZIP
(212) 555-5555
mary@goodstorycompany.com

Bolded Manuscript Title
By Mary Kole
Words

———

NOW THAT THE LOGISTICAL INFORMATION IS OUT OF THE WAY, let's move on to formatting the text itself. First, we'll start with a prose manuscript. On the following page, you'll find two versions of a prose manuscript draft, the first with an art note and suggested pagination, the second without the pagination. Notice the difference in formatting. Also, pay close attention here to how both dialogue and narration are handled, and to the .5" indents for each new line. (Note that I wasn't able to reproduce double-spacing, but your prose manuscript will ideally be double-spaced.)

Prose Version One (Pagination Suggested in Parentheses):

(1-2)

   Duck walks along the road, only to trip over a rock.
"Ouch!" Duck yells.
   "What's wrong?" asks Owl.
   "I broke my favorite shoe."

(3-4)

   Duck's never seen a rock like this before. (Illo Note: The rock is actually a turtle.)

(5-6)

> "Who dares disturb my slumber?"
> Duck and Owl jump back.
> "We didn't mean to surprise you," Duck says, "but maybe you shouldn't be sleeping out in the middle of the road ..."

(7-8)

> "Are you okay?" Owl asks.

Prose Version Two (No Pagination Suggestions):

> Duck walks along the road, only to trip over a rock. "Ouch!" Duck yells.
> "What's wrong?" asks Owl.
> "I broke my favorite shoe."
> Duck's never seen a rock like this before. (Illo Note: The rock is actually a turtle.)
> "Who dares disturb my slumber?"
> Duck and Owl jump back.
> "We didn't mean to surprise you," Duck says, "but maybe you shouldn't be sleeping out in the middle of the road ..."
> "Are you okay?" Owl asks.

Now let's talk about rhyming manuscript formatting. Notice that we're not using indents, but the formatting for page turns and illustration notes remains consistent with the prose examples.

The rhyming version of the story is also intended to be single-spaced, whereas the prose version, above, is meant to be double-spaced, but this formatting was difficult to achieve in this format.

Once again, I'll offer two examples, one with suggested pagination, and one without:

Verse Version One (Pagination Suggested in Parentheses):

(6-7)

> I'll write a rhyming story.
> I think it's very fun.

(8-9)

> I'll use a page break in it,
> So the lines don't start to run.
>
> (Illo Note: Mary cradling her MacBook Air, beating
> out the meter of her story with her fingers. Mary is a cat.)

Verse Version Two (No Pagination Suggestions):

> I'll write a rhyming story.
> I think it's very fun.
>
> I'll use a page break in it,
> So the lines don't start to run.
> (Illo Note: Mary cradling her MacBook Air, beating
> out the meter of her story with her fingers. Mary is a cat.)

I strongly recommend paginating your project, especially as you compose it. Even if you're not an artist, you can train yourself to think like an illustrator by considering how your project will be laid out on individual pages or spreads.

Pagination and Page Turns

It continues to amaze me that aspiring picture book writers type their stories out as if they're a big block of prose or a single poem and … call it done. In my manuscript formatting examples, above, yes, I did indeed offer versions that weren't paginated.

That can be okay for submission, but every aspiring picture book writer should at least commit to paginating the manuscript as they create it, or during the revision process. Without doing this part, you are missing a crucial step.

Picture books are not novels. As we discussed in very broad strokes in Chapter 1, they are spread across between 14 and 18 spreads, or 28 and 36 individual pages, for 32- and 40-page layouts, respectively. The rest of the pages are taken up by the title page(s), copyright and dedication page(s) (sometimes combined, sometimes separate), back matter page(s) (if applicable), and endpapers (if the layout is self-ended instead of separate-ended). I'm a visual learner, so it really helped me to do a mock up in order to visualize it. You'll see exactly what I mean in the next chapter.

All this being said, when you write your picture book story and you're starting to think of how it might be illustrated, you should absolutely do the exercise of breaking the text itself into a storyboard. This might not only change the way you're writing and thinking about the project, it might change your entire story itself.

Remember our discussion of structure in Chapter 12? A lot of frameworks introduced there—like Midpoint Shift and Three Acts—depend on breaking the story into spreads. You can't really think structurally without also thinking about pagination and page turns.

You can paginate by introducing page markers in the manuscript text (as seen in the previous section) or sitting down with a mock storyboard (see the following chapter). When you do so, think about how much story should appear on each page.

For example, if you have 300 words in your project, you don't necessarily want to have one spread with 50 words, since the rest will likely have fewer. You're looking to establish a pattern and find balance. You might want to set a goal of about 21 words per spread (300 divided by 14) and then see where you need to deviate.

Some spreads have more or fewer words than is average for a particular project. These tend to be spreads that feature story turning points, like the actual Midpoint Shift moment. Sometimes that means more text is required to really hammer out a character's emotional transition. Alternately, that can also mean a wordless spread. That's right—you can build in wordless spreads where illustrations do *all* the talking. *Dragonboy* does this kind of rhythm well, as do *Extra Yarn* and *Courage Hats*. I'll describe the five different types of illustration options you have in the next chapter, to jog your creativity.

Page turns can be used in several different ways. They help with the pacing of the story, which is the reader's perception of how quickly or slowly the narrative moves. They can offer a break or an opportunity to integrate some revelations.

Each spread should be considered a separate entity within the story. It should offer progress in terms of character, plot, or the reader's understanding of objective, conflict, relationship —or all of these combined. Otherwise, that unit of story does not earn its keep.

If it's just description, or witty banter, or something else indulgent, you may want to think about cutting it, as you have no time to waste. Remember to use a number of settings, and consider actions and activities for your characters to do that'll open your story to interesting and varied illustrations.

Consider composition as well. Will your images be engaging if the story is entirely set in one place, with characters talking? Each spread will end up visually redundant. You can also vary where the "camera" is placed as you're thinking about your story. This is technically called the "viewpoint." *The Encyclopedia of Writing and Illustrating Children's Books* defines it this way:

> Viewpoint is the position that you choose for the reader to view an illustration. Viewpoint can have a dramatic effect on the composition and mood.[6]

For example, if your characters are woodland creatures, can we see them in the treetops, looking down at the action from a branch? Or looking up at the tree from a lower vantage point? Zoomed in on a character's face? Zoomed out in a bird's eye view? The viewpoint (the reader perspective) doesn't always have to be placed looking at a composition head-on, at ground level.

Go back to Chapter 11 and review the types of conflicts available, and to Chapter 12 for your structure options. Each spread represents a larger ingredient meant to serve the story. Spreads do hard work, but so do the spaces between spreads, called "page turns."

Here are some effects you can achieve by intentionally using page turns:

---

6. Desdemona McCannon, Sue Thornton, and Yadzia Williams, *The Encyclopedia of Writing and Illustrating Children's Books*, 50.

- **Suspense**: End on an ellipsis, in the middle of a sentence, or after some exciting action. Readers will be compelled to turn the page and close the loop on an open question. *Gator, Gator, Gator* depends on this technique;
- **Surprise**: Sometimes, something completely unexpected happens, like the neighborhood party at the end of *Toad on the Road: Mama and Me*;
- **Perspective**: Picture books are often written from the perspective of one character, but as we saw in our discussion of Nesting Stories structure in Chapter 12 and POV in Chapter 13, sometimes we have multiple narratives in one story. For examples of page turns used to shift perspectives from one character to another, check out *The Worst Teddy Ever* and *Nell Plants a Tree*;
- **Momentum**: In some instances, you'll see time passing in a compressed way, as it does in a movie montage. This skips over a necessary logistical section of the story without dwelling on it. You can use page turns to create the same effect in picture books, when you need to move forward in time, as we do in *Mother of Sharks*;
- **Setting**: Sometimes a page turn is a great way to reveal a new setting. We have several setting shifts separated by page turns in *The Adventures of Beekle: The Unimaginary Friend*; and
- **Relief or Integration**: A page turn can provide breathing room between two actions or in the middle of a sequence. This is a great way to resonate on character emotions after a period of movement or plot excitement, or to set the character up for future action, both of which happen in *A Spoonful of Frogs*.

Now let's take your brainstorming into the physical realm and parcel your text out into a storyboard. My fellow visual thinkers might find that these concepts really land in the following chapter.

And again, don't just imagine doing this. Do it. As you move ahead with finalizing your manuscript, thinking in illustrations, and pulling all of these craft considerations together, you will want to translate your thought process into reality, and make a "picture book dummy" (and yes, this is the industry term) of your layout—no artistic talent required!

SIXTEEN

LAYOUT AND DUMMY STORYBOARDING

Don't be afraid or surprised to see your story change entirely when you storyboard it. This is really where you get to experience your picture book as a reader (or listener) might. This will reveal holes in your plot or character development, and maybe inspire you to change the whole narrative. The latter, if it happens, is not a bad thing.

If your idea doesn't pass the layout test, you will find out later, anyway, when it fails to get an agent or publisher. It's better that you learn this now, before submission, when you can still make intentional changes.

Picture Book Layout

First, let's discuss how picture books are put together. In the broadest possible terms, there is the cardboard cover, and the signatures, which are bundles of paper that are folded in such a way that they appear in multiples of eight and are sewn together. They are affixed to the cover in one of two ways.

Sometimes pages from the signatures themselves are pasted onto the cardboard. That's the self-ended format, and this means you can have fun, printed endpapers, because all of the pages are part of the same printing process. However, this also means that you lose two individual pages right off the bat, as those are pasted down to the cardboard cover. So instead of 32 possible pages, you now have 30. But you'll also need endpapers before and after the main material, then front matter (title page, copyright, dedication) and even back matter (discussed in Chapter 8).

That's why, anecdotally, a lot of the self-ended projects I analyzed were 40 pages long, instead of 32, because so many pages are already accounted for by the binding process.

Self-Ended Layout

Here's what I mean, laid out visually. The 11" x 8.5" trim size (with safety margins) is just an example. Other common trim sizes are routinely used. For a 40-page and 48-page layout, we simply add more content spreads in the middle.

The following is a 32-page self-ended landscape format picture book (with an explainer in the first image):

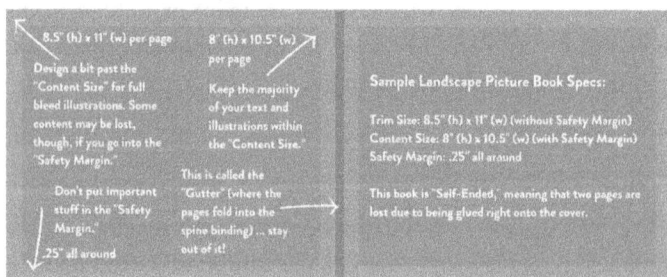

8.5" (h) x 11" (w) per page

Design a bit past the "Content Size" for full bleed illustrations. Some content may be lost, though, if you go into the "Safety Margin."

Don't put important stuff in the "Safety Margin."

.25" all around

8" (h) x 10.5" (w) per page

Keep the majority of your text and illustrations within the "Content Size."

This is called the "Gutter" (where the pages fold into the spine binding) ... stay out of it!

Sample Landscape Picture Book Specs:

Trim Size: 8.5" (h) x 11" (w) (without Safety Margin)
Content Size: 8" (h) x 10.5" (w) (with Safety Margin)
Safety Margin: .25" all around

This book is "Self-Ended," meaning that two pages are lost due to being glued right onto the cover.

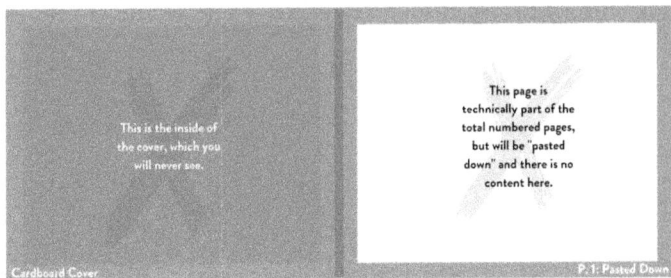

This is the inside of the cover, which you will never see.

Cardboard Cover

This page is technically part of the total numbered pages, but will be "pasted down" and there is no content here.

P. 1: Pasted Down

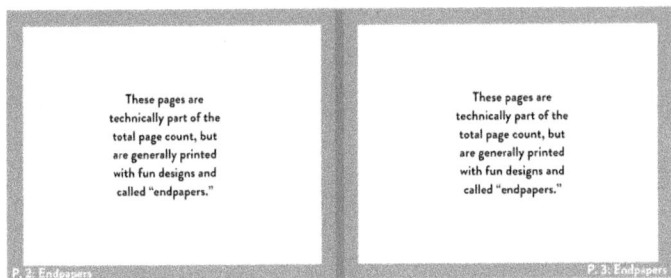

These pages are technically part of the total page count, but are generally printed with fun designs and called "endpapers."

P. 2: Endpapers

These pages are technically part of the total page count, but are generally printed with fun designs and called "endpapers."

P. 3: Endpapers

P. 4: Front Matter

P. 5: Front Matter

P. 6: Story Starts Here ...

P. 7: OR Here

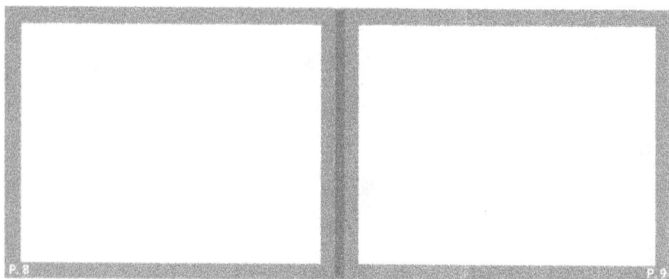

P. 16   P. 17

P. 18   P. 19

P. 20   P. 21

P. 22   P. 23

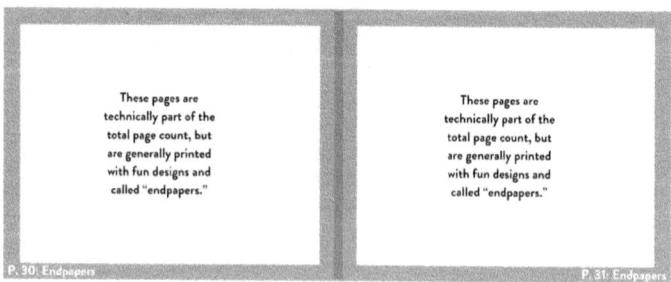

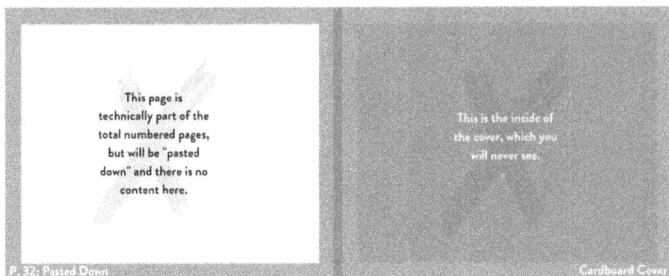

This page is technically part of the total numbered pages, but will be "pasted down" and there is no content here.

This is the inside of the cover, which you will never see.

P. 32: Pasted Down   Cardboard Cover

Separate-Ended Layout

The other popular picture book binding option is a separate-ended layout. Here, the signatures are glued to the cover using a separate piece of paper. Even though this leaf (generally solid, thicker colorful stock, which can be printed with up to one color) is technically one piece of paper, it's broken into four individual pages.

One is pasted down to the cardboard cover, we have a spread of colorful paper, and then the opposite page is affixed to the signatures with glue and comes before the title page. We haven't even reached the official first page in this configuration yet. The great news about a separate-ended format is you don't lose any actual printed pages.

Note that the 11" x 8.5" trim size (with safety margins) is just an example. Other common trim sizes are routinely used. For a 40-page and 48-page layout, we simply add more content spreads in the middle.

The following is a 32-page separate-ended landscape format picture book (with an explainer in the first image):

8.5" (h) x 11" (w) per page

Design a bit past the "Content Size" for full bleed illustrations. Some content may be lost, though, if you go into the "Safety Margin."

Don't put important stuff in the "Safety Margin."

.25" all around

8" (h) x 10.5" (w) per page

Keep the majority of your text and illustrations within the "Content Size."

This is called the "Gutter" (where the pages fold into the spine binding) ... stay out of it!

Sample Landscape Picture Book Specs:

Trim Size: 8.5" (h) x 11" (w) (without Safety Margin)
Content Size: 8" (h) x 10.5" (w) (with Safety Margin)
Safety Margin: .25" all around

This book is "Separate Ended," meaning that the cover is separate from the printed pages. The printed signatures are held in place by a single sheet that's pasted down to the cover on one side, folded in half, and pasted to the signatures on the other.

This is the inside of the front cover, which you will never see.

Cardboard Cover

This is a separate paper that holds the picture book materials in place. It is pasted to the inside cover. This is not included in the total page count. There is no content on this page, as you do not see it.

Separate Endpaper Pasted to Cardboard Cover

This is the opposite side of the paper that's pasted to the inside cover. This is not included in the page count. There is no content here. This is usually a solid color, or features one-color printing.

Separate Endpaper Pasted to Cardboard Cover

This is the opposite side of the paper that's pasted to the inside cover. This is not included in the page count. There is no content here. This is usually a solid color, or features one-color printing.

Separate Endpaper

This is still part of the endpaper holding the signatures in place. This is not included in the page count. There is no content here. This is usually a solid color, or features one-color printing.

Separate Endpaper

Usually a title page.

This is a separate bundle of paper that technically starts the actual printed story, and is the official first page.

P. 1: Front Matter

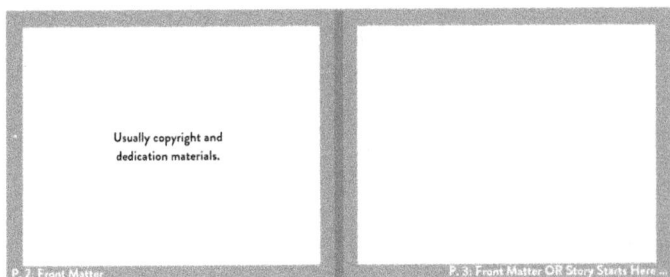

Usually copyright and
dedication materials.

P. 2: Front Matter

P. 3: Front Matter OR Story Starts Here ...

P. 4: OR Story Starts Here ...

P. 5: OR Here!

P. 6

P. 7

P. 8

P. 9

MARY KOLE

P. 26

P. 27

P. 28

P. 29

P. 30: Story Ends Here (OR Can Continue, If No Back Matter)

P. 31: Story Ends Here OR Back Matter

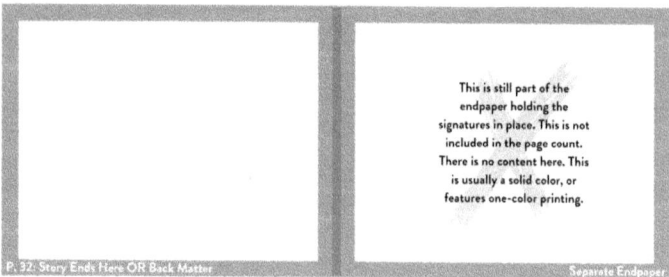

P. 32: Story Ends Here OR Back Matter

This is still part of the endpaper holding the signatures in place. This is not included in the page count. There is no content here. This is usually a solid color, or features one-color printing.

Separate Endpaper

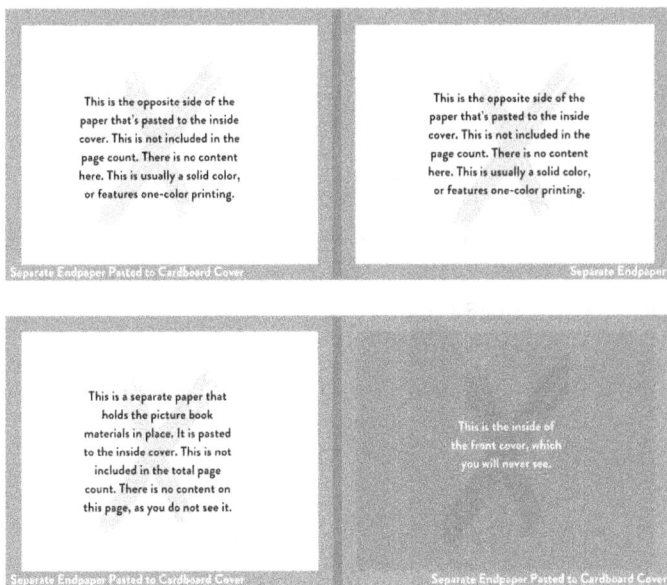

This is the opposite side of the paper that's pasted to the inside cover. This is not included in the page count. There is no content here. This is usually a solid color, or features one-color printing.

Separate Endpaper Pasted to Cardboard Cover

This is the opposite side of the paper that's pasted to the inside cover. This is not included in the page count. There is no content here. This is usually a solid color, or features one-color printing.

Separate Endpaper

This is a separate paper that holds the picture book materials in place. It is pasted to the inside cover. This is not included in the total page count. There is no content on this page, as you do not see it.

Separate Endpaper Pasted to Cardboard Cover

This is the inside of the front cover, which you will never see.

Separate Endpaper Pasted to Cardboard Cover

You can find a link to download these layouts as PDFs in Appendix B. I strongly encourage you to print them and use them to sketch out your picture book manuscript.

Once you've figured out how you will break up your text and have translated your ideas into a properly formatted and paginated manuscript format, per the previous chapter, you have a much more robust idea that has passed the storyboard test.

Perspective on Layouts

Out of the 154 books I analyzed from the shelves, I found a slight preference for self-ended projects. I also broke them down by total page counts in each category. Here's the data:

84 Self-Ended Projects (54.4%):

- 7 @ 32 pages (8.3%)

- 2 books @ 36 pages (2.4%)
- 2 books @ 38 pages (2.4%)
- 57 books @ 40 pages (67.9%)
- 3 books @ 44 pages (3.6%)
- 9 books @ 48 pages (10.7%)
- 2 books @ 56 pages (2.4%)
- 1 book @ 68 pages (1.2%)

70 Separate-Ended Projects (45.5%):

- 41 books @ 32 pages (58.6%)
- 2 books @ 36 pages (2.9%)
- 24 books @ 40 pages (34.3%)
- 1 books @ 44 pages (1.4%)
- 2 books @ 48 pages (2.9%)

Notice that we do have some page count outliers that don't fit into signatures of eight pages each. I emailed my former colleague and longtime friend, Chronicle Books executive editor Melissa Manlove, about this.

She explained that some houses that publish highly visual books—like Chronicle, or many Big Five publishers—can get price breaks from their printers that allow them to dictate specific page counts, if a project needs something non-standard. Is it probably still cheaper and easier to go for a classic number of pages? Sure, but sometimes even publishers make exceptions.

Still, the numbers don't lie. For the most part, there's a slight preference for self-ended projects, and within that category, a strong preference (almost 70%) for a 40-page layout, as this gives creators more usable pages. For separate ended projects, there's a stronger preference for 32-page layouts, but 40-page layouts are popular, too.

It's very important to remember that you cannot choose your book's format at this early stage. If you are an author/illustrator, and you've intentionally sketched your story out to be 32-pages, separate-ended, for example, you can make this compelling argument to a publisher during the acquisitions process, if you get that far. Otherwise, format and layout aren't fully decided until later, and these choices usually take heavy input from the editor, illustrator, and the design and production departments of the publishing house.

For your purposes at the manuscript stage, you can experiment by doing a storyboard exercise in a number of configurations, as you compose your project. See how your story might change if you're working within the constraint of 32 self-ended pages. Maybe it's worth trying 40 self-ended pages. Or you might want to play around with 32 vs. 40 separate-ended pages, to maximize the space available for storytelling.

Because I'm your picture book bestie, I have created the above templates for 32, 40, and even 48 pages, in both self-ended and separate-ended formats, in landscape and portrait configurations, and made them available as free downloads. See Appendix B for the URL.

Illustration Types

Now that we know the number of available pages you can use in a picture book, what can you do on that real estate? There are five different broad types of illustrations that you can play with. A lot of picture books generally use the first four types. The fifth one is specific to certain projects that have a more cartoon- or comic-inspired aesthetic. These are:

- **Spread**: Usually a full bleed illustration (the printing goes right beyond the edge of the page, and one illustration takes up both halves of a spread. Text is laid out over the image;

- **Page**: One full-bleed illustration that covers one page (half of a spread). The opposite page might shift to a different image, a different illustration type (except spread, which is no longer available), or be taken up by text;

- **Spot**: A spot illustration is a small illustrated vignette generally surrounded by white space on one spread or page. This style focuses the reader's attention on the moment being depicted, or zooms in on certain details.

- **Spots**: You sometimes see multiple spots on one page or spread. Multiple spots in sequence can be used to show physical actions or to move time forward. *Little Hoot* makes good use of spot illustrations; and

- **Panel**: Less common, but if you need to compress time, and your picture book lends itself well to a cartoon or comic illustration style, you can use panels to put several slices of a scene on one page or spread. *Moo Moo & Mr. Quackers Present What's Cooking Moo Moo?* uses a lot of panels.

Here are mock-ups of each type, including several options for spot illustrations:

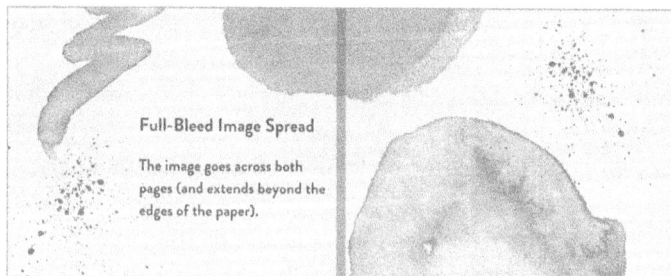

Full-Bleed Image Spread

The image goes across both pages (and extends beyond the edges of the paper).

Single-Page Image

The image occupies one page (half of a spread). The opposing side can contain a different image, a spot illustration (or several), or white space and text.

It cannot contain a spread, because one page is already used.

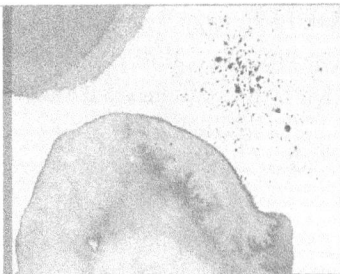

Spot Illustration

A spot illustration does not occupy an entire page or spread (it is not "full bleed"), and is usually surrounded by white space. The image can occupy one page (half of a spread), or a spread.

The opposing side can contain a different single-page image, another spot illustration (or several), or white space and text. It cannot contain a spread, because one page is already used.

Multiple Spot Illustrations

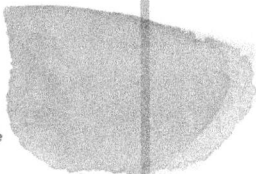

You can use several spot illustrations in sequence across one page or one spread. Sometimes, this effect is used to convey movement or the passage of time.

Panels

This illustration type is usually found in cartoon- or comic-style illustrations or stories. Like multiple spot illustrations, it can also convey action or the passage of time.

Here, you can see an example of one page that features five panels.

I did a little analysis, though with a smaller sample of books (because I couldn't go into that deep a rabbit hole on illustration type frequency). It seemed like, from studying 14 titles broken into 237 illustrations (an average of 17 illustrations per book), that the most popular options, in order, were:

- Spreads, by far. 123 out of 237 illustrations were full spreads;
- Spot illustrations, with 40 instances;
- Single-page illustrations, with either a spot illustration or text opposite, at 38 instances; and
- Two single-page illustrations next to one another, depicting different scenes on each page of a spread, at 36 instances.

As it happened, panel-style illustrations were not represented in this sample at all. I also didn't tally multiple spots (as opposed to single spots) separately.

This gives you a sense of what picture book layout looks like, and the kinds of illustrations that you can envision to tell your stories. Some projects stick to one type of illustration throughout (say, all spreads, like *Monster & Son*), while others mix things up.

Working with an Illustrator

Even though you've heard all of my arguments for leaving your idea "text only" before submission, you might decide to get your picture book illustrated anyway. If you're self-publishing, the reason is obvious: You need illustrations, so you have to make them happen. (I'll talk more about self-publishing a picture book in Appendix A, though this is not a comprehensive overview, by any means.)

If you're aiming for traditional publication, you might still very much believe that you want to enhance your submission package and present an illustrated version of your idea to agents and editors. You might want that exact illustrator to be part of the finished package, or just to give gatekeepers a sense of the finished product.

A lot of writers feel tempted to commission illustrations because they think having a dummy made will boost their odds for reasons discussed in Chapter 15. If you go this route, you are going to commission a version of the entire book, sketched out with quick illustrations, with text overlaid, just as it might appear in the finished product. Only two or three spreads will be "mock finishes," though, meaning they're done as if the pages are finalized and going to print.

The sketch dummy approach is actually smart (har har) and strategic because the story might change later in the publishing process, so there will be less to redo if the dummy consists mostly of sketches, rather than finishes. It's also cheaper, because it takes a talented illustrator much longer to do a finished spread, whether "mock finished" or actually finished, than it does to do a sketch treatment of the same image.

So, to recap, if you want to commission illustrations ahead of submitting to literary agents and traditional publishers, ask for a "sketch dummy with three mock finishes" (a standard request), instead of paying for every page to be fully rendered.

Remember, traditional publishers like to choose illustrators for the projects they acquire. If your existing illustrations are amazing, they might sign up the package deal—similar to the author/illustrator configuration discussed in the previous chapter.

If this is an illustrator you paid out of pocket, you might want to have an agreement in place that defines their art as "work for hire" in exchange for a flat fee. This means the illustrator was paid to create the images but is not entitled to any potential future advance and/or royalties if the project sells to a publisher. You also want to make sure they can be available to finish the project or revise current material if the project is acquired. This might trigger a new payment arrangement. You will want to hammer out terms *before* submission.

If you're true collaborators, you might enter into a profit-sharing agreement to split any future advance and/or royalties. Make sure to discuss this prior to submission as well.

All this being said, if the illustrations are *not amazing*, and you simply had them made to give agents and publishers "an idea of what the story was like" (I hear picture book writers say this all the time), **they won't consider the text separately**. They will assume that you're submitting what you intend to have published, even if you explain otherwise in the query letter.

You may want to save yourself the expense of commissioning illustrations before publication, as they could be a liability. And you get what you pay for, so if you want impressive illustrations to demonstrate your idea and get agents and publishers excited, this approach could easily get very expensive.

It *can* be possible for a writer and illustrator to collaborate and then submit to agents and publishers. But the illustrations have to be truly top-notch. To advise you comprehensively on this issue, I want to present how the picture book publishing process usually works for writers:

- Get literary representation for a text, or an offer from a publisher

- Sell text to publisher
- Do revisions
- Have publisher match your finalized text to an illustrator
- See illustrations, have varying levels on input
- Publish

And here's how the process usually works for children's book illustrators:

- Get representation from a literary agent or art representative for your illustrations, or get interest from a publisher
- Wait until a publisher has the right project for you
- Sign a contract to work on the project and turn in sketches
- Do revisions, if applicable
- Create finishes
- Publish

Most publishers have stables of illustrators they work with on a for-hire basis. They also have in-house designers and art directors, but they don't do illustration work. Instead, they put together a book's jacket, layout, and packaging, while the illustrator usually provides the cover and interior images.

If you decide to hire an illustrator for your children's book, you are, in effect, acting as the publisher, but without a publishing contract in place (unless you are self-publishing), and without any guarantee that the collaboration will be fruitful. That means you will have to find the illustrator, give them the specs for your project, do art direction, advise on layout and design, and offer feedback. Then you will present the entire project as an author/illustrator picture book to gatekeepers.

There are many venues to find an illustrator. The SCBWI (Society of Children's Book Writers and Illustrators), for example, has thousands of members working in all styles, even Harry.[1] This organization offers programming so that illustrators can grow their skills. Those artists also post their portfolios in the SCBWI member directory, and you can reach out to them individually. Picture book illustrators also keep their own websites, portfolios, and social media, so you can start Googling around to find artists. Ask for referrals at your local art school, if there is one. I'll share more resources for finding illustrators and other collaborators in Appendix B. The process of working with a hired illustrator is beyond the scope of this guide, but these ideas should at least get you started.

After you've finalized a project and produced at least a dummy, you will want to approach agents and publishers. If you've partnered with someone on the illustrations, the partnership should be disclosed in the picture book query letter.

Overall, I say you run one big risk with this arrangement, whether you're approaching an agent or a publisher: What if one component of the collaboration is better than the other? What if the text rocks, but your budget or artistic eye stopped you from getting a truly top-notch illustration result? Some collaborations are born of friendship, and if you have a close relationship with your co-creator and love the illustration results, you may have trouble evaluating the art's quality with an objective, critical eye.

Again, if you give a gatekeeper a package of text and art, the materials will be evaluated together. Agents and acquiring editors will see how you've currently executed the project and will have trouble imagining it any other way. So if you

---

1. This very bad joke is only in here to charm one person. He knows who he is.

present an agent or publisher with a complete picture book dummy, and one or the other component isn't working, the agent or editor will think, "Gosh, I really wish the text (or art) was stronger, but I guess this is how the creators envision it, so I think I'll reject." (In rare cases, the project may not work as a whole, but a wonderful agent or editor with lots of vision will see each component independently and offer revision suggestions, but I certainly wouldn't count on this.)

Of course, both text and art could be perfect, and work harmoniously together, in which case the agent could offer representation to either or both of you (if you are collaborating with the illustrator and want to continue working with them), and the publisher could issue each of you a publishing contract.

But, more often than not, I've seen collaboration only working when the writer and illustrator are well-matched in terms of talent. Often, they are not, and that's the risk. If you're dead set on publishing a project with a collaborator, that's fine. But you could be cutting yourself off from the possibility of selling the text separately, if you don't happen to be flexible. As a result, you might take a big swing with an illustrated text, but fail to sell that incarnation of the project. Or you might be a good candidate to self-publish.

When I was submitting picture books as an agent, I would prefer to submit just text, just art, or text and art from an author-illustrator client who has a great grasp of how their two mediums play together. I would be reluctant, for some of the above reasons, to consider an author and illustrator team of collaborators if the combination isn't sublime. I'd also be reluctant—again, unless I had a great match in mind—to pair a text with, say, one of my illustrator clients and present both to the publisher as a package deal.

The publisher has the final say in terms of picture book illustration. That decision has to do with the editor's vision, their own relationships, the imprint's brand identity, the prestige of either creator, and how the publisher's sales and marketing people might react to either component. There are a lot of moving pieces to keep in mind here with text and illustration alchemy.

In a competitive picture book market, where some Big Five titles aren't even getting picked up for distribution by the major bookselling chains, publishers often find themselves pairing a debut author with a name illustrator, or vice versa, to make the project more viable. If you're insisting on a debut text paired with a debut illustrator ... you may not have the most compelling case.

Don't cling. Don't be precious. Be flexible if you're considering teaming up with an illustrator before submission. How willing you are to entertain other illustrators for a specific project really could mean the difference between being published and not.

Speaking of which, now that we know what the manuscript looks like, and you've done all the hard work of writing and paginating your picture book project to refine your structure, you might want to engage in one or more rounds of revision. That's where the following chapter comes in, and it'll provide you with a comprehensive checklist of action items.

SEVENTEEN
PICTURE BOOK REVISION

THIS CHAPTER MAY SEEM like a bit of a cop-out, as I am going to bundle and reiterate various ideas we've discussed along the way. But I also know, from years of teaching writing, that repeating information isn't necessarily a bad thing, as not everything lands with someone the first one or two or even seven times they hear it.

Essential information, restated and reframed, can click in new ways. My intention with this chapter is to offer a revision checklist and summary of best practices, so that you can visit or revisit it whenever you're working on a project and want to make sure you've considered every relevant angle.

I could write an entire guide on revision (and knowing me, I probably will, just give me a few minutes). Revision is a very different beast from planning a book or drafting it, even for the picture book audience.

Many writers argue that books are actually made in *revision*, instead of in the initial creation phase. I would tend to agree. Revision is where you shape what you've come up with into something that fulfills your intention, then communicates that vision to your reader.

The first draft is just you telling yourself the story.

TERRY PRATCHETT

The above is one of my favorite writing quotes. It's after that first draft, once you know what you're actually writing, that you can start to think about how to tell that story to others. (And, in this case, a very specific audience of young listeners and readers.)

For over ten years, I've been delivering editorial notes to clients. I'm usually working with early drafts, but I can also come into the process much later, when a project has been revised many times already. Once I render my feedback, my writers or workshop participants start to revise. As such, I've heard about the ups and downs of the revision process from thousands of people.

The information in this chapter—condensed mostly into checklists—is a result of me learning what writers struggle with during revision, and how best to advise them through the process. You can take all of the thoughts in this chapter with a grain of salt and develop your own revision workflow. Don't be surprised if your revision style changes from project to project, or gets a complete overhaul over the course of your writing journey.

Revision is not a one-size-fits-all process that can be easily prescribed, and there's no one right approach. It can be incredibly fluid. Armed with these best practices, though, I hope you can find your way toward a final draft as intentionally as possible.

Revision Checklists: Big Picture Premise

First, let's attack the primary aspects of your picture book concept. My argument throughout this guide is that you don't have much of a story if you aren't following established market expectations or haven't taken the time to develop a strong premise. The below list covers all the main ingredients you need for both.

While you're working on this step, I give you permission to temporarily skip over this chapter, go to Chapter 18, and try writing your query letter. Even if you plan on self-publishing, which I discuss in Appendix A, write your pitch. See what happens.

Boiling your idea down into a logline can either clarify the essential points of your story, or confuse you. Writers find that doing this exercise can be very illuminating, especially in terms of how your premise comes across.

You then need to make sure that the actual story on the page reflects what you're pitching at a high level, and that includes adhering to contemporary picture book market guidelines.

Here's a checklist to make sure you're on track:

- The manuscript fits an established category of the picture book market (see Chapter 1).
- My word count is within standard expectations, but ideally less than 600 words for narrative picture books and 1,500 for nonfiction (excluding back matter).
- My manuscript can be laid out across a standard page count (32, 40, or 48 are the most common).
- My manuscript does not require any special formatting or expensive extras (interactive flaps, die cuts, paper engineering, etc., as defined in Chapter 7), unless there's a compelling reason for me to demand

these elements. If I still need them, I am aware that this might hurt my book's marketability.

- My project fits the target audience of three-to-five-year-olds (young picture book) or five-to-seven-year-olds (older picture book and nonfiction).
- My main character is either a child or a childlike animal or object avatar.

Now, as I discussed in Chapter 1, I'm not trying to cage your creative freedom. Not at all. But if you are looking to debut in the traditional picture book market, especially, you will want to work smarter, not harder, and present a project that plays within established expectations. If you're already well published, with a strong sales track record, or are self-publishing, you can pay less attention to what the main-stream market is doing. (But don't ignore it altogether.)

Next, let's make sure that you have all of the components of a strong picture book premise for your project:

- My narrative or narrative nonfiction manuscript (if applicable) has a strong thematic idea operating below the surface (see Chapter 4). The theme I'm working with is:

  _____

- My theme or concept is timely and/or noteworthy, and I have done some comparative title research (discussed more in Chapter 18). Three comparative titles—that share elements in common with my project, but are different enough from it that mine stands out—are:

  1. _____

2. _____

3. _____

- My concept or nonfiction manuscript (if applicable) has a specific topic or concept, which is:

_____

- My manuscript has at least three topics or sales hooks in addition to a theme or concept (see Chapter 6). They are:

1. _____

2. _____

3. _____

- My manuscript is character-led (for narrative and narrative nonfiction projects).
- My narrative or narrative nonfiction project has a structure.
- My concept or nonfiction idea has an organizing principle that gives it a structure or flow (as discussed in Chapters 7, 8, and 12).
- My idea is driven by a theme or message, but does not explicitly express or explain it in a way that condescends to my target audience (more about moralizing in Chapter 5).

In the following section, I'll break these elements down into more detailed checklists, arranged by topic.

Revision Checklists: Craft Topics

Because this guide goes from theme and topic to character, let's follow that same trajectory with the next revision checklist. Character is less important in a concept or nonfiction book, but you might want to review this checklist anyway. If you are writing a narrative or narrative nonfiction project, you'll want to make sure the following character ideas are part of your story:

- It is clear who the main character is, even if my story has multiple characters. (Some story structures, like Odd Friendship, can accommodate two protagonists with equal focus.)
- The main character is the one who either goes on a transformational journey (literal or figurative) or takes other characters on one (see Chapter 10).
- I only present the main character's or narrator's perspective or direct POV (point of view). Some structures, like Nesting Stories and Odd Friendship, can incorporate more than one POV, but this must be a very intentional choice.
- My character has an objective, or something that they're pursuing in the story. It is:

  _____

- My character has a reason for wanting the objective, which is known as their motivation (see more on these ideas in Chapter 10). It is:

  _____

- My character is proactive (moving the story forward) rather than reactive (having things happen to them).

- There are several characterizing details that define who my character is on a deeper level (that are more consequential than preferences, which everyone has). These important character elements are:

    1. _____

    2. _____

    3. _____

- My character is facing a conflict in the story. It is:

    _____

- The character's conflict relates to their objective, ideally creating an obstacle.
- If my character has an attribute that will help them save the day, it is:

    _____

- My character either has something they're struggling with about themselves, or something they celebrate about themselves. It is:

    _____

- My character relates to my story's theme and/or takes a position on that emotional idea, with a specific worldview.
- My character either changes over the course of the story (though not in an unrealistic of heavy-handed way, per Chapter 5), OR

- If there is no overt growth on the page for the protagonist, there are other characters in the story who change. They are sufficiently different from my protagonist, and offer layers of nuance, pertaining to my theme.
- Even if the character interacts with an older/wiser ally character, the protagonist still realizes the valuable lesson for themselves, or with very limited prompting/steering/explaining.

Now let's talk about plot and structure. Once again, this largely applies to narrative or narrative nonfiction projects. As you revise your plot and structure, make sure the following points are true:

- My story has a defined beginning, middle, and end.
- There is conflict introduced within the first few pages.
- Characters have tension or conflict with one another, rather than simply coexisting. This conflict drives the story forward, in addition to conflict from the story world.
- There is both internal and external conflict.
- The story incorporates stakes, or a reason *why* the story matters to the character, and therefore the reader. (See more about this craft idea in Chapter 10.)
- The initial conflict either escalates throughout, or the conflict transforms or transitions around the midpoint (see the Midpoint Shift structure in Chapter 12).
- The story has an engaging resolution that ends with a full circle moment, joke, twist, or final image that captures the theme (see Chapter 11).
- There's a clear reason that the story starts today, as opposed to yesterday or next week.
- The events of the story flow in a cause-and-effect sequence, rather than happening seemingly

randomly. My story's scenes cannot be rearranged into any other order.

- If anything is out of balance or I'm not using dialogue, I will try to incorporate more narrative storytelling tools and elements, if applicable.
- My story has a good balance of:

  description
  action
  scene
  character development
  dialogue

Now let's talk about the actual writing of the story. This is the part many writers get distracted by while revising, when they should actually be finalizing bigger story structure elements first. There is no compelling reason to work on the prose part before the larger idea and framework are set.

If your story ends up significantly changing, then the writing you've polished will be rendered moot. This is also why I advise writers to finalize the manuscript before commissioning illustrations (if you're taking that route, as discussed in Chapter 15).

Only once you've done the big structural work should you start messing around on the sentence level. You can obviously always change the story later (and you should, if you have nagging feelings that something's not working, because your writing intuition is powerful, even if revision means more work for you). Building a strong foundation first, before you erect the walls, and certainly before you put up pictures and buy throw pillows, is working smarter, not harder.

Otherwise, it's like rearranging deck chairs on the *Titanic*.

On that cheerful note (!), this is the revision checklist I'd recommend when you're finally ready to tackle the sentence-level writing of your picture book manuscript:

- I've read my work aloud.
- I've had someone else read my work aloud to me (both discussed in Chapter 14).
- I've actually done both of the above instead of sitting there, thinking it's a good idea, and then *not* doing it for reasons of dread or anxiety.
- I've properly formatted my manuscript according to the guidelines in Chapter 15, because it's so much easier to do it now than later.
- My sentences are about twenty words or fewer, depending on my target reader age.
- I've worked hard to write clearly, rather than indulging in formal phrasing or unnecessary wordiness.
- My sentence syntax is not complex or confusing.
- I have run my story through the readability level checker in Appendix B and know that the language is age- or grade-appropriate for my target audience.
- Even if my character is not a child, their word use and dialogue reflect the voice and sensibility of my target audience.
- If I'm writing in rhyme, I have kept my stanza lengths and line counts consistent.
- If I'm writing in rhyme, I have kept my end and/or internal rhymes to a specific pattern.
- If I'm writing in rhyme, I have determined my syllabic counts for every line.
- If I'm writing in rhyme, I've ensured that my syllabic counts have a consistent rhythm throughout.
- If I'm writing in rhyme and I depart from my

established rhyme or rhythm, there is an intentional story reason for doing so.

- If I'm writing in rhyme, I haven't twisted my sentences into any strange pretzels just for the sake of end rhyme.
- If I'm writing in rhyme, I have made a conscious effort to let the story drive the style (the rhyme and word choice), rather than the other way around.
- If I'm writing in rhyme, I have tried to remove the rhyme to make sure there's still enough story substance for a prose version. If not, I won't put it back into rhyme until I'm clear on all of the premise and story points in the above checklists.

Great! Now that you have done the premise and theme work, the character and plot work, and the writing work, you're done with revision!

Just kidding. Sorry. You're not.

Next, you will want to make sure your story makes room for illustrations (as discussed in Chapter 15). A picture book text, as we now know, is an incomplete product, just waiting for a collaborator. Here's how you ensure that you are leaving the door open:

- I've removed most of the physical or visual descriptions from the text.
- My story doesn't micromanage the illustrator by explaining overly granular or obvious details that are either irrelevant, a personal preference, or clear in the text itself.
- I keep my setting, clothing, furnishing, and character descriptions to a respectful minimum in the narrative.
- My story doesn't spend a lot of time describing emotions, facial expressions, limb positions and

movements, or body language. The emotions come from the story itself, or are expressed in other ways, like dialogue.

- If I need to convey something related to illustrations (which is not already clear from the text), I've used a respectful number of illustration notes (see Chapter 15).

Okay, now we're actually done with revision! Phew!

Just kidding. Again.

Before you move on to the recommendations in the rest of this chapter, go back to Chapter 16 and learn how to paginate your project. Lay out your story and make a storyboard or dummy. It can be for your eyes only—you don't even have to sketch anything, you can simply distribute your text. Doing this might completely upend what you thought your story was all about, and how you want to tell it.

If you haven't done this yet for your picture book project, you are not even close to done with revision. Now go. Actually do it. I'll wait. I can be very patient.[1]

Great. Now, if you can *honestly* say that you have revised and paginated and analyzed your picture book project again, there are a *few more* best practices that I would recommend.

Revision Next Steps

Your first, most important, and scariest next revision step is to get feedback from other sources. This doesn't have to cost money. You can join a critique group or writing workshop or otherwise cultivate productive relationships with fellow writ-

---

1. An absolute pants-on-fire lie. I outed myself as very impatient in Chapter 2.

While specifics for doing this are outside the scope of this guide, I have an article with more information for you, linked in Appendix B. (Picture book writers in particular should join the SCBWI, or Society of Children's Book Writers and Illustrators, also linked in Appendix B.)

Outside feedback is important because, while you know what you're doing—you hope—you need to make sure it tracks with a third party. You have a vision, you have written your project with intention, you know every comma and word choice that you're using to get your idea across, and you know the rhythm and tone that are so clear in your head.

An outsider does not.

When you give your story to someone who doesn't know it, that's the real test of whether it's ready for an audience. However, this other person should be qualified to give you constructive feedback. You don't want to just give your manuscript to any random person off the street, or a literal child. In fact, please don't give it to a child. You'd think this would be a good way to get feedback from your target audience, but it won't work.[2]

The best person to give picture book feedback is actually either an adult who has read a lot of picture books recently

---

2. I know this sounds counter-intuitive, but kids are not good at commenting on manuscripts. First of all, remember the layers of gatekeepers you have to impress? During the submission phase, you have to gear your project more to agents and publishers. Kids won't be able to give you notes in this regard. Second of all, you have to consider your relationship to the child. If it's your own kid, of course they're going to read your work and approve. They want dessert tonight. Same goes for other kids in your family, friends' kids, and kids you teach, if you have access to a focus group, I mean, classroom. Invariably, they will be biased by your relationship with them. Also, feedback like "It's good!" doesn't actually tell you anything, even if it feels temporarily nice. Most children the same age as your target audience won't have the critical understanding tools or language to go beyond broad value judgments.

(an exhausted parent, a librarian, a teacher) or another writer who specializes in children's books. That's the feedback you're after, not your mother's[3] or your published erotica writer buddy's.[4]

I'm obviously a freelance editor—I make my living when writers show up to ask me for feedback on their manuscripts. That makes me biased, because I have a vested financial interest in recommending that you get outside feedback. But I am plenty busy, and that's not why I'm giving this advice. Whether you pay for feedback or not, it's very possible to cultivate critique relationships for free (as long as the writers who will be evaluating your work know something about picture books, otherwise, their advice is not going to be that helpful).

Of course, you *can* guarantee that you're getting qualified feedback that will be very useful to you if you hire a picture book expert to edit your work. As they say, you can either get something cheap, something fast, or something good. You can even get two of those qualities at once, but never all three. So if you want something good, you're probably not going to get it by also trying to get it cheap or fast.

If you want to speed up your learning curve and challenge yourself, get a review or edit from a freelance editor who specializes in picture books. I've put some links in Appendix B for resources, including my own website, of course. (Marketing is all about having a captive audience, after all!)

---

3. Other non-child people you're close to, like parents, siblings, and spouses, make for terrible critique providers as well. Your mom will either love it unconditionally or ask you what you're doing with your life, depending on the kind of relationship you have.
4. Fellow writers are a good option, but if they don't know the picture book craft or market, they are going to be of limited use.

Making the Most of Feedback

Should you decide to get editorial, workshop, or critique group feedback, make sure you're considering the notes you get with an open mind. Some feedback might not be worthwhile (especially if it comes from a clueless-about-your-genre-or-category reader), but outside opinions can often, at the bare minimum, point out parts of the project that aren't working. I was reading a book of essays by the novelist Haruki Murakami, and he talks about sometimes working with editors whose suggestions or proposed revisions he has *really disagreed* with.

Instead of sulking, though, he goes back to that part of the story and tries to revise it, because clearly *something* isn't working. He may not agree with the suggested solutions, but he now knows he needs to fix that portion of the manuscript. Here's the quote:

It seems that when a reader has a problem, there is usually something that needs fixing, whether or not it corresponds to their suggestions. In short, the flow of their reading has been blocked. It is my job, then, to eliminate the blockage, to unclog the pipe, as it were. How to do that is up to me, the author.[5]

As long as you're considering the feedback you get from a place of flexibility instead of ego, you can figure out your own solutions to identified problems. The more qualified the person giving the critique, the better and more useful their notes will be. They might even help take your work to the

---

5. Haruki Murakami, *Novelist as a Vocation*, 101.

next level, especially if they understand the integrity of your idea and consider your intentions.

Whether and how you address those suggestions is your own decision. You have, after all, a clear sense of the vision behind the project. Sometimes getting multiple reads and rounds of feedback from different people helps clarify your revision next steps. Sometimes it does not. I've heard endless stories of writers getting diametrically opposed feedback, which left them more confused than ever. Remember that art (and publishing) is incredibly subjective, and everyone has an opinion.

After you've gotten additional feedback and made a plan that feels good, revise accordingly. Perhaps go back to some of the checklists in this chapter to make sure all elements of the story are clicking along nicely.

Then shove it in a drawer for two weeks. (Or close the computer file. You know what I mean.)

That's right.

Put it away.

Stop thinking about it. Take some time to rest and reflect. Let your back brain operate below the level of conscious awareness and keep turning the story over and over. This is your last-ditch effort to manufacture a sense of fresh eyes and a new perspective for yourself. Once you come back to the project two weeks after you've already "finalized it," then you'll know whether or not it is done.[6]

If it is, then you can move on to polishing your pitch, and,

---

6. In the vein of setting expectations, you should know that even published authors often wish they could tinker with books already on shelves. "Done" is relative.

after that, submitting it to literary agents and publishers, or self-publishing.

EIGHTEEN
PICTURE BOOK SUBMISSION

You ARE ALMOST to the finish line with this version of your project, and I am so proud that you have come this far! Here, I'll discuss submitting to literary agents and publishers, the pitch, the query letter, submission strategy and research resources, and more.

A few things to keep in mind first.

You will ideally be submitting your strongest picture book project, but you will want to have a few more ideas in reserve. At this point, you might be thinking about your overall "author brand," and how you will come across to gatekeepers. (We discussed authorial tone in Chapter 14.) Consider whether there's a thematic or style element that pulls together the picture book stories you want to tell. Are there any common threads?

If an interested agent or publisher asks to see more work, you can present two projects that are in the same vein, and maybe another that's a departure. For example, if you are thinking of telling funny picture book stories, but you also have a more poignant concept book in mind, it's okay to deviate from your "type" without worrying about being pigeonholed. At the submission stage, the projects you showcase should be as strong and finished as you can get them, but you don't yet have to worry about career steering (discussed a bit later in this chapter) or getting stuck in one category. Anchor into your current interest area, or depart from it. As long as you have more than one idea, you should be in a good spot if someone asks to see more of your work.

For the strongest project, which you'll submit initially, you will have, in a perfect world, intentionally crafted your picture book from the ground up, using all of the principles in this guide. Writing your pitch should come naturally, as you've already thought through your themes, topics, sales hooks, character, and plot.

If this isn't the soft landing you expected, maybe revisit the bulk of this guide, especially Chapter 17, and do a few more revision passes. There's no one answer to when a project is ready for submission. If you find that you've reached the fullest possible expression of your intentions for your leading picture book idea, then it's probably time to get out there with it and see what happens.

Here's a submission order of events:

1. Get clarity on your goals
2. Decide whether to approach a literary agent or publisher (or both!)
3. Do your submission research
4. Work on your logline and hook
5. Write your query
6. Get your assets in order
7. Submit!
8. Analyze the results
9. Regroup and consider next steps

Let's get after that first step. What are your goals for submission? Here are some questions you can use to get clarity on your writing and publishing goals as you prepare to submit:

1. What is your primary aim for this project? (Try to be more specific than "get published." You can think about your ideal path to publication, what you want this project to do for your career, where you are in your writing journey, etc.)

2. What is the exact picture book audience you're envisioning for this project? (Try to be more specific than "everyone.")

3. Is your project pretty straightforward, or does it have special requirements (die cuts, flaps, paper engineering, etc.)? What form do you imagine the final product taking? Check out Chapters 7 and 16 to metabolize your options.

4. How much help and guidance do you want from a potential agent or publisher? Do you want to communicate with them often, or do you want to be left to your own devices?

5. How much control and input do you want during the publication process? (Your answer here might point you firmly toward either traditional or self-publishing. Picture book writers, in particular, need to be prepared to cede control over the illustrations in the traditional publishing process, as discussed in Chapter 15. The writer is almost always completely excluded from this part of production.)

6. What size of agency or publisher feels right to you? (Imagine a large corporation with many clients versus a cozy boutique with smaller lists and more individual attention. Keep in mind that most publishers and agencies occupy a space somewhere between these extremes.)

7. What relationship do you envision with your agent or publisher? (Imagine a lifelong partnership or a quick, sales-based transaction.)

8. What kind of peers do you envision surrounding yourself with? Do you care about other writers or names at that agency or house? (Most writers don't think about this aspect of publishing, but the prominence of the agency's existing clients helps its agents establish precedent for favorable contract terms after a blockbuster deal negotiation.)

9. How many projects do you have in you as a writer? How often do you imagine coming up with a book that's ready for publication? (There is no right or wrong answer here, but having too many projects that you'd like to publish all at once—as some picture book creators do—can actually be a liability, as very few houses will do more than one book every year or two.)

10. How important is money? How important are subrights (movie, merchandising, audio, foreign etc.)? Are you more comfortable with an advance, a royalty-only deal, or some combination thereof? (You might not be able to choose, but you should have a bottom line in mind.)

Should You Work with an Agent or Directly with a Publisher?

Submitting to a literary agent seems to be a standard starting place for today's writers, so some aspiring authors don't realize that using an agent is a choice. There are pros and cons to working with an agent. (Yes, I was an agent for a number of years, but I try not to be biased. Agents aren't for everyone, or for every project.) Submitting directly to a publisher can be a viable alternative, depending on your goals. There are pros and cons to working with a publisher without a middleman as well.

The pros of working with an agent are:

- Agents have access to publishers that are closed to unsolicited submissions, like the bigger players (HarperCollins, Penguin Random House, and other Big Fives, etc.) There aren't many loopholes to get you there otherwise, unless you connect with an acquiring editor at a conference and they're amenable to direct submissions (usually for a set period of time after the event).
- Agented submissions go to the top of the pile. Even houses that accept unagented submissions (those who open themselves to hearing directly from writers) will receive projects from agents—and read those first.
- Contract negotiations are off your plate. You'll have an expert in your corner, fighting for your interests. (This can be replicated with an intellectual property attorney, but that individual might not have the same clout as a publishing-specific agent, and you will pay for their services out of pocket.)
- The agency will have precedent-filled boilerplates with each publisher and use the leverage developed during previous negotiations to work for you when it comes to clauses, royalty percentages payout schedules, escalators, bonuses, etc.
- Agents act as buffers between you and your house if problems arise over the lifecycle of your book. You never want to think this will happen, but you want to be protected in case it does.
- Most agents will help you revise projects and advise you on bigger picture questions and your overall career trajectory.

- Agents are connected to foreign publishers and film agents, so their professional networks can help your project get more opportunities worldwide and in the film world, should your work be a good fit for those markets.

The cons of working with an agent are:

- Agents charge for their services. 15% is standard commission for domestic sales, and 20-25% is standard for subrights and foreign sales, as agents often use an in-house or partner co-agent to make deals. They take a commission from each royalty check, too.
- If you part ways with your agent, they are still the "agent of record" on the projects they sold for you and will continue to receive commission. There's no easy way to sever this provision without taking legal action, and even then, you'd need cause.
- Agents are easily excited about exciting projects, but if you've had some obstacles to success, or your books haven't sold well historically, depending on the agent, their enthusiasm might wane. Not all relationships last forever. People don't like to talk about this side of the industry, but break-ups happen.
- Some writers get lost in the shuffle on a big agent's list, within a big agency, or if the agent is dealing with a big deal on behalf of another client. Self-advocacy can still be required, even after you've gone over your first big gatekeeper hurdle and secured representation.
- Even if an agent is championing your work, they might be slow to respond. Agents can get overwhelmed with other projects (see above), and delays can arise due to stuck gears elsewhere in the

process. Sometimes, publishing can feel like "hurry up and wait," even after getting representation.

It's perfectly possible to connect directly with publishers and secure a contract. I'll offer some resources for finding these targets later in this chapter.

That said, the pros of working directly with a publisher are:

- If you approach a house directly, you cut out the middleman and can have more control over the process of submission. This means the onus of research is on your shoulders, but if you thrive on picking through your options, you won't have an agent telling you what to do, how to pitch your project, or who you should sell to. (Your options will be more limited, though, so it's a balance.)
- You can potentially cultivate a strong relationship with a publisher and editor, without an intermediary. Some wonderful partnerships have resulted from this kind of direct connection.
- You can feel freer to bring your ideas to a publisher without worrying about an agent's feedback or submission timeframe. Agents often juggle other clients and submissions on behalf of multiple parties, so this might influence their choices about where to send projects. For example, the agent might already have two picture book submissions each with their favorite editors in that category. (Agents actually try not to have more than one project under consideration with a specific editor at any one time.) Those editors don't want to see any more picture books from that agent until they resolve their existing backlog.
- All the money that's coming to you is yours alone. You don't pay a commission to anyone when you sell

directly to a publisher. (But don't forget to put a percentage aside for taxes! Agented or not, all writers are equal in the eyes of Uncle Sam.)

The cons of working directly with a publisher:

- Many publishers that are considered larger (like the Big Five) simply don't accept unagented submissions (with very few exceptions). Your choices are limited to smaller or regional publishers. If you have a niche project that might do really well at a modest or independent house, this might be ideal. But if you believe your project has what it takes to be a national or international bestseller, a smaller house is not ideal.
- It's up to you to negotiate your contract. The publisher will be fighting for their bottom line on each deal point with terms that are advantageous to them, not you. Many writers report fearing that the offer will be withdrawn at every turn, which might make you feel pressured to capitulate.
- The monetary terms and the advance, if any, tend to be more modest for writers who approach a house independently. Not just because you're working with a smaller publisher, but because you have less leverage than an agent, who might represent other writers at the same house—incentivizing the editor to keep everyone happy.
- If you hire an intellectual property lawyer to look over your contract or to settle any disputes with the publisher, this costs you money. If problems arise, you will have to navigate these waters with diplomacy, and likely without knowledgable advice. Relationship maintenance will be entirely your responsibility.
- You get to make your own decisions, but you are also on your own for big-picture steering and career

guidance—and you might be learning as you go, so you could make more mistakes and wrong turns as you forge forward.

It's important to note that you can submit to agents and publishers simultaneously. Some resources will tell you not to do this, but I don't mind it. The only issue happens when you get interest from an agent and publisher at the same time, which is extremely unlikely.

If a small or medium publisher expresses their desire to acquire a direct submission, you are completely within your rights to tell them that you are also talking to agents and will respond to their gracious offer within two weeks. Some writers believe this will get the offer withdrawn, but publishers know that writers often work with agents, or are simultaneously looking for one as they query houses, so it's not an insult or surprise to say that you're on submission.

Agents like to make sales, so they will generally respond favorably if you email them to say that you have a publishing offer in hand (but this situation can also be a double-edged sword, explained below). However, make sure you *don't accept any offer terms* before you do this—simply thank the publisher for their enthusiasm, communicate your update about currently querying agents, and say that you will get back to them soon. If you've already accepted the offer, an agent will be less interested in coming aboard because there's nothing for them to negotiate.

Agents, in general, can sometimes be less enthusiastic about coming into an existing offer because they may have wanted to send the project to bigger houses, or those they consider a better fit for the book. It's unlikely that they will withdraw the book from the offering publisher, or that you will want to give up the "bird in the hand" of a contract, but this situation does limit your option to place the book elsewhere.

Generally, as long as both parties (the offering publisher and the prospective agent) are aware of what's going on and all cards are on the table, it's perfectly possible to entertain interest from both a literary agent and publishing house simultaneously. With forthcoming communication, you will end up with a configuration of parties for the sale at hand, whether you accept the offer and work directly with the publisher, or whether you bring on an agent as an intermediary in this deal.

If you are able to get a contract yourself and you don't end up connecting with an agent this time around, you can always stay in touch with any interested parties for your next book. There will ideally be other projects, and other directions you want to take. Agents can be very patient if they see you as a promising creator. (They have to be patient, working in publishing.)

A final consideration here: Whenever you submit to either an agent or a publisher, you need to be okay with that person or house accepting the work. You need to be at peace with the idea that you will then publish the project with the smaller house you're submitting to directly, for example, or being represented by the agent you queried.

This seems like a bizarre point to be making, but think about "safety schools." Sometimes writers will have "dream agents" and "fallbacks," and submit to both. I cannot tell you how many writers have emailed me in a panic, saying something along the lines of, "I submitted to Agent X and … they want to represent the project!" But they're upset. When I ask why, they tell me that they don't actually want to work with Agent X, they are holding out for Agent Y.

Well, they've made some bad decisions. (But that feedback isn't helpful, so I usually keep it to myself.)

Don't submit to an agent or publisher unless you are okay working with them. Don't do it as a back-up plan. Yes, there will always other projects, and you can try to work with someone else in the future, but the project at hand will be locked in. Don't harbor resentment or bitterness or engage in endless what-ifs because you actually wanted someone else. (This is why I suggest submitting to your A List first, instead of your B List, later in this chapter.)

By asking yourself the questions that kick off this submission discussion, and getting a sense of what you want to do with your writing career *before* clicking *Send*, you can prevent a lot of these fraught situations from happening to you.

Be intentional about who you submit to and how you handle this process. Spend time here, just like you've spent time on your manuscript. A lot of the dramas and mistakes I hear about after submission actually stem from shortsighted or ill-informed decisions made in the submission *planning* stage.

If you're clear on what you're doing before you approach agents or publishers, you can save the conflict for your manuscript. Submission research is a big part of setting yourself up for potential success, and I'll talk about that next.

Submission Research

Below you'll find a list of books and websites that will be helpful to you with the agent and publisher search. There are some great resources here, and all are worth a skim, whether you're actively searching or merely looking ahead and learning what's out there.

One important thing to note is that you might find tons of companies by Googling "publisher for my book," or similar. Be careful with this approach, and wary of what you'll find. Most of the results you'll uncover this way will be vanity or hybrid publishers, which will issue your book (and provide all of the production services you'd expect from traditional publishers, with the potential to add marketing and distribution services), but for a fee.

Make no mistake, these services are "pay to play," which is why these companies shell out money to advertise and show up at the top of Google search results, hoping to attract vulnerable writers who just want a publishing contract. When I hear that a writer has several offers on the table, I make sure to learn whether these are advance and/or royalty offers (from traditional publishers), or vanity press contracts where *you* owe money to have the company produce the work.

There's nothing inherently wrong with this business model. But some of these publishers are predatory because they know writers are emotionally invested in their projects. They will offer to print anything, without any quality control. Others do a good job of producing professional, compelling work, and will not automatically take everyone who inquires.

You need to be clear that this vanity arrangement is what you really want when you approach one of these publishers. As long as you are aware that this route to market is different from the traditional publishing model, you can pursue it (and invest your money). Make sure to vet every publishing offer and contract you receive, just to make sure you understand what you're getting yourself into with a publisher, and what they will do on your behalf. If an offer seems too good to be true, most times, unfortunately, it is.

The resources below are more geared to finding traditional-model publishers and literary agents:

Manuscript Wish List: manuscriptwishlist.com

- A great and frequently updated resource that collects "wish list" mentions from agents and acquiring editors at publishing houses This means that gatekeepers will indicate on social media, or elsewhere, that they are *especially* looking for certain categories, themes, or topics. Some of these might have a timely bent.

- Add this aggregator to your research and see if you can catch the right gatekeeper at the right time, especially if they're seeking something similar to your work. Also check out the #mswl hashtag. This is where you'll find agents and editors posting their desires live.

Association of American Literary Agents: aalitagents.org

- The Association of American Literary Agents (formerly the AAR) features a list of member agencies that have agreed to abide by certain ethics codes and standards.

Literary Rambles: literaryrambles.com

- This blog features a roundup of agent interviews, web presence, and submission information. It's a careful analysis of an agent and their reputation in the marketplace, organized by individual names.

Agent Query: agentquery.com

- A searchable database of agents that allows you to sort the data by category and genre. Want someone who represents both picture books and young adult fantasy? Check the boxes and see who fits your criteria. Results give you contact information and examples of recent sales (which are sourced from Publishers Marketplace).

Writer's Digest: writersdigest.com

- Writer's Digest is a great resource for writers, and its various platforms (magazine, blog, webinars, conferences, etc.) often profile agents, introduce new agents to the writing community, interview writers about their agents, talk about the process of being published, and the ins and outs of the industry. I highly recommend their *Writer's Market* guide, edited by Robert Lee Brewer, and *Children's Writer's and Illustrator's Market* resource, edited by Amy Jones, which are frequently updated and contain names, agencies, and other salient details (**including lists of publishers that accept submissions directly from writers**).

Query Tracker: querytracker.com

- This is a similar website to Agent Query (above), but it also lets you organize and track your query and submission status. You don't have to use a spreadsheet anymore (though I have one I'll share in Appendix B)! There's also a community element, where you can interact with other writers, read about agents' response times, and otherwise go down rabbit holes, trying to guess what your favorite agents are up to, what they might say about your own submission, and when.

Duotrope: duotrope.com

- A subscription submission tracker and resource for finding agents and publishers.[1] It pulls together a lot

---

1. As of this writing, it costs $5/month (with a price break for annual

of information and offers a way to stay on top of submissions, timing, and everything else you need to know. For all my spreadsheet lovers, this interface will please you.

Publishers Marketplace: publishersmarketplace.com

- As mentioned in Chapter 6, PM is a paid resource for agent and publisher research. They have lists of top dealmakers (agents who have a track record) in many different categories and genres. You can see who's selling what, the types of books they gravitate toward, who they're selling to, and more. I recommend that everyone join for at least a month while doing research (you can always cancel after you make your submission list). Agents sound great on paper and on their websites, but I think a demonstrable sales record is much more telling. Same for publishers. Which ones are doing deals in your category? How many deals? What are the dollar amounts[2]? Most people in the industry are on PM every single day, looking at all of the latest sales and trends.

The list above is intended to be a starting place for your own research. Once again, do not skimp on this step. You will regret it if you don't put the same care and attention into researching potential publishing partners as you do into the creative part of the process.

So many writers, understandably, are focused on the

---

subscriptions).

2. You can't predict your specific advance level, as there are many factors involved, some of which are discussed in Chapter 6. There is a resource for curious writers, called Publishing Paid Me, which I'll share in Appendix B.

endgame of submission—seeing their books published and available on bookstore shelves. It takes a lot to get there, though, and you can't rush through any stage, no matter how impatient you are to reap your potential future rewards.

Submission Rules and Guidelines

There are many resources that will tell you which agents and publishers are out there. However, I would always recommend comparing the submission guidelines reprinted on any aggregator site (like Agent Query, Query Tracker, and Duotrope) against the agent or publisher's own website or social media.

Guidelines are copied and pasted into so many resources that it's like a giant game of telephone. You can use a source like Agent Query or PM to get names and general details, but then you should head over to each agency or publisher's website to cross-reference and double-check. Sometimes you won't know that an agent has closed to queries until this last step, which is always disappointing, but you want to make sure you are working with the latest and greatest information.

Below are my best practices for strategizing a submission round to publishers or agents (or both at the same time). To reiterate: Submitting to agents and publishers simultaneously is totally okay. As advised, make agents aware of any publishing offers, and make publishers aware that you're also looking for an agent *before accepting any contract terms*. Gatekeepers are generally very understanding during this process[3].

Here's the strategy and approach that I recommend to all of my clients:

---

3. And if they aren't, that's a data point. Consider whether you want to work with such a person or organization.

1. Ideally, your first round of research will result in 20-30 names that seem compelling to you, whether those are publishers that accept unagented submissions or individual literary agents.
2. From there, you will dive deeper and segment your targets into an A List of 10-15 names and a B List of 10-15 names. If you find even more people you'd like to pitch, but are maybe lukewarm about, then you can also create a C List and keep it in your back pocket.
3. Remember the golden rule: *do not* simultaneously pitch more than one editor at a publishing imprint, and more than one agent at a literary agency.
4. It is perfectly acceptable (and beneficial to the writer) to send all your submissions at once (in rounds to your A List first, then your B list). This is called a "multiple submission" or "simultaneous submission." Just make sure to mention that you're doing so somewhere in your query letter, which we'll discuss in the next section. It's considered industry standard at this point, unless you've forged a very specific relationship with one gatekeeper (explained below) and an exclusive read is expected.
5. Do not grant exclusivity unless you have a compelling reason to do so. It does not earn you any additional favor with an agent or publisher. But if someone asks you to submit exclusively, you can decline, with one exception …
6. If you are revising for an agent or publisher based on extensive notes (called a "revise and resubmit"), you should grant them exclusivity (for a specified period, like two to four weeks). This is considered the right thing to do. If they pass, you are welcome to go out to a larger list, even if the revised manuscript reflects their notes.

7. Do not contact an agent or editor with a revised manuscript unless you have done significant work since submission. If so, you can withdraw your project from consideration and send the new version. Do not do this more than once, or you will look unprofessional. (Try not to do it at all, of course, but agents and publishers are used to writers who keep revising after submission. You're not the first person to do this. No need to panic.)

8. Notify everyone who has responded favorably to your submission if you receive an offer of representation or an offer from a publisher. Don't notify people about a manuscript request (this is less of a concern with picture books, because you're going to be sending the manuscript in the same email as your query, in most cases). It's only news if you have an offer of representation by an agent, or the manuscript is being taken to acquisitions by a publisher (that's the step before an offer). If you have that concrete interest in hand, absolutely let everyone else know, and give them time to respond (a week or two is fine).

9. Follow all submission guidelines for agents and publishers, with, perhaps, the exception of the "query only" rule (where they don't request any material with the query). Sometimes it pays to take a risk and send the manuscript itself alongside the pitch. Otherwise, follow everyone's guidelines to the letter, as outlined on their websites.

10. Submit according to those guidelines (whether that's an email query or query form), even if you can find an agent's direct email address online. Most agents will specify a different email address for queries. Sending a query to their non-submission email doesn't make you clever—it makes you look like you

don't follow instructions. Allow them to consider your project how they want to, or you risk annoying or alienating them.

11. **DO NOT SEND ATTACHMENTS**, unless they are *specifically* requested. (Illustrators or writers who have commissioned illustrations can send a link to a website, password-protected page, or file to transmit a large sample image or picture book dummy. Some agents and publishers will not open links, in which case, you have to wait until they request more work and provide instructions for sending illustrations.)

12. Send to your A List first. That's right. Go for the brass ring right off the bat. Why? Because if you send to your C List or B List first, and someone offers, you will always be wondering whether someone on your A List would've responded favorably. This is the dreaded "What if?"

13. Wait six to eight weeks (some agents will specify a response time on their websites). In most cases, if you haven't heard back within this timeframe, that's a no. Sometimes, if they say they respond either way, you can send a polite check-in after this period to make sure they received your inquiry. While it's rare, emails can go to spam or get otherwise lost.

14. Most gatekeepers will consider a manuscript again after they've rejected it, but only if considerable revision has taken place. Be honest that it's a resubmission in your query when you re-approach.

Now let's drill down to the submission materials themselves, and tackle that query letter.

Hone Your Pitch and Logline

A "pitch," "logline," and "elevator pitch" are related terms for a quick written or verbal summary of your story, meant to be communicated in an enticing way. While the terms and definitions can differ, the point of a pitch is the same: To make listeners or readers want to know more, or to request your manuscript.

To write a compelling pitch, you need to think about the following:

- Who your character is and what they want;
- The biggest challenge or conflict they face;
- The personal stakes of this obstacle; and
- Anything interesting about your setting or premise (or any curriculum or sales hooks that might make your project attractive for the educational market, which is especially relevant for nonfiction picture books).

We get a sense of the **world**, the **character**, and the primary **conflict**. You'll also want to convey the theme and topic, of course. These are the primary ingredients of a strong pitch. Think of your logline as the beginning of a conversation.

Especially if you're pitching in person, don't just rattle this off and take all your available time reciting a prepared statement. Make sure to leave room for reactions and questions from the gatekeeper, if appropriate.

The above pitch ingredients are great for narrative projects, but not all picture books fit that category.

If you're writing a nonfiction or concept book that doesn't follow a narrative structure, focus instead on your sales hooks. Remember how I broke topics down in Chapter 6? Do that with your work. Why does the world need a nonfiction picture book about your topic (especially if others already exist)? What fresh angle are you bringing to your concept?

A standard pitch or logline combines all of the above. Here's a fiction example:

> Benny doesn't want to go to bed. No way, no how. So he decides to stay up all night. But when his younger brother has trouble falling asleep, Benny has a change of heart, with surprising results.

And a nonfiction pitch:

> If you've ever looked at the light switch faceplate on your wall and wondered whether it has a story, this book is for you. Did you know that this common household item was actually the topic of hot debate that raged for centuries? You'll never take the familiar for granted again.

Okay, so I totally made up the faceplate one, but it's an example of how to make a potentially dry or boring nonfiction topic sound fresh, appealing, undiscovered, and maybe a little mysterious.

You can use a "meets" structure (see my example in the next section) or a "What if?" or rhetorical question format to phrase these, too. If you've built your idea from the ground up by following this guide, you should have no problem identifying these key elements. Once you have a pitch, you can expand it into a query letter.

Query Components and Formatting

Query formatting confuses a lot of writers, but it is actually quite simple. Queries have several moving parts, and those components can be arranged in different configurations. Let's dive into some definitions of these basic ingredients.

The great news for picture book writers is that the query should be short, because in most cases, the manuscript is going to be included as part of your submission. So don't overthink the query, and use the pitch as a launch pad to generate interest instead.

Personalization: If you have a personal reason for contacting the agent or publisher, use it! For example, "I'm querying you because you represented my favorite book, *Title*." This is specific and speaks to that agent or publisher's experience.

- If you have a personal connection with the agent or acquiring editor, that's always relevant here, too. An example of bad personalization would be, "I'm querying you because of your passion for literature." This is vague and can be said of anyone working in publishing (one would hope). Agents and acquiring editors, of all people, can recognize a form letter.
- If something vague is the best you have to offer, omit the personalization element entirely. As you research the agents and publishers you're targeting, try to find some personalization details to use in your submission.
- Some publishers or agencies will direct you to a general submission box, so personalization is not always possible.
- **The personalization section is optional, but it can help you stand out in the slush pile.**

Comparative Titles: If you find that your work has something in common with books or authors already on shelves, feel free to use comparative titles, or "comp titles."

- Over the years, comp titles have grown in perceived importance. Writers obsess over them and ask about them at conferences. The belief is that good comps can make or break a query, but that's taking it a bit far.
- Compare your work to projects that have come out in the last three years, make sure at least one of those titles is in your category or was written for your audience (don't invoke two adult novels if you're writing a board book).
- Feel free to use different elements of a comparative title, for example, "The heartfelt quirk of Oliver Jeffers and the earnestness of Susan Verde."
- You can do a deep dive into this topic,[4] but make sure you're not procrastinating or getting distracted, as the comp title sentence is not the end all, be all.
- **This section is optional as well.**

Logline: The logline or elevator pitch, is defined above.

- You include your comps to make your point—"It's *Mr. Tiger Goes Wild* meets *Mel Fell.*"
- Or you can write a one-or-two sentence summary of the finer sales hooks of your story, including the character and primary conflict.
- **Loglines are also largely optional**, because you are going to be pitching the story in much more detail with the query meat, defined below.
- But if you are not using personalization or comparative titles, which are some other optional query ingredients, you may want to consider creating a logline.

---

4. There are some articles that dive deeper into comparative titles linked in Appendix B.

Manuscript Logistics: This section of the query is where you mention the title, word count, and anything else relevant to your manuscript, like whether it's in verse or not.

- For example, "TITLE is a 600-word bedtime story told in rollicking rhyme."
- **The title and word count are the bare minimum here.**
- You should include this section as close to the beginning of the query as possible, so gatekeepers can set their expectations.

The Query Meat: The most substantial part of the query is the one-to-three-paragraph description that present the character and plot of your fiction project.

- If you're a vegetarian or vegan, you can call this the "heart" of the query.
- For picture book manuscripts, which will likely follow the query in their entirety, this meat can be shorter. Picture books will focus on character, plot, any interesting or timely sales hooks, and the universal theme or lesson learned.
- Read the backs of published books and their sales page marketing copy. This is roughly the length and tone you're going for.
- The most well-crafted queries, in my opinion, are ones that make me care about the story and characters. They make me feel something. They make me want to know what happens next to characters that I've invested in.
- Keep your query letter to 250 to 400 words, or up to one single-spaced page. Picture book queries tend to be shorter, so if you're at 400 words, this is unusual (and likely unnecessary).

- Agents and editors want to hear from writers. They want good projects. They simply can't do their jobs without them. So present the juiciest, most compelling points of your story or concept, mention the important details outlined above, and, finally, have fun and be yourself. (But don't get too gimmicky or write *as* your character.[5] If it feels like a cheap trick to you, it'll come across that way in the slush pile.)

Biographical Information: This refers to information about you and your qualifications or writing experience.

- It's strange when this section is entirely missing, so think of at least one sentence to include. On the other hand, don't go overboard with voice, jokes, or personality.
- Don't make your bio longer than the query meat. Include only professional-sounding and relevant details.
- If you have writing credits, publications, or contest wins, make sure to cite the publication or contest name and year. Be specific, or readers will assume that your credits are self-published.
- If they are, say so. It's okay. There's no stigma here. (You may encounter a problem if you're pitching a project that was previous self-published, in an effort to have it reissued. See Appendix A for more on that scenario.)
- Avoid being too cheeky with your biography. Seriously. The number of cats you have is probably not going to be relevant, for example, unless you are working on a cat book. Focus on writing experience

---

5. Unless you're writing an autobiography, of course. Then you have no choice but to write as your character.

and life experience that relates to the book project at hand.

Query Logistics: This is your breezy sign-off to the query letter itself.

- It can literally be: *Per your guidelines, the complete manuscript is enclosed below. Please note that this is a simultaneous submission. Thank you very much for your time and consideration.*
- Simultaneous submissions (sending the pitch to more than one agent or publisher at a time) are considered industry standard, but they're still worth mentioning.
- That being said, remember not to submit to more than one agent at an agency or one acquiring editor at an imprint at a time! (Submissions to multiple agencies and publishers are fine, but you have to choose one name per target.)
- If one agent at an agency passes, you can submit to someone else there, but only once you no longer have anyone considering at the same venue.

Name and Contact Information: Exactly what it sounds like.

- Your real name, a pen name (if you're writing with one), the best contact info to reach you (ideally email and phone number minimum, no need for your mailing address), and then any web credentials, like your website URL and social media profiles.
- These can all go underneath the letter and your signature, on separate lines.

It's easy to get intimidated by queries. After all, you're condensing an entire story idea (and potentially months or years of work!) into a single page, putting it out into the world, and hoping it'll catch the eye of a busy agent of acquiring editor. I've been on the receiving end of tens of thousands of query letters, both as an agent and now as a freelance editor.

My book, *Successful Query Letters*, pulls together more than forty authentic letters that worked (and some that could use revision), and breaks them down, line by line, with comprehensive feedback on each. There's also a whole submission strategy section that gets very specific about how and where to send your work, and what to include in a compelling submission package. You're welcome to check it out for some more robust examples of entire picture book queries (this category is *very* well represented).

Organize Your Information

I've outlined the basic query elements above. You can rearrange them a bit, as you'll see. But for the most part, this is how they appear in queries. A few elements are optional. The more you can include (and the more correct and relevant your ingredients), the better. But keep that target 250-400-word total in mind. Just because queries are expected to cover a lot of ground doesn't mean they have to be long. To get you started, here are three perfectly valid versions of how you might want to organize your query letter. There is no one way of doing it "right," and if there was, some writers wouldn't get the memo anyway. These are my recommended options:

Example Query 1:

- Paragraph 1: Personalization
- Paragraph 2: Comps, Logline, Manuscript Logistics
- Paragraphs 3-5: Query Meat
- Paragraph 6: Bio Paragraph
- Paragraph 7: Query Logistics

- Name and Contact Info

Example Query 2:

- Paragraph 1: Manuscript Logistics and Comps
- Paragraphs 2-3: Query Meat
- Paragraph 4: Bio Paragraph
- Paragraph 5: Query Logistics
- Name and Contact Info

Example Query 3:

- Paragraphs 1-3: Query Meat
- Paragraph 4: Personalization and Manuscript Logistics
- Paragraph 5: Bio Paragraph
- Paragraph 6: Query Logistics
- Name and Contact Info

That's it. Try your query a few different ways and see what feels and reads right to you.

Putting Everything Together

First and foremost, write the best possible manuscript you can. This is really the most important part of the submission puzzle, so do not skimp on the time and energy it takes to perfect the project itself.

As mentioned at the beginning of this chapter, make sure you have two or three pretty solid picture book manuscripts revised and ready to go before you submit, too, as interested parties will usually ask what else you're working on. You'll be sending your strongest project first (and concentrating exclusively on it for the purposes of the query letter). Do not summarize all of your various projects in one query, though. They will ask for other pitches, if interested.

Get a strong sense of your project's sales hooks, and how you plan to pitch it. Is it a narrative story? A concept book? Make sure it fits the general expectations of your category, like word count. As discussed in Chapter 1, you can absolutely break category and genre rules, but it's harder to do so as an aspiring debut. You might want to save your total expectation-busting project for later in your career, unless you're certain that the market will respond positively.

Research your possible targets, from agents to publishers (if you want to submit directly to houses that are open to unagented submissions). Narrow down your final submission list of 10-15 agents and/or publishers (your A List), and keep another 10-15 in reserve (your B List).

Review the submission guidelines for each of your chosen targets. Then write and assemble your submission materials. For a picture book, agents and editors generally request a combination of these elements:

- Query letter;
- Manuscript;
- Dummy (if applicable): Make sure this can be accessed online via link or password-protected website, rather than sending this as a huge attachment.

Prepare your query and submission materials in a format that's ready to send. This is where some writers get tripped up because they have a beautifully formatted manuscript (thanks to Chapter 15), and now it has to go into an email or submission form text box. It therefore looks unfortunate—a mere imitation of its former glorious self. You worry that you'll seem unprofessional.

I suggest that you copy and paste your materials (the query and manuscript) into an email, send it to yourself, and copy and paste from *that* version of the document for all of those submission emails and forms. Copying and pasting from email to email or form preserves formatting more faithfully than copying and pasting from Word, Pages, or a Google Doc. You'll also want to keep that beautifully formatted manuscript file to send around, if one is requested.

It can be frustrating to send out materials according to slightly different requirements, as everyone has their own instructions. But following directions at this stage is worthwhile. I had an email slush pile for years. In fact, my first internship at a literary agency still had us reading paper mail submissions, so when I retire, my body will be put into a publishing museum, along with the other dinosaurs. If you start to feel anxious about your digital submission formatting, try to relax.

I guarantee—*guarantee*—that if you are trying, and you do the little copy-and-paste-from-email trick, above, you are going to be fine. Your submission might not preserve all of its formatting, but there is going to be someone else in that inbox that used Comic Sans font,[6] I promise. As long as you're not the least impressive (or unintentionally funny … there's a lot of that in the slush, too), you are right on track.

The Aftermath and Next Steps

Wait up to three months, or until you hear back from everyone who's going to respond to your submission round.

---

6. Resist the temptation of Comic Sans. Yes, it looks "juvenile" and seems "perfect" for a picture book. But this font is dated and uncool in a way that has made it the butt of Internet culture jokes. As discussed in Chapters 15 and 16, picture book visuals have leveled up considerably. Do not resort to Comic Sans, especially for a self-published project.

If you feel like your message was genuinely overlooked,[7] you can follow up after about six to eight weeks. Sometimes you won't hear back at all, and that's considered a decline.

Compile the responses you've received. Decide if you have enough new ideas to do a revision, and try resubmitting to a mix of agents who gave you feedback from your A List, and weave in some B List and C List targets this time around.

Perhaps you want to try independently publishing, or moving on to a new project while you consider what to do with your current work.

Decoding Rejections

It may surprise you to know that there are different levels of rejection. Each type means something specific, and I offer this explainer so you can see what the responses are *really* saying as they start to roll in.

Form Rejection: You are rejected but don't receive any feedback. Gatekeepers will sometimes personalize their response with your name and the title of your project, but they won't say anything specific about it.

- This is usually what people send when the writing isn't solid enough, the voice doesn't grab them, the idea doesn't resonate, etc. For whatever reason, it wasn't for them, and they knew that pretty quickly (if not immediately).
- They want to respond, so they send a template letter. You get one of these if your work is obviously not a fit or not polished enough for serious consideration.
- Watch out—sometimes rejections that *sound* personal

---

7. And you're sure it's not just denial over a "no response means no" rejection.

are actually still boilerplate verbiage. For example, "The voice didn't resonate with me as much as I would've liked." You think they're talking about you, but they probably send this same message 100 times a day. The craft concept of voice is nebulous enough that they can mention it without digging deeper, and some writers take this as custom feedback.

- It isn't malicious—they simply don't have time to go into detail with every submission, as that is the role of a critique partner or freelance editor.

Personal Rejection: The gatekeeper will still pass on the submission but provide general critique. They will use this rejection response either for a query that they thought had promise, or to call your attention to an easily articulated flaw in the writing.

- The project has potential, but issue X or Y is holding it back. Or maybe it isn't right for their list—which isn't something you, the writer, can control.
- Perhaps the agent or publisher will have thoughts on how it could be improved before they'd consider representing it—which you can take into account, if you wish.
- These rejections are a bit more specific but don't give detailed editorial notes. This type of decline is reserved for a project that has some spark but might require too much revision for the agent to seriously consider it at that moment.
- If you're getting a lot of these, that means you have some definite strengths, but there may be problems with the writing, plot, character, or overall premise.
- Sometimes these are the most frustrating rejections because they aren't detailed enough to guide you during revision, but you know the agent or editor

thought about the project for a while. They could've sent a form letter, but they didn't.

Revise and Resubmit: Also called an "R & R" in the industry. In this situation, the gatekeeper has spent some time with the project and will give you specific notes for revision.

- If you rewrite accordingly, the agent or editor would love to see it again.
- They will often ask to consider the project exclusively if you revise based on their notes.
- In this case, you may not end up getting representation, even if you do resubmit, but this is a very promising rejection. Those gatekeepers have hundreds of submissions to consider, but something about yours grabbed them.
- Keep submitting, even if the original gatekeeper has passed. This type of rejection means you're on the right track.

Some writers take rejection terribly, and I understand why. I don't blame anyone for resorting to some stress eating or squeezing out a few tears when a decline comes in.

However, keep in mind that rejections are *data*. As much as they seem personal, they are not. The gatekeeper isn't saying that *you* suck and should give up. They're saying that the project presented doesn't fit their list or their personal, subjective idea of what they think they can sell to their contacts in the industry.

Take the feedback and hold it until you can assemble a clearer picture of your submission round. I have clients who feverishly jump on every bit of critique they receive, rip their project apart, and do a major renovation after each rejection. They do this over and over.

If your project is that easy to dismantle and rebuild based on one piece of feedback, then it's not a strong or worthwhile project to begin with. It's much easier said than done, of course, to wait and stay the course, but you need to sit tight and focus on other things while you're out on submission, like your next project, or developing yourself and your platform.

Putting Things into Perspective

I initially started giving this advice to my picture book clients when I was an agent: Only one out of ten of your picture book ideas/manuscripts will be good enough for pitching to a literary agent or editor, *even if you're already represented.*

Writers with a stable of strong manuscripts might still face rejection from publishers or middling book sales once their work is available to readers. Traditional (and self-) publishing isn't about one amazing idea breaking through—it's an exercise in continuously improving your craft, staying on top of trends in the larger book and child-rearing worlds, and turning out dependable, lovely projects that hit several topics or sales hooks at once.

The entire process of publishing a picture book, having it released, and then marketing it, is obviously beyond the scope of this guide. However, it is never too soon to start building up your author platform, social media presence, and future marketing reach.

Work on your next project, develop your portfolio, create your online footprint, read writing reference books, take a class, go to a conference, and otherwise do professional development while you wait for the results of your submission round, or in the odd limbo period before a book is released into the world.

Writer Assets

The obvious stars of a picture book submission are the query letter and the manuscript itself. But you should know that agents and publishers are looking for all sorts of other things (hard assets and soft skills) when evaluating you and your work.

Here are some ideas for developing yourself as a writer and professional. You don't have to do all of these things at the same time, but if you ever find yourself stuck for ideas, consider pursuing one of these projects in parallel to working on your writing.

Remember to be professional in all of your dealings, especially online. If you want to be a professional writer, act like a professional writer, and present yourself well. Be sure to let everyone know about your successes by updating your social media—but be careful. People who only talk about themselves and their projects online don't gain a following. Be useful and helpful by sharing news stories and articles that your readers might find interesting. Remember to provide enriching content so that people see you as someone of value, not just an advertising channel for your own endeavors.

Here's what else you can be doing while on submission or alongside your active writing:

- Develop strong follow-up projects, whether part of a series or meant to stand alone. This is especially important for picture book writers, as agents and editors will generally always ask what other kinds of ideas you have. Remember, **I wouldn't suggest going on submission at all unless you have two or three projects polished and ready to go**.
- Pursue placing articles or short pieces in blogs, literary magazines, online journals, and trade

magazines. Whether they're relevant to your project topic or not, professional writing clips will help establish your experience as a writer and demonstrate that you're serious about your craft.

- Develop a strong informational website. Here's what to include:

  Compelling static homepage with info about you;

  A more detailed About page with links to clips and published work;

  A Projects page (avoid posting manuscript materials and focus on short summaries instead);

  A Contact page (with a form or email link); and

  A blog that's updated once a month to keep it alive (if time allows, though you might want to develop your social media presence instead).

- Nurture your social media footprint, or at least create some profiles for your brand on X/Twitter,[8] Instagram, TikTok, etc. Deliver good value and interesting content, rather than talking solely about yourself or pushing any existing books. Remember that marketing is a two-way street!
- Attend conferences and writing events. Go to as many as you can, both regional and in big media cities (New York, Los Angeles, etc., if you're able), and write about your experiences on your website or social media. Practice pitching your work at events or online so that you're always putting yourself out

---

8. Whatever this social media platform is called now, if it still exists when you're reading this.

there. Virtual conferences make this easier, in terms of both time and budget.

- Patronize local literary events. Get a feel for your immediate writing community. Network with other writers, if applicable, without being too self-serving.
- Participate in message boards and forums. Contribute to threads and build up a following in writing communities online. Other writers are going to be your biggest readers and supporters early on, so it's never too soon to connect with them.

The publishing marketplace, literary agent responses, and sales numbers are largely out of your control. Your own commitment to your work, learning your craft, and pushing the boundaries of your creativity, however, are within reach. Focus here as you forge your way forward as a picture book creator.

CONCLUSION

CREATING a picture book allows you to leave your mark on the world. It's about expressing yourself in a way that inspires a child, a family, and a larger community.

It's about reaching a person in one of the most dynamic stages of their existence, when they're learning all about being alive. The things you have to say to a child are some of the most essential and important ideas you'll ever express.

Doing so is an opportunity and a responsibility, and your picture book audience deserves nothing but the best. The seeds you plant in their minds and hearts at this incredibly fruitful and fertile time might blossom in ways you can't even imagine.

There is no more pure and powerful calling than writing for the picture book audience. Leave your reader with something incredible, give them the keys to a more successful and compassionate life, and take their creative spirits to new heights.

The great part is, as a picture book writer and/or illustrator, you get to go on one heck of a quest yourself, in order to take your young reader on a journey of their own.

I hope you've learned a lot and broken open in your understanding of the picture book market, its available opportunities, and how you can succeed in a way that's irresistible to everyone around you.

Writing is all about the process, not just the product, and I hope that this picture book pursuit takes you in the direction of your wildest dreams.

APPENDIX A: SELF-PUBLISHING

The complex topic of self-publishing a picture book is beyond the scope of this guide. There are, however, excellent in-depth resources, like *How to Self-Publish and Market a Children's Book* by Karen P. Inglis, and *How to Self-Publish a Children's Picture Book* by Eve Heidi Bine-Stock, if you want to do a deeper dive.

I will leave writers interested in self-publishing with a few considerations, though, which I've developed in my years of experience with both "trad" (traditional) and "indie" (independently published, not to be confused with a small or "independent publisher") picture book creators.

First of all, self-published projects live and die by two things:

- **Production**: The end product needs to be high-quality, from the story itself, to the writing style, to the choice of illustrator, to your paper and binding selection; and
- **Marketing**: When you self-publish, you will need to work hard for each sale, especially at the beginning, before your project gains natural momentum (though

there's no guarantee it will). I can't tell you how many people have said to me, "The project is so good, it'll sell itself!" It most certainly will not.

Every day, people press the *Publish* button on KDP and upload their work directly to the open market. "If you build it, they will come" no longer applies to self-published projects. To be a successful self-publisher, you need to be a marketer. If that notion makes you queasy, odds are good that self-publishing will not end up being the right fit for you.

Your picture book audience for self-published projects has largely had their expectations trained by traditionally published books. Yes, it matters less now *who* published something, because everything is lumped together in one giant marketplace online. However, while some barriers to favorable public perception are lower, reader expectations are higher than ever.

As I've said several times in this guide, you can do whatever you want, especially when you self-publish. But your odds of succeeding with a category-busting moonshot are going to be low if you don't also fulfill your audience's inherent expectations of what a picture book is.

Some of those expectations are forged by the traditional publishers and their products. They are:

- Contemporary-style illustrations and a good-looking jacket, because customers absolutely judge a book by its cover;
- A physical version of the book available for sale, as many parents read to their kids after school or at bedtime, and an ebook version would necessitate using a computer, phone, or tablet. Be aware that some families like to minimize screen time, even if the content on that screen is educational. Most picture

books are enjoyed in analog format, whether hardcover (preferred) or paperback, so you need to make this option available by purchasing a print run or via POD ("print on demand") to be competitive; and

- Distribution presence that allows you to reach schools, libraries, and bookstores. Many self-publishing platforms, like IngramSpark, will advertise that they can get you into distribution pipelines, but it's very rare to experience any kind of inroad into the physical brick-and-mortar space, without significant effort on your part to connect with schools, libraries, and booksellers directly.

The tools to self-publish have never been better or more robust. But self-publishing a picture book is still a pretty involved process, and picture books are perhaps the most investment-intensive of all the categories that you can choose to produce. When you self-publish, you need to pay for the illustrations—and any revisions, if you sequence your work-flow incorrectly and don't finalize the manuscript before you commission the art.

Strong picture book art, as discussed in Chapter 15, costs a lot of money. And you need appealing, stylish, contemporary, and consistent art in order to be competitive. Anecdotally, I can share that very few self-published picture book creators who have spent thousands of dollars on illustrations are able to recoup their investments through book sales.

Submitting a Previously Self-Published Project

Self-publishing can be great, but it can also be a lot of hard work (which I will hammer home in the next section, if I haven't made myself clear already). Self-publishing, however, is publishing. It's right there in the name!

I cannot tell you the number of well-meaning writers who have self-published a project, then show up to our consulting call and say, "Well, I tried it, and I think it's ready to go on submission!"

And I'm like, "Come again?"

They say that they tried self-publishing, realized it was pretty hard, but they still believe in their idea, and they'd like to try for a literary agent and a publisher now.

Except ... the book ... is ... already published.

Clicking *Publish* on the self-publishing interface should have been a dead giveaway.

But no, every day, writers try self-publishing, realize that it's a very specific skill set, and want to undo it and aim for traditional publishing again, with the same project.

To be perfectly clear, agents and publishers are unlikely to be interested in a project that's already published. They're even less likely to be interested in the follow-up installment in a series where the first book was self-published (because this would mean they'll need to republish the entire series, and that's an expensive proposition). Why?

They figure that you've already tapped your network, and anyone who's going to buy this project has bought it. If it took off, they would know, because you would have impressive sales numbers. But, more often than not, it didn't, and if they come in and republish it (which is, again, expensive), they might not be the magic bullet that turns the project around and makes it start selling.

If your self-published project has a solid track record—1,000 sales per year or more—then an agent or publisher *might* take notice. Still, unless you have a runaway bestseller on your hands, they might prefer to bring a brand-new product to market with you, rather than republishing a property that already exists for sale.

You are absolutely welcome to mention any previous self-publishing history in your query letter if you are submitting a new project to agents and publishers. That's fine. There's a lot less stigma now, and having previously self-published can even demonstrate that you are committed and have taken the time to complete a project and learn the industry.

But if you are submitting a project that has already been self-published, and you want it reissued by a traditional publisher, or you want a follow-up to a self-published book traditionally published, you are unlikely to get anywhere unless you have a serious sales track record.

Because the book is already published.

But Seriously—Marketing

When you self-publish, especially at the beginning of your career, when you don't have much of a platform or an email list or connections in the industry, you will be single-handedly responsible for every single book sale. The needle will only move when you move it.

Moreover, the Amazon algorithm will bury you within days of publication unless you learn strategies to rise on its fickle waters. You're also likely going to be invisible to the distribution pipelines that cater to school and libraries and book fairs, cutting you off from big potential sales opportunities for picture books.

If you're just starting out, you probably don't have money to spend on ads, but a lot of self-published books depend on ads to reliably bring in sales (as long as the cover, marketing copy, and existing reviews are doing their jobs and converting curious browsers into customers when they hit your product page).

I don't want to bum you out, but when you self-publish, you need to be very aware that you are now a marketer, selling a product. You are not an artist, you are not a writer, you are not a creative (at least not immediately).

You are now the sales and marketing department of a publishing house, and you need to have strategies in place for (ideally) the year before your publication date, lists of contacts to reach out to, and ideas for how to make the world sit up and take notice. (I'll mention my Marketing Mastery Toolbox resource in the next appendix, but I'm not saying all this to sell you anything. I'm saying this because I really need you to know what you're up against before you spend tens of thousands of dollars on illustrations to finalize an indie picture book.)

If you are clear-eyed and intentional about self-publishing picture books, you could make a lovely niche for yourself. But self-publishing is not the answer if you're resentful that the traditional publishing industry has rejected you, and you see going indie a shortcut or back door onto shelves. Self-publishing is also not the answer if you are hoping to be a runaway bestseller tomorrow.

It's a choice. There are so many amazing strategies to learn, and tools to use, when you self-publish. But to be clear, it's also swapping out one hat—that of creator—for another—that of marketer. The people who aren't expecting this, or can't get excited about it, are generally in for a rude awakening.

Self-publishing should be intentional, rather than seen as a fallback. There are some great resources, not specific to picture books, that can help you get acclimated. Two I've personally studied, in addition to the guides cited at the beginning of this section, are:

Kindlepreneur: https://kindlepreneur.com/

Mark Dawsons's Self Publishing Formula[1]: https://selfpub lishingformula.com/

In the introduction to this guide, I made a point to say that the writers who thrive in today's modern marketplace tend to be those who are open-minded and open-hearted, especially when it comes to learning new things. Nowhere is that truer than in self-publishing. I hope you're able to educate yourself, engage in some robust self-inquiry, and take the indie picture book market by storm!

---

1. I have purchased software and/or classes from both, and have no finan-cial incentive for recommending them.

APPENDIX B: RESOURCES

Articles and Resources Mentioned In This Book

- "Writing a Proactive Protagonist": https://kidlit. com/writing-a-proactive-protagonist/
- "Will AI Replace Creative Writers?": https://www. marykole.com/will-ai-replace-creative-writers
- "Comp Titles in a Query and Other Questions About Book Comps": https://kidlit.com/comp-titles-in-a-query-book-comps
- "Finding Comp Titles": https://goodstorycompany.-com/blog/finding-comp-titles
- "Finding Critique Partners": https://www. goodstorycompany.com/blog/critique-partners
- "Don't Be Fucking Precious" Sticker: https://www. goodstorycompany.com/shop/p/fucking-precious-sticker
- Readability Formula Checker: https://bit.ly/ pbreadability
- Printable Picture Book Layout Downloads: https:// goodstorycompany.com/pb-vip

- Manuscript Wish List: https://manuscriptwishlist.com
- Association of American Literary Agents: https://aalitagents.org
- Literary Rambles: https://literaryrambles.com
- Agent Query: https://agentquery.com
- Writer's Digest: https://writersdigest.com
- Duotrope: https://duotrope.com
- Publishers Marketplace: https://publishersmarketplace.com
- Publishing Paid Me Spreadsheet: https://bit.ly/pubpm
- Submission Tracker Spreadsheet: https://bit.ly/subspreadsheet (Go to "File" and then "Make a copy …" to repurpose it for yourself on your own Google Drive.)
- Marketing Toolbox from Good Story Learning: https://goodstorycompany.com/membership/

Resources to Find Illustrators, Editors, and Other Collaborators:

- Deviant Art: https://www.deviantart.com/
- Reedsy: https://reedsy.com
- 99 Designs: https://99designs.com/
- Upwork: https://www.upwork.com/
- Fiverr: https://www.fiverr.com/
- SCBWI: https://www.scbwi.org/
- Good Story Editing: https://goodstoryediting.com

Additional Useful Articles

- "Books That Teach Life Lessons": https://kidlit.com/books-that-teach-life-lessons

- "How to Write Child Characters With Their Own Wisdom": https://kidlit.com/how-to-write-child-characters
- "How to Write a Picture Book Query": https://kidlit.com/picture-book-query
- "Writing Nonfiction Picture Books": https://kidlit.com/nonfiction-picture-books
- "Including Illustration Notes In Your Children's Book Manuscript": https://kidlit.com/childrens-book-manuscript
- "How to be a Good Critique Partner": https://www.goodstorycompany.com/blog/how-to-be-a-good-critique-partner

Webinars

I've spent over a decade creating educational materials for writers and designing courses, books, and services on writing and publishing topics. I regularly teach free webinars about query letters, character, plot, and first pages. Some webinars offer the opportunity for live feedback.

Please check out a current list of my upcoming workshops here:

https://goodstorycompany.com/workshops

I'm also available to Zoom into your critique group or design a presentation or workshop for a writing retreat or conference.

Editorial Services, Ghostwriting, and Writing Workshops

If you enjoyed this book, consider getting personalized one-on-one advice from me. My specialty is deep developmental editing on your entire manuscript. Alternatively, I am happy to step in as a ghostwriter or offer ghost revision for your project. We can also work together in a small group writing workshop intensive setting.

Developmental Editing Services:

https://marykole.com

Ghost Revision and Ghostwriting Services:

https://manuscriptstudio.com

Story Mastermind Small Group Writing Workshops:

https://storymastermind.com

Books and Courses

It is my (perhaps manic) goal to create as many writing resources in as many formats as possible. I hope you find these books and courses useful. I'm always so grateful when a written or recorded version of me can be of service.

***Writing Irresistible Kidlit* Book:**

https://bit.ly/kolekidlit

***Successful Query Letters* Book:**

https://amzn.to/46gJr9i

Writing Mastery Academy Character Class:

With by Jessica Brody, of *Save the Cat Writes a Novel* fame!

https://www.writingmastery.com

Writing Blueprints Submission Resource:

If a deep dive into the submission process sounds helpful, this self-paced course contains over ten hours of instruction. There will definitely be some information overlap between the class and this book, but you'll also get access to agent interviews, over thirty handouts, and a comprehensive step-by-step submission guide.

https://bit.ly/kolesub

LinkedIn Learning:

https://www.linkedin.com/learning/crafting-dynamic-characters/

Udemy:

These budget-friendly classes cover assorted writing and publishing topics in an easy-to-digest format.

https://www.udemy.com/user/mary-kole/

Good Story Company

In 2019, I decided to create Good Story Company as an umbrella brand so that my amazing team and I could collaborate in the service of writing and writers. GSC is where you'll find our most comprehensive library of resources and services.

Good Story Company:

https://goodstorycompany.com

Good Story Podcast:

https://goodstorypodcast.com

Good Story YouTube Channel:

https://youtube.com/goodstory

Writing Craft Workshop Membership:

https://www.goodstorycompany.com/membership/

Good Story Marketing:

https://goodstorycompany.com/marketing

Picture Book Downloadable Resources:

https://goodstorycompany.com/pb-vip

Workshops:

https://goodstorycompany.com/workshops

APPENDIX C: LIST OF CITED WORKS

ANALYZED WORKS

I'm putting each analyzed book's word count in parentheses after the project's listing. These numbers are as accurate as I could get them. The word counts do not include title pages, copyright pages, or back matter.

CONCEPT BOOKS

Berger, Samantha. *What If...*. Illustrated by Mike Curato, Little, Brown Books for Young Readers, 2018. (255)

Brown, Margaret Wise. *Goodnight Moon*. Illustrated by Clement Hurd, Harper & Row, 1947. (141)

Catalanotto, Peter. *Ivan the Terrier*. Simon & Schuster Books for Young Readers, 2007. (183)

Curry, Jessica and Parker Curry. *Parker Looks Up: An Extraordinary Moment*. Illustrated by Brittany Jackson, Aladdin, 2019. (404)

Daywalt, Drew. *The Day the Crayons Quit*. Illustrated by Oliver Jeffers, Philomel Books, 2013. (1,019)

Deeley, Cat and Laura Baker. *The Joy in You*. Illustrated by Rosie Butcher, Random House Books for Young Readers, 2022. (227)

Haneline, Tiania and Scarlett Gray. *I'm Going to Have a Good Day!* Illustrated by Stephanie Dehennin, Zonderkidz, 2023. (382)

Hitchman, Jess. *All Kinds of Awesome*. Illustrated by Vivienne To, Feiwel & Friends, 2021. (113)

Karst, Patrice. *The Invisible String*. Illustrated by Geoff Stevenson, DeVorss Publications, 2000. (540)

Klein, Cheryl and Katy Beebe. *Thunder Trucks*. Illustrated by Mike Boldt, Little, Brown Books for Young Readers, 2019. (459)

Kuipers, Alice. *Violet and Victor Write the Most Fabulous Fairy Tale*. Illustrated by Bethanie Deeney Murguia, Little, Brown Books for Young Readers, 2016. (469)

LaRochelle, David. *Monster & Son*. Illustrated by Joey Chou, Chronicle Books, 2016. (163)

Llenas, Anna. *The Color Monster*. Little, Brown Books for Young Readers, 2018. (297)

MacLeod, Mrs. & Mr. *How to Eat a Book*. Union Square Kids, 2022. (411)

McGhee, Alison. *So Many Days*. Illustrated by Taeeun Yoo, Atheneum Books for Young Readers, 2010. (251)

McPike, Elizabeth. *Little Bitty Friends*. Illustrated by Patrice Barton, G.P. Putnam's Sons, 2017. (96)

Mora, Oge. *Thank You, Omu!* Little, Brown Books for Young Readers, 2018. (864)

O'Leary, Wendy. *The Monster Parade : A Book about Feeling All Your Feelings and Then Watching Them Go*. Illustrated by Noémie Gionet Landry, Bala Kids, 2022. (285)

Pearlman, Robb. *Dolls and Trucks Are for Everyone*. Illustrated by Eda Kaban, Running Press Kids, 2021. (224)

Peterson, Ellie. *How to Hug a Pufferfish*. Roaring Brook Press, 2022. (230)

Petrus, Junauda. *Can We Please Give the Police Department to the Grandmothers?* Illustrated by Kristen Uroda, Dial Books for Young Readers, 2023. (617)

Rosenthal, Amy Krouse. *Duck! Rabbit!* Illustrated by Tom Lichtenheld, Chronicle Books, 2014. (210)

Rosenthal, Amy Krouse. *Little Hoot*. Illustrated by Jen Corace, Chronicle Books, 2010. (367)

Rosenthal, Amy Krouse. *Plant a Kiss*. Illustrated by Peter H. Reynolds, Harper Festival, 2015. (92)

Rosenthal, Paris, and Jason B. Rosenthal. *Dear Boy,* Illustrated by Holly Hatam, HarperCollins, 2020. (274)

Sainte-Marie, Buffy. *Still This Love Goes On*. Illustrated by Julie Flett, Greystone Books, 2022. (240)

Scanlon, Elizabeth Garton. *All the World*. Illustrated by Marla Frazee, Beach Lane Books, 2009. (194)

Shang, Wendy Wan-Long. *The Rice in the Pot Goes Round and Round*. Illustrated by Lorian Tu, Orchard Books, 2021. (326)

Shumaker, Debra Kempf. *Tell Someone*. Illustrated by Tristan V. Yuvienco, Albert Whitman & Company, 2021. (344)

Soundar, Chitra. *Holi Hai!* Illustrated by Darshika Varma, Albert Whitman & Company, 2022. (651)

Sutton, Sally. *Wheels*. Illustrated by Brian Lovelock, Candlewick Press, 2020. (169)

Thomas, Jan. *Rhyming Dust Bunnies*. Simon & Schuster Books for Young Readers, 2010. (126)

Vamos, Samantha R. *Alphabet Boats*. Illustrated by Ryan O'Rourke, Charlesbridge Publishing, 2018. (271)

Verde, Susan. *I Am One: A Book of Action*. Illustrated by Peter H. Reynolds, Abrams Appleseed, 2022. (184)

Wade, Cleo. *What the Road Said*. Illustrated by Lucie de Moyencourt, Feiwel & Friends, 2021. (759)

Wenzel, Brendan. *They All Saw a Cat*. Chronicle Books, 2020. (207)

Wheeler, Lisa. *Even Monsters Need to Sleep*. Illustrated by Chris Van Dusen, Balzer + Bray, 2017. (259)

Willard, Christopher, and Daniel Rechtschaffen. *Alphabreaths*. Illustrated by Holly Clifton-Brown, Sounds True Publishing, 2019. (573)

Willems, Mo. *Don't Let the Pigeon Drive the Bus!* Hyperion Books for Children, 2003. (125)

Woodcock, Fiona. *Look*. Greenwillow Books, 2018. (38)

Yamada, Kobi. *Maybe*. Illustrated by Gabriella Barouch, Compendium, 2019. (345)

Yolen, Jane. *How Do Dinosaurs Say Good Night?* Illustrated by Mark Teague, Blue Sky Press, 2000. (152)

Yolen, Jane. *What to Do with a Box*. Illustrated by Chris Sheban, Creative Editions, 2023. (150)

Yoshitake, Shinsuke. *The Boring Book*. Chronicle Books, 2019. (634)

Yulo, Nic. *Patch of Sky*. Dial Books for Young Readers, 2022. (395)

Zommer, Yuval. *The Lights that Dance in the Night*. Doubleday Books for Young Readers, 2021. (225)

NARRATIVE

Aronson, Kate. *Clovis Keeps His Cool*. Illustrated by Eve Farb, Page Street Kids, 2021. (730)

Ashman, Linda. *Maxwell's Magic Mix-Up*. Illustrated by Regan Dunnick, Simon & Schuster Books for Young Readers, 2001. (685)

Barnett, Mac. *Extra Yarn*. Illustrated by Jon Klassen, Balzer + Bray, 2012. (565)

Beaton, Kate. *The Princess and the Pony*. Arthur A. Levine Books, 2014. (479)

Beaty, Andrea. *Iggy Peck, Architect*. Illustrated by David Roberts, Abrams Books for Young Readers, 2007. (702)

Berger, Barbara. *Grandfather Twilight*. Philomel Books, 1984. (98)

Bernstrom, Daniel. *Gator, Gator, Gator*. Illustrated by Frann Preston-Gannon, HarperCollins, 2018. (531)

Bernstrom, Daniel. *Good Night, Little Man*. Illustrated by Heidi Woodward Sheffield, HarperCollins, 2023. (454)

Brown, Peter. *Children Make Terrible Pets*. Little, Brown Books for Young Readers, 2010. (374)

Brown, Peter. *Mr. Tiger Goes Wild*. Balzer + Bray, 2013. (198)

Burach, Ross. *Pine & Boof: The Lucky Leaf*. HarperCollins, 2017. (364)

Carzoo, Breanna. *Lou*. HarperCollins, 2022. (197)

Chapman, Ty. *Sarah Rising*. Illustrated by Deann Wiley, Beaming Books, 2022. (565)

Cooper, Elisha. *Beaver Is Lost*. Schwartz & Wade, 2010. (4)

Cronin, Doreen. *Click, Clack, Moo: Cows That Type*. Illustrated by Betsy Lewin, Simon & Schuster Books for Young Readers, 2000. (408)

Cummins, Lucy Ruth. *Stumpkin*. Atheneum Books For Young Readers, 2018. (401)

Desierto, Derek. *Oddbird*. Feiwel & Friends, 2021. (363)

Dewdney, Anna. *Llama, Llama, Red Pajama*. Viking Children's Books, 2005. (226)

DiPuccio, Kelly. *Zombie in Love*. Illustrated by Scott Campbell, Atheneum Books For Young Readers, 2011. (380)

Donaldson, Julia. *Room on the Broom*. Illustrated by Axel Scheffler, Puffin Books, 2001. (837)

Elliott, David. *Finn Throws a Fit!* Illustrated by Timothy Basil Ering, Candlewick Press, 2009. (105)

Fliess, Sue. *Race!* Illustrated by Edwardian Taylor, Little Bee Books, 2017. (193)

Forsythe, Matthew. *Mina*. Simon & Schuster Books for Young Readers, 2022. (460)

Goodrich, Carter. *Say Hello to Zorro!* Simon & Schuster Books for Young Readers, 2011. (308)

Gordon, David. *Smitten*. Atheneum Books For Young Readers, 2007. (788)

Henkes, Kevin. *Kitten's First Full Moon*. Greenwillow Books, 2004. (250)

Hoefler, Kate. *Courage Hats*. Illustrated by Jessixa Bagley, Chronicle Books, 2022. (452)

Higgins, Ryan T. *We Don't Eat Our Classmates*. Scholastic, 2018. (427)

Jeffers, Oliver. *The Heart and the Bottle*. Philomel Books, 2010. (285)

Jeffers, Oliver. *Lost and Found*. Philomel Books, 2005. (498)

Jenkins, Emily. *Sugar Would Not Eat It*. Illustrated by Giselle Potter, Schwartz & Wade, 2009. (920)

John, Jory. *The Bad Seed*. Illustrated by Pete Oswald, HarperCollins, 2017. (485)

Kaufman, Suzanne. *Confiscated*. Balzer + Bray, 2017. (197)

Kerascoët. *I Walk with Vanessa: A Story About a Simple Act of Kindness*. Schwartz & Wade, 2018. (0)

Klassen, Jon. *I Want My Hat Back*. Candlewick Press, 2011. (254)

Klassen, Jon. *We Found a Hat*, Candlewick Press, 2016. (214)

Krause, J. R. *Dragon Night*. G.P. Putnam's Sons, 2019. (588)

Kuefler, Joseph. *The Digger and the Flower*. Balzer + Bray, 2018. (288)

Lerch. *Swim! Swim!* James Proimos, Scholastic Press, 2010. (199)

Lies, Brian. *The Rough Patch*. Greenwillow Books, 2018. (366)

Lyall, Casey. *A Spoonful of Frogs*. Illustrated by Vera Brosgol, Greenwillow Books, 2022. (219)

Magruder, Nilah. *Wutaryoo*. Versify, 2022. (806)

Mahy, Margaret *Bubble Trouble*. Illustrated by Polly Dunbar, Clarion Books, 2008. (834)

Meddaugh, Susan. *Martha Speaks*. Houghton Mifflin Harcourt, 1992. (637)

Miller, Tim. *Moo Moo & Mr. Quackers Present What's Cooking, Moo Moo?* Balzer + Bray, 2018. (335)

Muhammad, Ibtihaj and S.K. Ali. *The Proudest Blue*. Illustrated by Hatem Aly, Little, Brown Books for Young Readers, 2019. (620)

Murguia, Bethanie Deeney. *Buglette: The Messy Sleeper*. Tricycle Press, 2011. (382)

Murray, Diana. *Grimelda and the Spooktacular Pet Show*. Illustrated by Heather Ross, Katherine Tegen Books, 2017. (878)

Napoleoni, Fabio. *Dragonboy*. Little, Brown Books for Young Readers, 2021. (575)

Norman, Kim. *Puddle Pug*. Illustrated by Keika Yamaguchi, Sterling Publishing, 2014. (408)

Olsen, Elizabeth and Robbie Arnett. *Hattie Harmony: Worry Detective*. Illustrated by Marissa Valdez, Viking, 2022. (1,008)

Otis, Chad. *A Little Ferry Tale*. Caitlyn Dlouhy Books, 2022. (521)

Parappukkaran, Sandhya. *The Boy Who Tried to Shrink His Name*. Illustrated by Michelle Pereira, Abrams Books for Young Readers, 2023.

Paulson, Norene. *Benny's True Colors*. Illustrated by Andy Passchier, Imprint, 2020. (606)

Peacock, Lou. *Toby Is a Big Boy*. Illustrated by Stephanie Christine Pym, Schwartz & Wade, 2018. (446)

Perez, Nomar. *Coqui in the City*, Dial Books for Young Readers, 2021. (735)

Petty, Dev. *I Don't Want to Be a Frog*. Illustrated by Mike Boldt, Doubleday Books for Young Readers, 2015. (384)

Petz, Moritz. *Badger Is Bored!* Illustrated by Amelie Jackowski, NorthSouth Books, 2022. (780)

Pilgrim, Eva. *Walter Does His Best!* Illustrated by Jessica Gibson, Tommy Nelson, 2021. (401)

Reul, Sarah Lynne. *Nerp!* Sterling Publishing, 2019. (55)

Rex, Adam. *On Account of the Gum*. Chronicle Books, 2020. (471)

Rex, Michael. *Eat Pete!* Nancy Paulsen Books, 2018. (237)

Rosenthal, Amy Krouse. *Uni the Unicorn*. Illustrated by Brigette Barrager, Random House Books for Young Readers, 2014. (282)

Rubin, Adam. *Dragons Love Tacos*. Illustrated by Daniel Salmieri, Dial Books for Young Readers, 2012. (506)

Santat, Dan. *The Adventures of Beekle: The Unimaginary Friend*. Little, Brown Books for Young Readers, 2014. (289)

Sauer, Tammi. *Your Alien*. Illustrated by Goro Fujita, Sterling Publishing, 2015. (321)

Sendak, Maurice. *Where the Wild Things Are*. HarperCollins, 1963. (338)

Shojaie, Rosemary. *The Snow Fox*. Starfish Bay Children's Books, 2020. (213)

Sima, Jessie. *Not Quite Narwhal*. Simon & Schuster Books for Young Readers, 2017. (458)

Small, David. *Imogene's Antlers*, Random House Books for Young Readers, 1985. (294)

Smith, Sydney. *Small in the City*. Neal Porter Books, 2019. (302)

Song, Mika. *Tea with Oliver*. HarperCollins, 2017. (358)

Tabor, Corey R. *Mel Fell*. Balzer + Bray, 2011. (289)

Taylor, E. Dee. *Lots of Cats*. HarperCollins, 2018. (309)

Underwood, Deborah. *Interstellar Cinderella*. Illustrated by Meg Hunt, Chronicle Books, 2015. (543)

Urbanovic, Jackie. *Duck Soup*. HarperCollins, 2008. (414)

Valentine, Madeline. *More Than Fluff*. Knopf Books for Young Readers, 2021. (327)

Verdad, Marcelo. *The Worst Teddy Ever*. Little, Brown Books for Young Readers, 2022. (312)

Watkinson, Jocelyn. *The Three Canadian Pigs*. Illustrated by Marcus Cutler, Sleeping Bear Press, 2022. (570)

West, Wallace. *Mighty Red Riding Hood: A Fairly Queer Tale*. Little, Brown Books for Young Readers, 2022. (835)

Willems, Mo. *Knuffle Bunny Too: A Case of Mistaken Identity*. Hyperion, 2007. (426)

Wulfekotte, Dana. *Rabbit & Possum*. Greenwillow Books, 2018. (367)

Wynter, Anne. *Nell Plants a Tree*. Illustrated by Daniel Miyares, Balzer + Bray, 2023. (237)

Yerkes, Jennifer. *A Funny Little Bird*. Sourcebooks, 2013. (186)

Ying, Jonathan. *Take a Ride by My Side*. Illustrated by Victoria Ying, HarperCollins, 2018. (276)

Ying, Victoria. *Meow!* HarperCollins, 2017. (21)

Yolen, Jane. *Owl Moon*. Illustrated by John Schoenherr, Philomel Books, 1987. (770)

Yoon, Helen. *Sheepish (Wolf Under Cover)*. Candlewick Press, 2021. (109)

Yoon, Salina. *Found*. Bloomsbury Children's Books, 2014. (214)

Zhang, Kat. *Amy Wu and the Warm Welcome*. Illustrated by Charlene Chua, Simon & Schuster Books for Young Readers, 2022. (559)

Zimmerman, Andrea and David Clemesha. *Smashy Town*. Illustrated by Dan Yaccarino, HarperCollins, 2020. (277)

NONFICTION

Barton, Bethany. *I'm Trying to Love Garbage*. Viking, 2021. (1,051)

Fishman, Seth. *A Hundred Billion Trillion Stars*. Illustrated by Isabel Greenberg, Greenwillow Books, 2017. (512)

Holub, Joan. *Zero the Hero*. Illustrated by Tom Lichtenheld, Christy Ottaviano Books, 2012. (1,273)

Kyung, Hyewon. *Bigger Than You*. Greenwillow Books, 2018. (53)

Messier, Mireille. *Sergeant Billy: The True Story of the Goat Who Went to War*. Illustrated by Kass Reich, Tundra Books, 2020. (843)

Sayre, April Pulley. *Thank You, Earth: A Love Letter to Our Planet*. Greenwillow Books, 2018. (158)

Shetterly, Margot Lee. *Hidden Figures: The True Story of Four Black Women and the Space Race*. Illustrated by Laura Freeman, Greenwillow Books, 2018. (1,301)

Winter, Jonah and Jeanette. *Oil*. Beach Lane Books, 2020. (367)

Yolen, Jane. *On Gull Beach*. Illustrated by Bob Marstall, The Cornell Lab, 2020. (218)

NARRATIVE NONFICTION

Chen, Eva. *I Am Golden*. Illustrated by Sophie Diao, Feiwel & Friends, 2022. (461)

Erdrich, Louise. *The Range Eternal*. Illustrated by Steve Johnson and Lou Francher, The University of Minnesota Press, 2002. (1,261)

Ho, Joanna. *Eyes that Kiss in the Corners*. Illustrated by Dung Ho, Harper-Collins, 2021. (399)

Marquez, Melissa Cristina. *Mother of Sharks*. Illustrated by Devin Elle Kurtz, Penguin Workshop, 2023. (1,842)

McDonnell, Patrick. *Me … Jane*. Little, Brown Books for Young Readers, 2011. (222)

Norman, Lisette. *Platanos Go with Everything*. Illustrated by Sara Palacios, HarperCollins, 2023. (702)

Nyong'o, Lupita. *Sulwe*. Illustrated by Vashti Harrison, Simon & Schuster Books for Young Readers, 2019. (863)

Parra, John. *Growing an Artist: The Story of a Landscaper and His Son*. Simon & Schuster Books for Young Readers, 2022.

Patel, Meenal. *Priya Dreams of Marigolds & Marsala*. Beaver's Pond Press, 2019. (693)

Yang, Kao Kalia. *From the Tops of the Trees*. Illustrated by Rachel Wada, Carolrhoda Books, 2021. (1,183)

Wagon, Brad and Alex Stephenson. *The First Fire: A Cherokee Story*. Seventh Generation, 2020. (919)

NOT ANALYZED BUT CITED

WRITING GUIDES

Bine-Stock, Eve Heidi. *How to Self-Publish a Children's Picture Book: The Easy and Inexpensive Way to Create a Book and eBook: For Non-Designers*, 2016.

Brewer, Robert Lee. *Writer's Market*. One-hundredth ed., Writer's Digest Books, 2021.

Brody, Jessica. *Save the Cat! Writes a Novel: The Last Book on Novel Writing You'll Ever Need*. Ten Speed Press, 2010.

Ferguson, Margaret W., Tim Kendall, and Mary Jo Salter. *The Norton Anthology of Poetry*. Sixth ed., W. W. Norton & Company, 2018.

Inglis, Karen P. *How to Self-Publish and Market a Children's Book*. 2018.

Jones, Amy. *Children's Writer's & Illustrator's Market*. Thirty-third ed., Writer's Digest Books, 2021.

Karr, Mary. *The Art of Memoir*. HarperCollins, 2015.

Kole, Mary. *Successful Query Letters*, 2023.

Kole, Mary. *Writing Irresistible Kidlit*. Writer's Digest Books, 2012.

Marcus, Leonard S. *Dear Genius: The Letters of Ursula Nordstrom*. HarperCollins, 2000.

Murakami, Haruki. *Novelist as a Vocation*. Alfred A. Knopf, 2022.

Paul, Ann Whitford. *Writing Picture Books*. Second ed., Writer's Digest Books, 2018.

Snyder, Blake. *Save the Cat! The Last Book on Screenwriting You'll Ever Need*. Michael Wiese Productions, 2005.

BOOKS

Ahmed, Roda. *Mae Among the Stars*. Illustrated by Stasia Burrington, HarperCollins, 2018.

Andreae, Giles. *Giraffes Can't Dance*. Illustrated by Guy Parker-Rees, Orchard Books, 2001.

Arena, Jen. *Acorn Was a Little Wild*. Illustrated by Jessica Gibson, Simon & Schuster Books for Young Readers, 2022.

Barnett, Mac. *Sam and Dave Dig a Hole*. Illustrated by Jon Klassen, Candlewick Press, 2014.

Bemelmans, Ludwig. *Madeline*. Viking Children's Books, 1939.

Blake, Quentin. *Three Little Monkeys*. Illustrated by Emma Chichester Clark, HarperCollins, 2017.

Boisrobert, Anouck. *Under the Ocean*. Illustrated by Louis Rigaud, Tate Publishing, 2014.

Brown, Peter. *My Teacher Is a Monster! (No, I Am Not.)* Little, Brown Books for Young Readers, 2014.

Burach, Ross. *Pine & Boof: Blast Off!* HarperCollins, 2018.

Burton, Jeffrey. *The Wheels on the Fire Truck*. Illustrated by Alison Brown, Little Simon, 2019.

Chapman, Gary. *The Five Love Languages: How to Express Heartfelt Commitment to Your Mate*. Manjul Publishing House, 2001.

Clark, Karla. *You Be Mommy*. Illustrated by Zoe Persico, Feiwel & Friends, 2020.

Cline-Ransome Lesa. *Before She Was Harriet*. Illustrated by James E. Ransome, Holiday House, 2019.

Colleen, Marcie. *Love, Triangle*. Illustrated by Bob Shea, Balzer + Bray, 2017.

Dalton, Angela. *To Boldly Go: How Nichelle Nichols and Star Trek Helped Advance Civil Rights*. Illustrated by Lauren Semmer, HarperCollins, 2023.

Frazee, Marla. *Boss Baby*. Beach Lane Books, 2010.

Gorman, Amanda. *The Hill We Climb*. Viking, 2021.

Greening, Rosie. *Never Touch the Monsters*. Make Believe Ideas, 2020.

Hegedus, Bethany. *Alabama Spitfire: The Story of Harper Lee and To Kill a Mockingbird*. Illustrated by Erin McGuire, Balzer + Bray, 2021.

Jeffers, Oliver. *This Moose Belongs to Me*. Philomel Books, 2012.

Krause, J.R. and Maria Chua. *Poco Loco*. Two Lions, 2013.

Leaf, Munro. *The Story of Ferdinand*. Illustrated by Lawson, Robert. Viking Children's Books, 1936.

Martin, Emily Winfield. *The Wonderful Things You Will Be*. Random House Books for Young Readers, 2015.

Novak, B.J. *The Book with No Pictures*. Rocky Pond Books, 2014.

Numeroff, Laura. *If You Give a Mouse a Cookie*. Illustrated by Felicia Bond, HarperCollins, 2015.

O'Connor, Jane. *Fancy Nancy*. Illustrated by Robin Preiss Glasser, HarperCollins, 2015.

Paul, Ann Whitford. *If Animals Kissed Good Night*. Illustrated by David Walker, Farrar, Straus and Giroux Books for Young Readers, 2008.

Rash, Andy. *Ten Little Zombies*. Chronicle Books, 2010.

Raczka, Bob. *Guyku: A Year of Haiku for Boys*. Illustrated by Peter H. Reynolds, Clarion Books, 2018.

Rockliff, Mara. *The Busiest Street in Town*. Illustrated by Sarah McMenemy, Knopf Books for Young Readers, 2009.

Rosenthal, Amy Krouse. *Little Oink*. Illustrated by Jen Corace, Chronicle Books, 2010.

Sadler, Marilyn. *Elizabeth and Larry*. Illustrated by Roger Bollen, Aladdin, 1992.

Salas, Laura Purdie. *Clover Kitty Goes to Kittygarten*. Illustrated by Hiroe Nakata, Two Lions, 2020.

Schertle, Alice. *Little Blue Truck*. Illustrated by Jill McElmurry, Clarion Books, 2008.

Schertle, Alice. *Little Blue Truck Leads the Way*. Illustrated by Jill McElmurry, Clarion Books, 2009.

Shaskan, Stephen. *Toad on the Road: Mama and Me*. HarperCollins, 2018.

Stead, Philip C. *A Sick Day for Amos McGee*. Illustrated by Erin E. Stead, Roaring Brook Press, 2010.

Thomas, Jan. *A Birthday for Cow*. Clarion Books, 2018.

Thomas, Jan. *The Doghouse*. Clarion Books, 2018.

Tokuda-Hall, Maggie. *Love in the Library*. Illustrated by Yas Imamura, Candlewick Press, 2022.

Underwood, Deborah. *The Quiet Book.* Illustrated by Renata Liwska, Clarion Books, 2010.

Witek, Jo. *In My Heart: A Book of Feelings.* Illustrated by Christine Roussey, Abrams Appleseed, 2014.

WAIT! BEFORE YOU GO!

If you enjoyed this book, there are **three small things** you can do which would make a big difference to me and Good Story Company. Thank you so much for your time, kind attention, and consideration!

Subscribe to Our Newsletter

Our respectful, short, and non-spammy newsletter features all of our latest and greatest free resources, workshops, events, and critique opportunities. Go here to sign up:

https://bit.ly/hellogsc

Leave an Honest Review

Please also consider leaving a review for this title on your retailer of choice, as well as Goodreads. I love getting feedback of my own, and testimonials help greatly with our discoverability and marketing efforts, so that we can reach more writers.

Reach Out

Finally, I'd love to hear your experience and celebrate your accomplishments. If you run into some trouble in the writing and publishing worlds, don't be a stranger, either. Drop me a line:

mary@goodstorycompany.com

ACKNOWLEDGMENTS

This picture book guide started out after a phone consultation client said, randomly, "Hey, you should write a picture book guide." (If you recognize yourself here, reach out—I'd love to officially acknowledge you! I couldn't reconstruct the conversation and peg it to a specific call.)

I wasn't planning on it. I didn't think I had more than 30k words of stuff to say.

But then I became obsessed with picture books for, like, six months straight. (If you know me, you know I don't do anything lightly.) To be clear, I've always loved picture books, and specialized in editing them. However, I'd never turned my entire heart and soul over to them before.

It was a lovely experience.

The project quickly ballooned to 150+ books analyzed, several spreadsheets, 1,000 book deals catalogued, and a guide clocking in at over 100,000 words.

I hesitate to call anything my "magnum opus," because I have a feeling I'll become just as obsessed with another category or craft topic soon. (In fact, the surest way to guarantee that I'll write another book is to have me say, to anyone who will listen, "I am *never* writing another book. Oh my god, why do I do this to myself?????")

But this project really was an incredible labor of love and

quite literally consumed my every waking thought. I hope it's fruitful for you and your work.

A note of deep gratitude to everyone who had supported my work over the years, whether by reading one of my books, watching a video, working with me directly, showing up at book club, or checking out the podcast.

My team at Good Story Company allows me to do the work I love. Thank you to Kristen Overman, Amy Wilson, Rhiannon Richardson, Jenna Van Rooy, Kaylee Pereyra, and Kate London.

To all of my marvelous clients: Thank you for letting me cheer you on from the sidelines, and teaching me about your ideas and passions. I'm not talking about *you* when I make some of my more critical points, though.

To my business partners, the amazing John Cusick and Julie Murphy: Our work is why I get out of bed in the morning.

My gorgeous, smart, and funny best friends, Lauren Burris and Scott Marasigan: This one goes out to Scott, who schlepped a late-stage manuscript version of this book across Berkeley and Oakland for me while I was technically supposed to be on "vacation."

To Todd, Theo, Finn, Ella, Gertie, Olive, and Luna: I love you with my entire heart.

ALSO BY MARY KOLE

Writing Irresistible Kidlit: The Ultimate Guide to Crafting Fiction for Young Adult and Middle Grade Readers

Writing Irresistible Picture Books: Insider Insights Into Crafting Compelling Modern Stories for Young Readers

Successful Query Letters: 40+ Real World Query Letters With Literary Agent Feedback

How to Write a Book Now: Craft Concepts, Mindset Shifts, and Encouragement to Inspire Your Creative Writing

Writing Interiority: Crafting Irresistible Characters

www.ingramcontent.com/pod-product-compliance
Lightning Source LLC
Chambersburg PA
CBHW070050030426
42335CB00016B/1843

PRAISE FOR MARY KOLE

"Mary truly is amazing! Thanks to her, I have learned so much about writing. She made me laugh. She made me cry. She made me a better writer!"

M. CHURCHILL

"I've read many books on the craft of writing, and *Writing Irresistible Kidlit* is among the best. I've never been so excited to get to the keyboard."

ALAN HARELL

"The advice is wonderful, thoughtful, and so clearly written that no writer could read *Writing Irresistible Kidlit* and not walk away with something gained from it."

ASHLEE W.

"*Writing Irresistible Kidlit* is hands-down the best writing book I've read in years. It's a masterclass in a book."

ALISON S.

"I can't begin to say how helpful *Writing Irresistible Kidlit* has been for my own writing journey."

JOEL A.

"*Writing Irresistible Picture Books* is insightful, invaluable, and incredibly thorough! It's a must-have for anyone who aspires to write picture books and a great resource for those who are looking to hone their craft. I've already sent the link to writers I know."

ELLE

"After writing a novel, unpublished writers inhabit an unguided middle space between not being important enough to warrant industry attention, and needing professional feedback to see how they stack up in the market. That is where Mary Kole lives. Her advice is sound, she pulls no punches, and if you listen to her, your work will improve."

ANDRES FAZA

"I would highly recommend learning from Mary Kole to anyone seriously looking to improve their writing."

KATE K.

"Mary is a top professional in the industry and her advice is on-point and actionable. Having Mary on your team will no doubt improve your pitch, manuscript, query, or whatever you're writing."

ELANA I.

"Mary Kole brings years of solid experience and insight to the art of writing literature for younger audiences."

ROBIN

"From now on, if I see a writing craft book with Mary Kole's name on it, I will hit the 'one click purchase' button without a second thought. She respects writers. She feels for writers. She understands writers. She knows exactly what insights writers need as they work. *Writing Irresistible Kidlit* is possibly the very best book on writing craft I have read in twenty-five years."

SPROCKET

"Mary Kole made me feel a renewed enthusiasm towards my writing goals."

SUSAN

"*Writing Irresistible Kidlit* is quite simply, the best 'how to' book on novel writing that I've ever read and probably ever will read in my life."

CAROL

"Mary Kole helped me to find my way. Her suggestions on my query letter are just what I needed to begin fearlessly searching for a place to call my own. I now consider Mary Kole my secret weapon."

TRACY

"*Writing Irresistible Kidlit* is the perfect blend of technical 'how to' guidance mixed with a healthy dose of encouragement. If anything I write in the future ever sells, I feel I may owe Ms. Kole a royalty for her shaping input from this book."

A. GABLE

"Mary Kole knows all that a story needs to be to be successful in today's market."

"I'm a big fan of everything Mary Kole does and this book was no exception. I learned so much reading Mary's feedback on the various components of each query letter in *Successful Query Letters*."

JAMIE L.

"Kole is clearly passionate about her work and the world of kidlit, and that passion spills over the pages of *Writing Irresistible Kidlit*."

ASHLEY B.